ANN ROBINSON

An Interesting Journey

Best Wishes
Ann Robinson

MADDINGCROWD PUBLISHING
MELBOURNE

First published in 2006 by MaddingCrowd Publishing, Level 1, 696 High Street Road, Glen Waverley, Victoria, 3150, Australia. Email: info@maddingcrowd.com.au.

The National Library of Australia Cataloguing-in-Publication data:

Robinson, Ann Elizabeth Pollen.
An interesting journey.

ISBN-13: 978-1-921158-00-1
ISBN-10: 1-921158-00-X

1. Robinson, Ann Elizabeth Pollen. I. Title.

920

Designed and typeset by MaddingCrowd Publishing
Edited by Rosie Scott
Printed by BPA Print Group

Photography courtesy of iStockphoto (agency) and with thanks to photographers: Sam Aronov, Christian Tschui, Julian Barkway, Brad Daily, Michel Mory, Roberto Adrian, Bryan Busovicki, Rafael Laguillo, Marcel Pelletier, Denis Babenko, Andrew Chambers, Spencer Doane, Alban Egger, Mark Howells, Tony Tremblay, Allen Johnston, Natalia Bratslavsky, Joanne Harris, Natalia Bratslavsky, Spencer Doane; Dreamstime (agency), photographer: Allan Grosskrueger, 'Prestong', 'Alexvu', Joan Coll, 'Olgalis', Ron Sumners; Fotolia (agency), photographers: Gael Roty, Zeev Lieber, 'Albo'; Stock.xchng (agency), photographer: Jean-Marc Labbe, Paul de Bruin, Jordi Boix; Wikimedia Commons, photographer: 'ReneS'; PDPhoto.org, photographer: Jon Sullivan; Flickr, photographer: Eric Titcombe; ibiblio.org; Creatas Images.

The author and publisher are grateful for permission to reproduce the following material: 'Their Love of Travel Drew Them On' an article published in the Australian newspaper *The Age* on 22nd June 1955, 'Travel On A Shoestring' an article published in the Australian newspaper *The Listener-In* on 24th–30th December 1955, 'Two Britons Saw The World On Typing, Teaching, Thrifting' an article published in the Hong Kong newspaper *The Standard* in April 1958. Every effort has been made to obtain permission to reproduce material from other sources. Where permission could not be obtained, the publisher welcomes hearing from the copyright holder(s) in order to acknowledge that copyright.

To dear friends along the way.

Acknowledgements

I am very grateful to Rae Anstee for her encouragement and advice, my cousin Jane Williams who provided some information for the family tree; Rachel Roberts, the archivist of Cheltenham Ladies' College, for her assistance in obtaining a photo of the College; Cathy Dewar for the reproduction of the photo taken by her late husband Bob Dewar of Her Majesty Queen Elizabeth II and Dame Pattie Menzies; Nick Carr of Little Bookham who sent some photographs of Little Bookham Church and grounds, and particularly to Besharl Hein (MaddingCrowd Publishing) for her great personal interest in the preparation and publication of this story.

Foreword

If you enjoy books of travel that describe with exquisite skill the lands being visited and the people the author meets along the way, then you will enjoy *An Interesting Journey.* This book is a delightful account of three young women: Ann Robinson, the author and her companions, Jane McCreath and Helen Gibson, who leave secure positions in post-war Britain to travel first in Europe and later in Canada, the USA, New Zealand and Australia, and many other countries. On these travels, over a period of thirty-three years, they visit many exotic places, have many amusing, and at times scary, experiences and meet many delightful people.

It is generally assumed that to travel overseas one must have a lot of money. Not so for Ann and her companions. Writing about the trip to Switzerland in 1952 with Jane, Ann commented: 'I again held true to what was becoming a trademark of my journeys—we left home with very little money on which to survive.' Again, in 1953, when Ann and Jane arrived in Canada, they had only twenty pounds between them to start life in their new environment. But survive they did, and along the way they had a wonderful working holiday.

Many and varied were the jobs they took. Having applied for employment at a bungalow camp in the Banff National Park, Canada, they received a reply from the proprietor saying, 'It would appear that your qualifications are sufficient for cabin girls.' Ann and Jane were greatly amused to think that a Sister Tutor from the London Hospital and an Administrative Assistant from the BBC, London, should just meet the intelligence required for cleaning bungalows.

A highlight of their time in Canada and the USA was the seven thousand mile bus trip down the east coast of the USA, through New York and Washington and on to Miami and back again to Canada. Most of the trip was on the famed Greyhound buses. Ann's powers of description are such that, as you read, you feel you are there on the trip with her, seeing what she is seeing and sharing her experiences.

After two years of travelling, Ann and Jane's thoughts turned to home, but instead of returning immediately, they decided to see the west coast of the USA and many other places, including Australia. Soon after arriving in Melbourne, the ABC radio station, 3LO, asked Ann to give a series of talks on her travel experiences. *The Listener In* of 24th–30th December 1955, in an article on those talks said: 'Her story is an inspiration to any penniless but travel-hungry girl who is willing to work.' It certainly is and much more beside. When they arrived at Hong Kong in 1958, they were interviewed by the *Hong Kong Standard* which headed its account of Ann and Jane's travels, 'Two Britons Saw The World on Typing, Teaching, Thrifting.'

Five years after setting out on their travels, Ann and Jane eventually arrived home. But the travel bug had bitten deeply as it wasn't long before many more exciting travels were being undertaken.

An Interesting Journey is an excellent book in every way. It is very well written and makes for easy and enjoyable reading. It is the kind of book that having once started, you don't want to put down. I have enjoyed reading it very much—twice—and I know you will too. I heartily commend it.

Geoffrey Blackburn
Assistant Minister
Scots' Church, Melbourne

An Interesting Journey

TRAVEL ON A SHOESTRING

Former BBC behind-the-scenes organiser Ann Robinson, who is working in Melbourne during a world tour, is looking forward to her first Australian Christmas.

Her story is an inspiration to any penniless but travel-hungry girl who is willing to work.

About three years ago, Ann and a nursing friend decided to desert the BBC and a London hospital respectively. They set off for a year in Canada.

They landed with £20 between them and got jobs in Quebec, Ann as secretary in a Canadian electrical company. By the end of that year, despite touring and living in a luxury flat, they had saved 1200 dollars.

They went on a 7000-mile bus spree right down the east coast of the U.S., through New York and Washington to Miami, flew across to Nassau for a week, then to New Orleans and returned to Canada through Oklahoma, Colorado Springs and Salt Lake City.

Their next job provided them with a lifetime of amusement — they cleaned cabins in a holiday camp in the Canadian Rockies for four months.

Then they moved on to Vancouver where in four months they saved their fares to Australia.

They took a ship to Seattle, then travelled by bus down the Oregon coast through the Californian redwood forests to San Francisco where they were entertained for two weeks by an American woman they had met in Switzerland.

They stayed ... luxury hotel, which pro... breakfast trays, ... in Hollywood.

Now they are ...

Ann is workin... and giving free... ABC; her frien... tralian College ...

Ann doubts ... down again. ... tour of Queen... Territory — t...

She hopes ... put their exp...

Ann joined ... retary on th...

From 1945 ... to the head ... sponsible fo... details durin...

Until 1953 ... sistant to ...

Their Love of Travel Drew Them On

AN impulse to take a job in Canada for a year has led to wanderings much further afield for English visitor Miss Ann Robinson, who is at present in Melbourne in the course of a long working holiday which is taking her round the world.

After working with the British Broadcasting Corporation in London, for 13 years, Miss Robinson and a friend (Miss Jan McCreath) arrived in Quebec with 55 dollars between them. In 12 months work there they saved 1200 dollars which enabled them to set out on a Greyhound bus tour of the United States and Canada.

They travelled 7000 miles by bus, finishing up in the Canadian Rockies, where it was time to find some work again. Both took jobs as domestics at a holiday camp between Lake Louise and Banff.

"We were right out in the backwoods among the big timber and the bears," Miss Robinson said.

... Work

... in charge ... ed holiday ... ad to be ... rviced. As ... 10 check- ... there was a ... routine of ... d remaking and polishing floors.

... 40 cabins in ... each with two ... oms, large sit- ... with big open ... chen with elec- ... d stove and well ... athroom.

... he staff were stu- ... vacation or school children earning some extra money in this mountain resort during their holidays.

After four months of working and saving the girls travelled by lorry "with seven wood stoves for company" to Vancouver, where they found jobs and saved a little more money.

To Australia

Having long overstayed their 12 months intended visit, they decided to travel on to Australia, where Miss McCreath had accepted a job as tutor at the College of Nursing, Australia. Miss Robinson found herself a secretarial job in Melbourne, and they expect to remain for at least a year.

"We arrived with £20, as we intend to return to England, via Rangoon, you can imagine we shall have to stay a good while to get our fares saved up.

For five years of her term with the B.B.C., Miss Robinson was private secretary to the officer in charge of all outdoor broadcasts, such as large sports meetings, big ceremonial functions and the like.

One of her most strenuous, but interesting, jobs with him was working at Wembley during the Olympic Games there—"among many other odd jobs I organised a 24-hour laundry service for the team of commentators, as well as attending to 101 other jobs," Miss Robinson said.

Another great event where she was very much on the inside of the scene was the Queen's wedding, another of the B.B.C's. major assignments.

For her last few years with the B.B.C., Miss Robinson was an administrator of children's programmes. Five producers and an administrative assistant were employed full time in this department.

Although she had not participated in any TV productions for children, she said that when she left the B.B.C. was giving 55 minutes daily to televised children's shows. This was a mixed programme of popular entertainment, including talks, plays and specialty features.

Two Britons Saw The World On Typing, Teaching, Thrifting

If you find travel too expensive—or unsettling—then hear the tale of two Britons.

The pair, ladies of 30-plus years (one has escaped the post-40 rut), have roamed the world now for five years, and their run-of-the-pence bank accounts are just what they were when they left home—plus interest.

Yet the[illegible] well [illegible] hair perm'd, their dress fashionable. They have used regular-price trav[illegible] tickets throughout the trip. They have even entertained some of the more friendly hosts along the [illegible]oute.

Their secret? Making between-trips count—but heavy.

"We've earned two incomes ther[illegible]—and lived on one," Miss Ann Robinson, for 13 years a BBC assistant, said with a twinkle. "We've found life can be thrifty—and people kind."

Take their first crisis, early in 1953.

They have just t[illegible]rown up their jobs in London—where the other tourist, Miss Jane McCreath, was a nursing tutor—to Go West. They made it to Quebec with just £10 betw[illegible] them.

While Miss McCreath had a job awaiting her at a hospital, Miss Robinson had to look around on the spot. Canadian General Electric came through—made her a secretary.

Things were rosy again, except that in another 13 months they couldn't hold still any longer. But that was long enough. The two-in-one economics had paid off, and with their savings they survived bills for a gay trip to Florida, a flight to the Bahamas, and back via New Orleans and the southwestern US to the Canadian Rockies.

"What a place to stop—Lake Banff and Lake Louise!" enthused Miss McCreath. Her partner nodded.

In this ambiance they took courage and became housemaids—fir[illegible] time ever. The houses were well-to-do, of course, and the folks in charge took their two greenhorns on a raft of excursions through the northwest.

Sights all seen, the junketers pushed on to Victoria. What they missed of Banff's beauties they made up in restuffed purses—after just four months of work.

They had three weeks of southern California sun. Then in San Francisco they climbed aboard the luxury liner Orsova and cruised the enchanted isles of the South Pacific, to arrive a month later in Australia. That was in March 1955. By Melbourne they had to dig in again. For 14 months, using their three tested talents—typing, teaching, thrifting—they salted away the stuff that makes dreams come true.

Finally came the call of the open spaces. They chugged off for Adelaide, had a spot of camping at Alice Springs, a look at Ayers Rock—seven miles around—and a longer one at Darwin and the east coast.

"We staggered into Townsville in bad shape," Miss Robinson confessed. "Just £3 left. But I managed a waitress' job for ten days, and that got us right again." Which meant that £3 became £13—even with Miss McCreath jobless.

It remained for Hayman Island, on the Barrier Reef, to see them bring off their biggest coup. Hooking on with the work staff of a luxury hotel, they translated the £13 into £300 in three months. That one made ears perk up at the Australian Broadcasting Corp., and the pair recorded a dozen programmes on their adventures.

Arriving here last Sunday on s.s. Taiping (first class), the two globetrotters agreed it was finally time to head home (also first class, on the Chusan). No Japan? No China?

"Sure—next time," they chorused. "We'll get jumpy in another couple years—you watch."

Any takers?

Introduction

Travel gives a character of experience to our knowledge,
and brings the figures upon the tablet of memory into strong relief.

Henry Tuckerman (1813–1871)

How true is Henry Tuckerman's quote? For me, as I contemplate the time I spent travelling to so many different places, and just how much I have learnt in doing so, I realise just what a very large part people do play, even on the shortest of journeys. Going home on a crowded tram, for instance, a cheerful conductor seems to make the discomfort far less acute, and when we reach home, instead of talking about the number of people who trampled on our toes, we are far more likely to remember the conductor whose courtesy or witty remarks made us all laugh.

People make the whole process of travel much more colourful, and my journeys would not have been so memorable if I had not been blessed by the many people who touched my life along the way. Similarly, as I look further back, my thoughts take me home to my beloved England and the many faces of family and friends, back to the beginning of the longest journey I ever took—the journey of my life.

GROWING PAINS

1918–1948: An Eventful Time

I was only nine years old. I had no idea of what had eventuated. In fact, I was excited because the Headmistress had told me that Grannie was coming to see me and that I had been given permission to leave school for the night. I can remember standing by the window watching for her arrival; I didn't even notice that she was dressed all in black. She waited until we had arrived at home before breaking the news to me; I sat cuddled on her lap while she tried to explain what had happened. We remained like this for some time, but it was then suggested that I should go with my aunt to feed the chickens and the four ducks.

I don't remember anything about the next twenty-four hours, but on my return to school, the other boarders had a set of jacks for me (a popular game at the time) and I quickly joined some of them for a game.

Speaking about my mother's death in 1927.

I was born on the 29th April 1918 in Westminster, England, with the end of World War I in sight, and later christened Ann Elizabeth Pollen Robinson at All Saints Church, Little Bookham in Surrey where my parents had been married in 1917. I believe my christening was rather a solemn occasion as my mother's illness had been diagnosed as tuberculosis and she was shortly after admitted to a sanatorium where she stayed for the first two years of my life. This was very distressing news for the family.

During the time of my mother's illness, I was cared for by my father's parents and sister, together with a nanny. We continued to reside in Surrey, later going to live in Effingham which was situated only a short walk across the fields from the Little Bookham Church where I had been christened.

All Saints Church, Little Bookham, Surrey.

I have few early memories, but I recall that as a very small child I was given a small, brown teddy bear to care for—a friend that still sits proudly on my bed to this day. I can recall receiving 'Bear' from 'Bun-pa', my maternal grandfather, who had just purchased him from a shop while I had been waiting in the dickey seat of the car. Shortly after this time, we went by sea to Scotland. I was seasick and can still remember seeing Bear pegged on the clothes line after our arrival, blowing in the wind after having been bathed. Bear has since lost most of his fur, but he now has a beautiful knitted red suit to wear, made by my friend 'Tip' from Quebec, and he and I have seen and done much together.

'Bear' in his red suit.

We spent every summer at my maternal grandparents' house. Grannie was a keen golfer and spent every summer at her house at Lossiemouth in Scotland, just a few minutes walk from the golf club with its three courses—eighteen-, nine- and eight-hole. When my parents and I visited, my job was to go down each morning and book her in for the eighteen-hole course, both morning and afternoon. From about the age of four, I was expected to play a round of the eight-hole course twice a day. The routine was: golf at ten o'clock, home for a glass of milk and a doughnut, then to the beach. Next came lunch, a short rest and then golf, followed by the beach again. We shared a hut at the beach with a family of five children, and our first job was to empty the hut, ready for anyone who decided to be naughty so that they might be shut in the dark for a while!

In 1926, my favourite uncle—Uncle Lestock—wed his wartime sweetheart, Dorothy. Happily, I was asked to be a bridesmaid, something I had not done before. I remember wearing a beautiful bright green frock and was strictly told by my mother, upon getting into the taxi that was to take us to the church, to make sure that I sat on the tissue paper placed on the seat so as not to crush my dress. I enjoyed every minute of that special day, even though I was requested—being such a grown up girl of nine years—to look after the pageboys and make sure that they didn't get into any mischief.

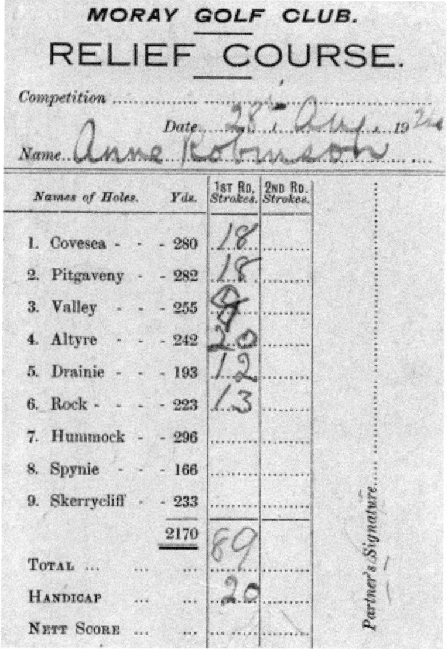

MORAY GOLF CLUB.

RELIEF COURSE.

Competition ....

Date 28th Aug. 1924

Name Anne Robinson

Names of Holes.	Yds.	1st Rd. Strokes.	2nd Rd. Strokes.
1. Covesea	280	18	
2. Pitgaveny	282	18	
3. Valley	255	9	
4. Altyre	242	20	
5. Drainie	193	12	
6. Rock	223	13	
7. Hummock	296		
8. Spynie	166		
9. Skerrycliff	233		
	2170	89	
Total ...			
Handicap ...		20	
Nett Score ...			

Partner's Signature ....

A golf card from one of my daily rounds. I was six years old.

Uncle Lestock had always been a favourite of mine. At the time of my birth, he was a soldier in the British Army actively involved in the hostilities taking place in France, yet he still found the time and the energy to send me a letter. Even now, I cherish this note, though I was only a baby at the time.

Shortly after Uncle Lestock's wedding, my father, who was employed by the Treasury, was posted to Khartoum in the Sudan. To enable my father to take up his posting in good time, my parents left for Khartoum on New Year's Day 1927. At the time, I had whooping cough and they could only put their heads around the door and say goodbye because of the fear of infection.

Upon my recovery, I was sent to boarding school at Coed-bel in Chislehurst, Kent, where I was the youngest boarder, together with the Headmistress' niece. I cannot remember much about the next few months, but I do remember being excited about seeing my parents again, as they were to return to England in order to avoid the intense heat and humidity of a summer in Khartoum. It had been arranged that my mother, whose health had been badly affected by the tuberculosis, would return in early July, and my father would follow a little later.

We passed a pleasant summer together, spent mainly at Lossiemouth, but before long it was time for me to resume my schooling, and for my parents to go back to Khartoum, travelling by easy stages. They both left England in October—with many farewells from me—but this was to be the last time that I saw my dear mother. Sadly, she developed pneumonia during the trip and died on 27th October 1927 in Cairo.

My mother was buried in, what was then, the British Cemetery in Alexandria. As a remembrance, Bun-pa, who was the Lord of the Manor of Little Bookham, had the electricity installed in the church in memory of my mother.

My mother, father and me at our home in Effingham in 1924.

In 1926, my parents had decided that I was to attend The Cheltenham Ladies' College in Gloucestershire for my senior years. My father had written, requesting my enrollment—which was accepted—and I became a pupil in 1932. I remained a student of this hallowed institution until 1936, but as I recall, never excelled as I was neither a scholar nor an athlete—the two talents that were important at that time.

My 1936 summer holiday was spent in Austria with friends of my father and their delicate daughter. One day, while out walking on my own, I met Elizabeth, and over the remaining weeks of my holiday and the years to follow, we became good friends. In the war years, Elizabeth took up a post as a driver with the Women's Royal Navy Service and I saw quite a lot of her as she often transported VIPs to London and, needing a place to stay, she often shared digs with me. It was during this time that she met Cedric, the great grandson of Charles Dickens, whom she eventually married.

Fly fishing in Scotland with my father in 1927.

On leaving school in July of the same year, it was decided that I might do well in art and so I started at the Chelsea School of Art in September. This was where I met Helen, who was soon to become not only a dear friend, but one of my travelling companions.

At the time, Helen was living with her Aunt Mabel in Holland Road, Kensington, and as I was situated in South Kensington, we often went out in the evening together. I also spent a few weekends with her at her family home in Petersfield where I came to know her family. I still remember being

Cheltenham Ladies' College.

impressed by the antics of Helen's brother John, swinging his way around the upstairs landing and hanging by the tips of his fingers from the picture rail. Their father, who had died in the early years of World War I, had been a keen mountaineer and had climbed with the famous George Mallory[1]. It was obvious that John, and to a lesser degree, Helen, had inherited his love of climbing.

In 1937, my father, who had previously been appointed Financial Secretary to King Edward VIII, was then appointed as Financial Secretary to King George VI. The coronation of King George and Queen Elizabeth took place at Westminster Abbey in May, and as a royal retainer, my father and his new wife Marjorie attended the ceremony. I also saw this magnificent event; my aunt and I were on a stand facing Buckingham Palace.

Shortly after his appointment, my father was granted a 'Grace and Favour Residence'[2]—Sheen Cottage—a beautiful home in Richmond Park where he and Marjorie lived until the early months of World War II. All official functions for the Royal Family then ceased and so my father's position came to an end (he was responsible for the financing of these functions). My father and step-mother continued to live in Richmond for a while, but finally felt that the continuous travelling in and out of London was too difficult, so they moved into an apartment in Central London. Shortly after their move, a gun site was set up close by Sheen Cottage. The German targeting of this military location destroyed the Cottage and devastated its grounds. My father had by this time been posted to the War Damage Commission of the Ministry of Works and was responsible, among other things, for dealing with bombed buildings and

1 Famous British mountaineer who was lost on Mount Everest in 1924.

2 A system of providing accommodation to royal retainers at the 'grace and favour' of the sovereign.

Sheen Cottage: the grace and favour residence granted to my father.

the temporary housing of people left homeless by the war, something of which he had certain knowledge!

The term break in the summer of 1938 was spent in Switzerland with Helen and her family. Our studies at Chelsea were progressing, and before the break, our teachers had requested all students to spend some time during their holidays painting so that we had something prepared for exhibition at the start of the next term. So, Helen and I spent hours painting the beautiful scenery of Arolla—the small village where we stayed in the Bernese Oberland, high in the Swiss Alps. With no road connecting the valley to the village, it was unique to have to walk all the way up through the beautiful mountains to the only hotel the village boasted, and just the right environment to provide inspiration for, in our opinion, some wonderful masterpieces. Unfortunately, the judge of the exhibition did not agree. He waved our paintings to one side saying, 'Never, never paint snow-covered mountains!' and went on to congratulate the student who had a painting of a dreary street with large windows and chimneys out of proportion with the buildings.

In the summer of 1939, I again went to the Bernese Oberland with Helen and her family, this time to the village of Saas-Fee. We were quite a party with Helen's brother John; mother Hester; aunts Mabel and Winnow; two elderly cousins Bertha and Maud; and two of John's friends John and David.

One day, when the men went off climbing, some of us took a lovely walk along a path through the woods. We came to a small bridge over a very inviting stream, and believing there was no one around, we all undressed and jumped into the wonderfully refreshing water. Anyone who knew Winnow would remember her giggle and this attracted a middle-aged couple who suddenly appeared on the bridge. The gentleman bowed to us and in French said, 'In this country we only look at the view,' and then the couple continued on their way.

The war clouds were gathering at the end of our holiday and we began to get somewhat concerned. We had travelled by car and felt it unlikely that we would be able to get on an earlier ferry than our original booking of 1st September and we didn't want to leave the cars in France. So we decided to move nearer to the coast in case we had to make a dash for home. We stayed overnight on the outskirts of Paris and were disturbed a good deal by heavy army vehicles making their way to the coast. Because of a lack of accommodation, Helen and I had to share a double bed and in the middle of the night the bed started rocking. Thinking that maybe war manoeuvres were in process, I sat up quickly ready to jump out of bed only to find that Helen had spilt a bottle of pills in the bed and was searching for them!

My family in 1932. Top left: Father, Aunt Marion and GP. Bottom left: Me, Gran and Marjorie.

With the war imminent, my father decided that art school was not for me and decreed that I should take a secretarial course, a decision which distressed me greatly at the time. I soon realised that it was the right decision and offered great opportunities for me. So, in September 1939, I began a six month course with Mrs Hoster's Secretarial College, which was located in the city; however, due to the air raids, we were all eventually evacuated to a large country house in Tunbridge Wells, Kent.

During my time at the college, I made many friends, particularly Mary, Irène, Elizabeth and Frieda. Frieda had, unbeknown to me, attended Cheltenham Ladies' College with me, but with over 300 pupils at the college, we didn't meet until we both lived in the same digs during our secretarial course. Frieda went to Singapore when she qualified and was later posted to Hong Kong as Secretary to the British Consul. When taken prisoner by the Japanese, she applied for a transfer to Shanghai where her parents had lived for a number of years. This was finally granted and they all became prisoners of war there. We used to exchange messages via the Red Cross and guessing what she was trying to say was sometimes quite a problem. One I remember said, 'On the march again with mug and plate, all the young and old together.'

On completion of my secretarial course, I was accepted by the British Broadcasting Corporation (BBC) as a shorthand typist in the Engineering Administrative Department, where I remained throughout the war. Elizabeth, who had completed the course at the same time, went to the Air Ministry and we used to meet for lunch every week. One day during the Blitz, her boss rang me to ask if I had heard from her as she had not turned up for work. I replied that I hadn't, striking fear into both our minds as we knew that bombs had fallen in her area during the night. Sadly, we soon discovered that Elizabeth and her parents had been killed, leaving her thirteen year old brother unharmed.

One of the many volunteer jobs during the Blitz—aircraft spotting on the roof of a London building.

Life went on. I rode my bicycle from Kensington to the BBC most days, but after night duty there, I went home on the tube to wash and have breakfast before returning to work. The tube platform at Oxford Circus was always busy with the night's sleepers tidying up their beds, often leaving them in place ready for the next night. When the V2 bombs started, I happened to see the first one coming over London, but had no idea what it was as it was quite different to the V1.

During this time, I learnt that Helen was ill and that she and her mother were to go and live with her Aunt Winnow at *Mylors* in Church Hanborough. Fortunately, Helen's illness was of short duration and it wasn't long before she had joined the Land Army and was employed by her farming neighbour Mrs Chitty. I well remember receiving a letter from her, humorously telling of her experience in trying to milk Mrs Chitty's cow, Lucy. According to Helen, she started off well, but was soon kicked by Lucy and landed with the stool and bucket in the muck. Poor Helen went to find Mrs Chitty and say that she was afraid she could not cope with Lucy, to which Mrs Chitty replied, 'From which side did you try milking her? If it was the left, she only likes to be milked from the right, so go back and try again!'

I spent many happy times with Helen at *Mylors* and came to know how much she loved her animals. If you did not want to share your bed with 'Assisi' the cat, you knew you must be sure to shut your bedroom door at night. She also had a few chickens in the walled garden and knew them all by name. I remember when 'Trousers' became ill—she wrapped her in a towel and put her in a box in the kitchen where she could be kept warm and then watched over her until she died.

Returning from one of these visits with Helen in the early days of the Blitz, I arrived to find that a bomb nearby had cracked the digs where I lived and as a result, we were not allowed into the building. All of our possessions were brought out and piled up in the closed-off street so that we could go and pick out our own belongings.

I then moved to a similar establishment in Queens Gate where I had a room on the very top floor. Outside my window was a plane tree, and hiding within its branches was a pigeon, sitting on her nest. Some nights, gun carriages would go up and down with the guns blazing and despite the noise, the pigeon would still be sitting there in the morning—a sure sign that life must go on.

I used to have several telephone calls with a BBC Receiving Station in Kent and I would often get the message that German planes had just flown over them so I was advised to keep away from windows. Shortly after, the London sirens would wail. During all this time, I carried out night time fire watching duties in my street and also first aid duty at the BBC.

For a short while, I boarded with a couple who had a flat in a modern building near the Westminster Hospital. The gentleman of the house was in the army, guarding the Bank of England, and was only occasionally allowed to sleep away from the bank. They had a fox terrier—Judy—that heard the planes coming up the Thames long before we did, and being a little frightened of the noise herself, she came and sat close to us. She became our early warning signal, as we knew that when she did this, it was time for us to go down to the hall for safety.

My next abode was shared with Molly, my godmother's niece. She had been looking for accommodation in London and we decided to rent a basement flat in Harrington Gardens, South Kensington. With our marmalade cat, Rowley Parker Robinson–Sheppard ('Rowley' because we liked the name, 'Parker' because he was always nosey, 'Robinson' after my surname, and 'Sheppard' after Molly's), we lived there for the greater part of the war and until I left for Canada in 1953.

After the war, when I was free to move away from my reserved occupation[3], I joined the Outside Broadcast Department of the BBC as Secretary to the Head of the Department. We covered a number of big events, including the 1948 Olympic Games in London. Later, I took up the position of Administrative Assistant in the Children's Hour Department, where the program of the same name was produced and broadcast each weeknight to the millions of young listeners across Britain. This was indeed a busy time for me, but also one of great enjoyment.

A Children's Hour Department meeting (me on left).

3 'Reserved occupations' were jobs vital to the war-effort and as such, could not be abandoned.

Paris
FRANCE
Vierzon
Vichy
Clermont-Ferrand
Royat
Saint-Flour
Le Puy
Mende
Langogne
Rodez
Millau
Albi
Toulouse
Beziers
Narbonne
Perpignan
Port-Vendres
Cerbere

Have Passport, Will Travel!

1949: Central France

In the summer of 1949, Helen posed the question of a visit to France. Motivated by her recent reading of Robert Louis Stevenson's book, Travels with a Donkey in the Cévennes, *she felt that a trip following the route mentioned in the book—a 120-mile journey through the Cévennes mountains in south-central France—would add another dimension to the trip.*

Having previously travelled with Helen and her family to Switzerland in 1938 and 1939, I knew that Helen was a wonderful travelling companion, and as we were both due for holidays—Helen from the Ashmolean Museum of Art and Archaeology in Oxford where she was a calligrapher, and I, from the BBC—we decided to go. We even managed to impart a touch more authenticity to our Travels trip when we found ourselves awake one night while in Le Puy, listening to a disgruntled donkey braying.

After planning our holiday to France earlier in the year, 5th August soon arrived—being the day for departure—and Helen came to our flat in time for supper. After she and Molly had more or less repacked her entire suitcase and discarded large quantities of clothes, we set out for Victoria Station where Helen, unusually concerned about the gourmet food we were likely be offered on our travels, weighed herself and made a mental note to revisit the scales on her return.

Except for Helen experiencing a bout of agonising indigestion that even a swig of brandy did not move, our train ride to the coast was uneventful. Fortunately, we moved quickly through Customs and left Dover, with its twinkling lights on the hill and its blinking lighthouse, on board a ferry bound for Dunkirk. It being a lovely night, we in our innocence, thought we should be able to sleep on deck and hence, had two deck-chairs put up in the bow just outside the area that was covered.

After exploring the ferry a little, we found the pilot standing near us and so started talking to him. He was most interesting and told us how the dock gates worked and pointed out the power house. He said we should have a calm crossing and that when daylight arrived, we should be able to see some of the wrecks on the Goodwins. We then settled down to sleep, but soon realised that it would be far too cold outside, so we gathered up our chairs and invaded the covered fo'rard, but by this time there was only room in the gangway and we were still suffering from a howling draught until I thought of shutting the door! After this, we dozed on and off until we reached Dunkirk in the early hours of the morning. Even though we knew it would be some time before we actually arrived at our destination, we couldn't resist getting up and watching.

We got off the ferry and through Customs, and having found our nice corner seats in the train bound for Paris, we revived ourselves with hot cups of coffee from our thermos flask and some egg sandwiches.

We slept most of the way to Paris and arrived there mid morning on a very hot day. We had excellent coffee and croissants for two francs at the buffet and then went out with our baggage to find a bus to the *Gare d'Austerlitz*[4]. We were very much flummoxed by a slot machine at the bus stop and felt sure it must be some sort of fire alarm or police warning. Eventually, a man came up and pulled down a handle and out came a ticket, so we asked him in halting French what was the meaning of the machine. He explained that when there were more than four people waiting for a bus, you took a ticket and so showed your rightful place in the queue—a very sensible practice we thought.

Having deposited our luggage at the station, we went out to have a look around, but after a very cursory glance at the gardens next to the station, we decided that it was really too hot to do anything but drink, so we sat ourselves down at a café in the middle of the crossroads where we both had a St Raphael[5] aperitif.

Our train left at noon and we were pleased to get settled. We were in a carriage with two of the most overweight people I had ever seen and a most amusing lady who was on her way to Royat to drink the mineral waters. Thoroughly enjoying her witty conversation,

---

4 Austerlitz Station.

5 A proprietary French fortified red aperitif wine of the quinquina type.

cordial entente[6] was maintained by the lady lending us her fan and plying us with fruit sweets in return for our smelling salts and squashed chocolate biscuits!

At Vierzon, there was great excitement when a man fell off the train steps as the train moved off. In true French fashion, everyone screamed and yelled and it was difficult to believe that everyone was not a near relative of the man in question. The pace was so great that we could not attempt to understand what was happening, while Madame made remarks such as, *'Il n'est pas mort.'*[7] About half an hour later, in the middle of an enormous corn field, whistles blew again and we stopped. A fireman walked slowly down the train with an enormous spanner and everyone hung out of the windows and screamed yet again. We didn't know if a wheel was coming off or something else, but we continued after some little time and eventually arrived at Clermont-Ferrand.

The hotel was straight opposite the station and after a certain amount of excitement—we had been put into the wrong room and Helen's suitcase had emptied itself onto the floor—we were left to have baths and revive. We had a very good dinner of soup, fish, York ham and vegetables, cheese, greengages and peaches, and we drank a whole bottle of red wine between us. This revived us considerably and we thought that a short stroll before bed would be a good thing. Unfortunately, we window shopped to such an extent that we lost our way and ended up walking a good three miles before at last finding the hotel again, quite exhausted.

The French seemed to drink until the early hours of the morning and would then rise a couple of hours later, so as a result our night was somewhat disturbed. After *café au lait* and croissants while sitting outside the hotel, we went up to the cathedral and entered just as the Father came around with the offertory. We put a five franc piece into a tray full of notes, and then after standing and sitting for no apparent reason for ten minutes, most people left and so we followed suit, feeling that we had at least made the effort.

We were quite intoxicated by the shops and spent the rest of the morning wandering around with our noses pressed to the windows, finally having an aperitif before finding a small and slightly scruffy café in the street behind the hotel. The café advertised a two franc lunch, but in fact, it came out to about three francs. We had artichokes, stewed steak,

---

6 Friendly agreement.

7 'He is not dead.'

a hotchpotch of vegetables, and dessert, with half a bottle of wine and water to mix with it (we lowered our standards somewhat after the first night).

In the afternoon, we took a tram to Royat and tried to fathom the intricacies of whether it was cheaper to stand or sit, but still didn't get it clear. Royat was a large, health resort with vast hotels, and it was very, very hot. We seemed quite unable to find anywhere to sit in the shade and finally ended up climbing the hill behind the town and sitting on a rather dried-up hummock next to the cemetery. Even then, it was too hot to be happy, but we were amused by a large French family who arrived and settled down to a large meal, eaten out of billycans. The husband was most talkative; he could speak a little English—learned, I think, at Dunkirk during the evacuation—and we spoke enough French to enable us to converse. Although they were quite a large party, he invited us to share their wine, but we declined, feeling that they probably didn't need our company as well. Instead we went down into the town and got rooked for an ice-cream at a grand restaurant, and then shortly after, fell for a lovely fresh lemon and iced water drink a bit further down the hill. It was still very hot, but by this time the whole town came out from its afternoon rest and streamed up the hill towards us. We returned home and collapsed on our beds until it was time to go and look for dinner having decided that it was cheaper to eat out, rather than in the hotel.

We got up early the next day, and in the scorching heat, went on an excursion to the top of the Puy-de-Dôme[8]. There was a lovely breeze up there and quite a few alpine flowers. We climbed to the top of the tower and had a wonderful view away over the Auvergne, but it was very windy and so we soon came down and went and had a drink at the flourishing café on the top. We got back to Clermont at noon and had our everlasting aperitif before buying ourselves some lunch, which we proceeded to eat in our bedroom using Helen's headscarf as a tablecloth—so hygienic. We lay in a stupor on our beds after that until late in the afternoon when we again went shop crawling and decided on all the things we would buy if our money allowed. We laughed a lot over trying to buy toilet paper and being offered very soft handkerchiefs until Helen said, '*Non, non, pour le W.C.*'[9]

We had dinner at yet another restaurant, which consisted of soup, mashed potatoes in gravy, a week's ration of cold pork and salad, greengages and of course, wine. Then

---

8 An extinct volcano in south-central France.

9 'No, no, for the water closet.' (toilet)

Puy-de-Dôme mountain.

we went to the cinema and saw *L'Oeuf et Moi*[10] which starred Claudette Colbert and Fred MacMurray. We got lost on the way home and finally were helped by a charming soldier who walked most of the way with us, as the trams had all long since stopped.

We woke up to a wet morning, but it soon cleared and was rather muggy. We did our final shop crawl after vacating our room and bought a little aluminium pot with a collapsible handle for boiling eggs. We also bought our lunch and consumed it in some rather new gardens with practically no shade, just out of sight of the hotel. We then staggered up the town with our luggage, checked in and got good seats on the bus to Le Puy, and then sat in a café and drank *citron pressé*[11] until four o'clock when we set off.

The bus was a real country affair with mothers feeding their babies en route, and great leave takings and greetings at each village. Our driver was a huge burly brute who had a drink at each village and drove madly in between, with little regard for any cattle being driven homeward. The journey took four hours through lovely country and the colours were superb. We arrived at Le Puy in a thunderstorm and the rain just broke overhead as we got out of the bus in the main square. We took shelter in a bar and drank beer, and finally did a dash up to the hotel and fell giggling and dripping through the swing doors of a rather grand hotel, much to the amazement of an old man sitting in the hall. However, the hotel staff were quite pleasant and we were given a nice room with two double beds.

---

10 *The Egg and I.*

11 A fresh lemon juice drink.

The next morning was a lovely one and gave us a beautiful view from our window of the Rocher Corneille[12] and the statue of Notre-Dame de France, the amazing terracotta coloured statue of the Virgin Mary perched high on the top which we planned to visit later in the day. We did our usual shop crawl after breakfast, but did not find the shops as good as those in Clermont, and then we returned to the hotel to get ready for the day's outing.

It was a perfect day—sunny with a slight breeze—and we started by wandering up to the cathedral through fascinating cobbled streets, all built in steps. The cathedral was beautiful and Romanesque, and as we came out of a side door, a whole school of little boys in 'crocodile' went down the stepped street singing lustily. It really was a perfect sight against the background of old houses and dappled sunshine, with old ladies sitting in the shade of the cathedral selling postcards and Auvergne lace. This was very much a lace town and all the old ladies sat outside their houses making the lovely lace on velvet cushions. The speed with which they worked was quite amazing and we would have liked to have stopped and watched however, we felt that in doing so, we would be obligated to buy some of their beautiful work and we really could not afford to do so.

Auvergne lacemaking.

Our next visit was to the Rocher Corneille and its wonderful statue. One climbs up inside the statue and looks out of little windows all the way out, as you would inside a lighthouse. We understood that we could get right up into the statue's crown, but in fact, got to about her eye level. The panoramic views were terrific. We sat and ate our lunch under her skirts and then wandered down to the river and sat and watched the women washing and the men fishing. As it was a little smelly, we soon left there and climbed to the chapel of St Michel, perched on an even more precipitous rock.

Back in the town, they were putting up the decorations for the Feast of the Assumption, a religious holiday for the whole country that was to take place on the following weekend. We then ran into a man who was most anxious to air his English and assured us that he

12 Corneille Rock; a volcanic headland that rises 757 meters above sea level giving a view of the city and countryside below.

was 'at our disposal' during our stay. We felt that two double beds was a bit of a complication, so we declined. Altogether, we were so fascinated by the place that we decided to stay on a little longer.

The Rocher Corneille statue of the Virgin Mary.

We arrived back to the hotel at about five o'clock and did a small wash, despite the printed notice on the back of the door forbidding laundering in the rooms, and we hung the smelly cheese that we had bought earlier in the string bag on a hook outside the window. Later, we went out and had dinner for 180 francs at an amusing little restaurant full of toughs playing cards. They put a mat on the tables that resembled a bath mat before playing and plied their small offspring with highly-coloured drinks to keep them quiet. There were two rather sweet kittens that had taken up residence in the restaurant: one very wild and anyone who tried to catch it received no thanks for their pains; the other, very friendly and loving. Helen took the risk of a flea or two and had it on her lap throughout most of the meal. It was a good meal of tomatoes and egg done in oil, haricot beans cooked in butter, two large slabs of cold veal and two pears each. An enormous quantity of red wine completed the picture. Feeling very mellow, we then went into another café to sample a Verveine du Velay[13] which we both enjoyed. We stayed there for some time, gossiping with Madame and a patron. We really began to feel that our French was improving until I tried to talk about English shoes not being watertight, whereupon Helen came to my rescue by saying, '*l'eau arrive*'[14] and they comprehended all right!

When we arrived back at the hotel, the statue on the Rocher Corneille was floodlit and looked very lovely. We went to sleep to the braying of a most turbulent donkey near our window, which really reminded us of the theme of this holiday: Robert Louis Stevenson and his book, *Travels with a Donkey in the Cévennes.*

---

13 A herb liqueur, strongly flavoured with vervain, which gave the name to the liqueur. Besides the vervain, thirty-two other plants are necessary to produce the liqueur.

14 'Water arrives'.

Just before getting into bed, the telephone in our room went off with a loud buzz and I bravely carried on a conversation with Monsieur about our prolonged stay. Somehow, talking on the telephone seemed much harder than talking to the person when gesticulations did a great deal to help one on.

We awoke to another perfect morning. We had finished our breakfast by eight o'clock and set off straight away to get our lunch and go to the bank. We then decided to walk to the Château de Polignac, a lovely old ruin standing on a rock about four miles from Le Puy and visible from the Rocher Corneille. The sun beat down upon us and we could feel ourselves burning, so we had our lunch sitting under some trees, looking across fields to the village and the rock. After a short siesta, we walked up to the village and looked at the church, continued up to the fortified château where there were lovely views all around, and then finished our excursion by walking back to the hotel via the main road, all of which was a bit wearying in the heat of the afternoon.

Later that afternoon after a cup of tea and a rest, we visited the museum which was modern and very pleasant. After closing, we sat in the museum gardens and watched life go by until dinner time. On the way back to the hotel we bought some little bottles of liqueur at eight francs each and Helen remarked that they would make good '*gâteaux*'[15]. The madame in the shop said we spoke very well and had obviously studied the language, so feeling rather pleased with ourselves, we went back to the hotel and talked to Madame regarding the payment of the bill.

Rising early, the hotel concierge had breakfast ready for us when we came down. We caught the early morning bus from the central square to Langogne. It was rather cold and the bus very full, but we made friends with a commercial traveller from Marseilles who enjoyed using his English, and so, despite our preference for talking French, we had to let him have his fling. The conversation started because he was sitting facing me on the window side and he suggested that I change places with him so that I could see the view as we climbed out of Le Puy.

At Langogne, we had to catch a train and the commercial traveller bought us large cups of coffee in a café opposite the station and we gave him a slab of chocolate for his lunch. We all climbed into a third-class carriage until we reached La Bastide where we dismounted

15 Cake. Helen meant 'cadeaux' (gifts).

amid fond farewells and climbed into a real mountain car full of every sort of person off on their holiday. We managed to find two seats and had an uneventful journey up rather a fascinating valley, climbing and climbing. We arrived at Mende and thought that we were going to experience our first hotel difficulty, but we were finally directed to a very nice large hotel where we were given an excellent room for three francs each. We decided to eat out for lunch and so found a nice little place about a ten minute walk from the hotel. We then retired to bed under our duvets and slept until late afternoon. Poor Helen was suffering from diarrhoea, but a dose of brandy seemed to help, so we then decided to explore the town.

Later, we had dinner in the hotel; Helen, having said that she would toy with an omelette, ate the lot. After the meal we decided to go out for a short walk and wandered down to the river where we found a charming little bridge being crossed by an old man bringing home a flock of about twenty long-eared sheep with bells around their necks.

We had a wonderful night in our deluxe beds, and after a breakfast of rather sickly croissants made with an unbelievable amount of lard, we climbed up above the town and wandered around a large cemetery with a number of German war graves. As Helen was still feeling rather rotten, we sat in the sun in a field and looked at a perfect view of the village in a dip between great green hills with the two spires of the cathedral sticking up from the middle of the houses. We ate our lunch there and then returned in time to catch the bus to St Enimie.

We started on our trip with a very young boy as the driver, but after we had been through one village he suddenly stopped and backed down a perilous route to the village again, the reason being that he had forgotten to deliver the provisions to the village shop. This exhausted him to such an extent that he climbed into the back seat and went to sleep while the conductor did the driving for a bit. He took over again before the perilous descent to St Enimie—and was it some descent! At one point we met a large lorry and only just got by. Helen and I were exclaiming a bit and the conductor turned round and said, '*Il est fini, mademoiselle!*'[16]

16 'It is finished, Miss!'

St Enimie was right down in the valley, surrounded by enormous walls of rock. It was no more than a small collection of houses gathered around a lovely old bridge that had been built over The Tarn, a river of a deep brown colour running over pure white stones.

The village boasted three hotels and we couldn't get into any of them, so we were directed to the local convent. At first the nun said she could only offer us a hut in the garden, but when we were halfway up the vegetable garden in a solemn procession, she remembered that there was a room available. We were then shown a large bare room with five beds, five washstands with tin basins and jugs. She was obviously not keen to give us sheets so we said that we could manage with the blankets on the beds, and having told us that they had just accommodated fifty school children, she assured us that it was all *bien propre*[17]. The Mother Superior came to see us and presented us with little medallions as mementos of our visit, and we had an awkward time deciding what we should give her for our night's lodging.

After a good meal in one of the hotels, we went for a short stroll, but soon had to return to the convent as the doors shut at nine o'clock. Helen mentioned that the atmosphere in the convent made her feel very religious, and as if to reinforce her comment, the nun located in the next room spent the next twenty minutes chanting her prayers in a sing-song voice. I did not fancy the blankets on the bed very much, so I went to bed in my slippers and dressing gown, laid a chiffon scarf on the pillow, and used my petticoat in place of a sheet. It was a good thing I did as Helen was covered in mysterious bites the next day.

Breakfast was at seven o'clock and was provided by the nuns just as they went off to Mass. It consisted of rather stale bread and tepid coffee, so as soon as they had gone out of the front door, we took out our butter which improved the bread.

The staff at the hotel where we dined the night before were most helpful and undertook to put our luggage on the afternoon bus to Millau for us, and so, with our night things on our backs in case of emergency, we set off to walk down to the magnificent Gorges du Tarn. We walked about eight miles along a very good road made out of rock, above the river, past the Château de La Gaze and arrived at La Malene at about noon. While waiting for a boat, a lovely woman in black came out of her little postcard kiosk and blew a few long blasts on a real horn. This call quickly brought two men on bicycles, with long punt poles over their

---

17 Quite clean.

shoulders, and the four of us went down to the river. We climbed into a flat-bottomed boat, something like a punt but wider, and sat on seats which were balanced on slats across the punt. The men put their bicycles in the back, then one stood in the stern and one in the bow, and off we went. There was not a great deal of water in the river, but it was crystal clear; at times we were scraping the bottom and the next minute we were in twelve feet of water. We shot little rapids in a most exciting way and the sun beat upon us and burnt our bare arms and faces.

Towering high above us were tremendous rocks of all shapes, sometimes coming down sheer into the water from hundreds of feet and sometimes ending up in little pebbly beaches with surrounding silver birch trees. It was a magnificent sight.

The high cliffs in the Gorges du Tarn.

At the end of the five mile journey, the men rode back to the kiosk on their bicycles while the boat was picked up by a man and his horse and cart.

We sat by the water for a bit and paddled, and then, conscious of the time and our need to connect with the bus to Millau, we walked another four miles to Les Vignes. There we found that everyone had different ideas about what time the bus left, and in the end, we had to wait over an hour for it. When it arrived, there was our luggage stowed upon it and we felt very elated since we could hardly believe that everything could go sufficiently smoothly for it to be there. The driver was obviously in a hurry and we had a hectic journey down a dangerous road. At Le Rozier, a group got in amid much cheering and waving, and they and their friends sang lustily for the rest of their journey.

We did not arrive at Millau until mid-evening, when of course, all the hotels were full. We left our luggage at a particularly grand hotel located next to the station and walked around rather disconsolately until, in despair, we asked if there was a convent. We were directed to the Couvent de Saint Maria, but our informant did not think that they took people in. We did not despair, however, and rang the bell, having first walked past the door since Helen felt sure it was a brothel and not a convent. A sweet little Spanish nun came to the door and she said she would go and ask *Ma Mère*[18]. Luckily, she was willing for us to stay, but then came the question of an evening meal. Since we were both hungry and it was nearing nine o'clock, the time that the convent doors would be shut, Helen said that we had various tidbits, and if we could be given some bread to add to our small supplies, we would be very grateful. So we were taken to the basement to a very nice clean kitchen where we were given some bread and water. We rummaged in our rucksack and brought out a tin of *pâté de foie gras*, some radishes, and the everlasting butter, and with sponge bags and hairbrushes scattered around us on the floor, we set to with a will. Initially, the nuns stood outside the door and peeped at us, but soon they came in and stood around and asked who we were and from where we had come. We were then escorted upstairs to an enormous room with thirty-four beds, in two lines down each side. We were offered two beds, a quarter of the way down one of the lines; some nice clean sheets were produced, and we were asked if we liked air. When we said we did, the window shutters were thrown open and we were advised to sleep at the other end of the bed so as not to be in a draught. Four nuns stood and watched us make our beds, asking more questions, and I got slightly involved in explaining that I worked at the BBC because they had not heard of anything so worldly.

At the end of the room were two very comfortable-looking beds with spring mattresses, pillows and quilts. White curtains were drawn back at each side of the beds and there were two similar ones further down the room. We thought they must be occupied by the prefects during term time, but to our amazement four nuns went to bed in them wearing white cotton nighties and white cotton caps. They giggled behind their curtains, talked about the *jeunes filles*[19], and left their heavy black robes, lined with men's shirting, hanging on pegs outside the curtains. At the top end of the room were a row of basins with running water, and when I went to wash, there was a nun stepping out of her blacks, so I looked straight ahead and she popped behind her curtains leaving her skirts on the floor. Also at the top end was

18 My Mother (Mother Superior, nun).

19 Young girls.

a cupboard—which Helen accidentally locked herself into. All four nuns offered advice from behind their curtains which I didn't understand and Helen didn't hear. Fortunately, we managed to get her out with much fiddling with the lock. Finally, we didn't know who should turn out the light, so Helen advanced down the room, but out popped a nun who said that she would do it. She then said something to us and I, not understanding, said, '*C'est bien*'[20], and on went the light again. We realised shortly afterwards that she must have said, 'Would you like the light on all night?', so once again Helen advanced down the room, this time saying, '*Ma soeur...*'[21], and after much explaining, put the light out.

To our amazement, despite the Feast of the Assumption, the nuns did not rise very early. In fact, one was still snoring when we got up at a quarter past seven. We decided that it would not be 'the thing' to have a really good wash in a nunnery, so I did a very decent scrub under my nightie. In the middle of this, the nun who had let us in the night before came along and asked if we were going to Mass. I was slightly taken aback by this and got around it by saying that I would ask my friend. We decided that perhaps we had better go and so got dressed and put scarves on our heads and proceeded to the chapel, but the late rising nun appeared at that moment and led us downstairs and out the front door. Feeling slightly relieved, we went and had breakfast instead.

Due to the Feast, there was no bread anywhere, everything was shut, including, to our horror, the banks. After a certain amount of rushing around the town, we came upon a man on a street corner who thought he might be able to find a pal who would cash a sterling pound for us. This eventually fell through as the man in question was out, but in the meantime we discovered that we had sufficient funds to travel on to Beziers on the mid morning train. We then tore back to the convent, and feeling absolutely sacrilegious, called *Ma Mère* out of Mass to pay her and to explain our speedy departure instead of staying there a second night as we had intended. We then collected some lunch and caught the train.

We arrived at our destination at about one o'clock. There was a very nice-looking hotel next to the station with a balcony overlooking the station approach, and so we went in and were given a room with hot water and a French window looking out onto the station itself. We had a wonderful wash, both of ourselves and our clothes, in the first hot water we'd had

20 'It is well'.

21 'My sister...'

since our bath at Clermont, and then lay exhausted on our beds as the heat was terrific so far south.

Later, after the day had cooled to a simmering temperature, we wandered up the town and found a lovely cathedral built on a hill overlooking the river and a wonderful view away to the sea. We decided, at this point, that we wanted to go to the Mediterranean, and later when we returned to the hotel, we had discussions with Monsieur about hotels located on the seaside. He finally persuaded us to stay at Beziers and take the bus to Valras-Plage, five miles away each day. All this was rather a strain, so we went to bed and replanned the last week of our trip a few more times. We found our room a bit noisy, and for most of the night we were disturbed either by cows bellowing or by the voice on the station's loudspeaker saying, '*Ici Beziers! Ici Beziers!*'[22]

The following day, we gathered together some lunch, bought ourselves a pair of espadrilles[23] each, and eventually caught the lunchtime bus for Valras. It was very full, but the journey only took twenty minutes. Soon we were falling into the blue sea; it was perfect heaven. The heat was awful and we were careful not to get too burnt, but despite our efforts, we suffered a good deal by the evening. We caught the last bus back and felt quite whacked by the heat.

We were up much earlier the next morning, but narrowly caught the nine o'clock bus. There was a fete being held at Valras and the bus was packed tight. On arrival at our destination, we bought ourselves sun hats and our usual bottle of white wine for one franc, and then spent our time in and out of the sea until noon. Learning from experience, we did not sit for one moment in the sun without something over our shoulders and backs. Soon a mistral had started up and blew sand everywhere, so we made our way to the lighthouse for lunch. We were much bemused by a mother and her small son who came and sat near us and proceeded to eat cold mashed potatoes and cabbage, followed by sardines onto which they added large dollops of butter.

Descending again to the beach, we found that the mistral had—as was its habit—become rather bad, whipping sand around the exposed parts of our bodies and making us

22 'This is Beziers! This is Beziers!'

23 Espadrilles are casual sandals that originated in the South of France. They are often made of canvas or cotton fabric with a sole made of rope.

yearn to be away from its presence. So we raced back to the village and bought ourselves a double ice-cream cornet followed by a glass of lemonade each as a means of passing the time until the return bus arrived. It was so hot waiting in the square that I felt quite sick by the time I got into the bus, but Helen's smelling salts soon revived me.

Poor Helen suffered all night from her sunburnt back, so we were up quite early the next day and visited our usual shop for our picnic lunch. We both felt that we had had enough of the sea by this time and had no desire to go back to Valras. We decided to move on to Perpignan and had a lovely trip in a diesel car through extraordinary country, rather like we imagined Palestine to be—great rocky hills coming down to sandy scrub land with little vegetation and then large blue lagoons over which the railway went, either on narrow tongues of land or on viaducts.

Arriving at Perpignan, we started another hotel hunt. Everything around the station was full, but eventually we managed to find accommodation at a very grand hotel just off the main square and beside the canal. It was a very old-fashioned place with enormous aspidistras in the dining-room. The rooms were built around two wells, one housed the dining-room and the other the smoking room. Each landing consisted of a balcony with iron balustrade from which you could look down on the diners below or up to a glass roof above. Some of the rooms even had windows out onto the balcony as their only means of ventilation. We were on the third floor and had a window looking out onto the canal. As we already consumed our picnic lunch, we went out and found a small café where we sat outside and drank beer and ate croissants. We then caught a tram back to the station and collected our luggage and returned to the hotel for our usual siesta. Later, we set forth in search of the *Syndicat*[24] to organise a trip into Spain, but it was closed. A funny little man appeared and sent us to the top of the old tower, all 139 steps! We thought it was all to do with finding the man in charge of the *Syndicat*, but it was, I think, only to occupy us while we waited. When we returned, there was still no sign of life in the *Syndicat*, so we went and had a drink. Helen fell for the gendarme on point duty who was most concerned lest we should think that all the French were as vague as the man in the *Syndicat*; he assured us that it was the Spanish influence! He directed us to the *Palais Consulaire*[25] and there we found a rather

---

24 Office of Tourism.

25 Consular Office.

useless subsidiary *syndicat* where they said there were no excursions to Spain until Tuesday. So, sadly, we decided that the only alternative was to take ourselves by train to the frontier and look at the Spanish coastline, if nothing else.

We returned to the hotel for dinner and had a superb meal of soup, croquettes, roast veal, tomatoes and haricot beans, followed by coffee ices. Helen shocked the staid inhabitants by whistling down at me from our third floor balcony when she went up to fetch a hanky at the beginning of the meal, and we were much amused by a resplendent white-haired lady who talked at great length in French with a strong American accent.

After our meal, we went and saw *Vie passionnée des soeurs Brontë*[26] for one franc. We giggled a lot over the Warner Bros idea of the Brontës and the strange effect of French in amongst the Yorkshire Dales. After the film, we sat in the central square under the palm and mimosa trees, drank orangeade and thought how different it all was to England.

We set out the following day by train for Cerbere and had a lovely run down the coast through Collioure, Banyuls and Port-Vendres. As we approached Cerbere, Helen started talking to a man in the corridor who finally said that after he had completed a *petit commission*[27] he would be most delighted to escort us up the hill to the frontier post. First, he gave us black coffee in the station buffet lounge; next he went off to carry out his task, and then off we went. We started up rather a rough road with stone walls on both sides and steps at intervals leading up to the shops. Our escort explained that this was the bed of the river, but in summer it was always dry and used as a road.

We soon left the town and started climbing up the hillside which we found to be rough going in our espadrilles, but Monsieur carried some of our luggage and we talked in French all the way.

On arrival at the French frontier, Monsieur persuaded the guard to let us through, but they were quite strict and demanded to see our passports. We were told we could go into No Man's Land, but Monsieur walked us up to the Spanish Customs where we stood shivering on our side of the rope while he went in and saw the guards. Suddenly there was a flashing of white teeth and a great deal of bowing and waving and we advanced into Spain. They said we could walk thirty metres down the road from where we could see Portbou, the first

---

26 *The Passionate Life of the Brontë Sisters.* Released in English-speaking countries as *Devotion.*

27 Small errand.

Spanish town. We took some photos, but hastily had to hide the camera when a car was seen coming up the zigzag road. The guards were most friendly and insisted on having their photos taken with us; one of them gave me his address in order that I might send him a copy of the photo[28] and we all parted very amicably. Monsieur then walked us out onto a promontory from where we had a lovely panoramic view of the coast and its wonderful blue sea. Without a rest, we were rushed down to the town again and given aperitifs and then, much against his will, we insisted on eating our picnic on the beach and bathing, so he went off to the station buffet for his lunch. He was soon back, however, and before long was plying us with more drinks and hinting that he would get off the train at Perpignan on the way home, since he was in no hurry to get back to Narbonne where he was staying with his mother. We then nearly missed the train and had to run up a steep incline to the station with Monsieur well in front, calling out to us to hurry and Helen and I panting, 'Oh, Monsieur!' at intervals.

Once on the train, we shared a carriage with rather a charming couple and their five month-old son. The wife was Spanish and the baby was all grins and appeared to be very intelligent for his age. There were no formalities like nappies or knickers, and there was plenty of breast milk when necessary. We were somewhat tremulous as to their chances of remaining dry as the baby was bandied about from one to the other, however all was well. At Perpignan, we all descended from the train and as Monsieur assured us his train wasn't until late, we could have yet another drink. He lost his ticket coming out of the station and we stood outside the barrier and he inside, while we exclaimed, '*Oh, c'est terrible*'[29] a great deal and hoped that the ticket collector would have compassion for him. Fortunately, he soon found it again and rejoined us on the right side of the barrier. Monsieur said, looking very disgruntled, that they were not like that in France.

After more drinks, he walked with us to the hotel and we invited him to dinner, but he insisted on paying for his own meal. Periodically, we had to revert to *les petits designs*[30].

---

28 Unfortunately, the film was found to be missing upon our return, so we were unable to send him a copy.

29 'Oh, it's terrible'.

30 Small drawings.

Helen's sketch book was full of strange scribbles from turkeys to vegetable marrows. These drawings amused the people at the next table to no end.

After dinner, we went out to see some gardens, but they were closed, and as it was now dark and Monsieur had become somewhat flirtatious towards me, I was quite pleased. Instead, we stood beside the canal and had a lesson in the stars. Helen suddenly said, in a mellow voice, '*Voilà le passage du lait.*'[31] (I have always thought of that description since.) We walked back to the town square where we had yet more drink and then we had to walk to the station and wave Monsieur goodbye on his eleven o'clock train.

We were up early the next day, our need for two croissants made us have breakfast in one of the cafés in the town instead of the hotel, and then we caught the train for Narbonne. After a hastily eaten lunch in Narbonne, we then continued on to Toulouse on a very full train, standing for part of the way. Alighting from the train in Toulouse, we then became a little agitated about finding how we were to get to Albi, but eventually a kind man directed us to a train and told us to change at Tessoni'ere.

We finally reached Albi in the late afternoon and bespoke a room in the hotel, which was very modern and grand, but wondered what we would be charged as it displayed no prices on the door as other hotels were apt to do.

We went out for a short stroll before dinner and found a cobbler who mended the sole of my shoe, and then we had an aperitif followed by a wonderful meal. Feeling distinctly mellow, we wandered down to the cathedral which was a weird looking building, more like a fortified castle, but with terrific proportions.

The next day dawned very hot, and after spending the morning discovering all that Albi had to offer, we paid our expensive hotel bill (there was a reason for no prices on the door) and caught a bus to Rodez in the cool of the evening. After an excellent dinner, we walked down to the bus stop to make enquiries about our journey to Clermont the following day. To our horror, we found that the banks did not open in Rodez on a Monday and we were penniless. Madame rang the gendarmerie at Severac to find out whether they could help us, but we paid largely for giggles and in the end discovered nothing. Finally, we were introduced to a man who said he was the Rodez representative for the Banque de France and told us that our only hope was to go back to Millau as that was the only town in this area where the

31 'There is the passage of milk.' She had meant to say, 'There is the Milky Way.'

banks opened on a Monday. So we brazenly asked the hotel to trust us, and we caught the first bus to Millau the next morning.

Albi Cathedral and Palais de la Berbie seen from Pont Vieux.

It was a chilly start from Rodez, the only place in our holiday which we never saw. We arrived at Millau and stopped opposite a bank which was open, so with money in our pockets again, we had coffee and cake before going to the *Bureau de Poste*[32] and sending off the money for our hotel bill in Rodez. We didn't want to stay in Millau again, so we caught a train to Saint-Flour which ended up being a terribly hot and boring five hour journey.

Upon arrival, we ordered an early dinner and then went to catch yet another train back to Clermont. By this time it was cooler and we managed to get a carriage without too many other travellers, but apparently it was reserved and we were told to find another at the next stop, despite all the others being full to overflowing. Finding the least full, we settled down on our bags in the corridor, slightly worried by the only drunk we had seen in France, who was lurching up and down. Eventually, we were offered two seats in a carriage full of very jolly people who were travelling through the night to Paris. We produced a lemon which they squeezed into a cup by hand and they all had lemonade and were even jollier. One of the women had been in Paris throughout the Occupation and was full of stories of how they downed the Germans at every possible opportunity. We did not get to Clermont until late in the night and it was very pleasant to cross the road to the hotel and be welcomed as old customers.

32 Post Office.

We were up betimes the next morning and went out on our great shopping expedition; we had been looking forward to it all throughout our holiday as we had been told of the wonderful bargains that were to be had in this city. We both bought a considerable amount of merchandise—stockings, bags, gloves and various oddments—all at bargain prices.

Our train for Paris left at lunchtime, and to our horror, we found it full and so again settled in the corridor. With great relief we were told that extra coaches would be put on at Vichy, and as we were covered with soot from being next to the engine, we were very glad. In fact, we obtained seats first in an extra coach at Riom, but moved again at Vichy, and thereafter had a good journey through to Paris where we arrived with the beginning of rain.

After depositing our luggage and having a slight and unsuccessful hunt for the Thomas Cook representative, we went and had a beer before setting out on a terrific sight-seeing tour in the pouring rain. We were shown the Avenue de l'Opéra and the Palais Garnier; the state theatre of France, Comédie-Française; the Basilique du Sacré-Cœur, La Madeleine, where fashion meant more than religion; and finally, in an absolute deluge with thunder and lightning all around, the Place de la Concorde and the Champs-Élysées.

Quite drenched, we returned to the Avenue de l'Opéra by the Métro and had dinner at Le Rally, a wonderful restaurant in the area. It was an excellent meal and took most of our remaining money. By the time we emerged, the rain had stopped, but we were running late and so had to catch a taxi back to the *Gare du Nord*[33]. We collected our luggage, found the Thomas Cook representative with our tickets, spent the last of our money on two bananas and proceeded on our way back to Dunkirk via the half past nine train. After an unbelievably calm crossing to Dover, our tour of France as per *Travels with a Donkey in the Cévennes* had come to an end, and Helen, making a beeline for the scales at Victoria Station, found that she had lost a pound!

33 Northern station.

Paris
FRANCE
Toulouse
Narbonne
Perpignan
Port-Vendres
Cerbere
Portbou
SPAIN
Girona
Palafrugell
Begur
Callela
Barcelona
Sóller
Cas Catala
Palma

World on Wheels

1951: Spain

Shortly after our return from France, my life then took a turn for the worse. My father who had been ill for some time, died on 30th August 1949 and I was so sorry that I hadn't been able to spend more time with him in the last few months of his life. He was sixty-two years old. Fortunately, I was kept busy at work during this time of grieving, assisting with the many and varied activities involved in producing The Children's Hour *radio broadcast.*

In 1951, Helen and I decided that another trip would be amusing. We wasted no time in organising a tour of Spain after we read that the restrictions on travel to this country, which had been in place since the war, were to be lifted. Helen, a keen horticulturalist, had also read much about Spain's native plants and promptly organised a licence from the Ministry of Agriculture and Fisheries to enable her to bring some specimens home. So, despite the small currency allocation and our complete lack of knowledge of the language, we were very enthusiastic. I think our families wondered if they'd ever see us again!

After spending considerable time choosing the route we were to travel, the evening prior to departure quickly arrived and found Molly and I opening the door of our flat in South Kensington to Helen, who arrived laden with rucksack, suitcase and paper carrier bags. Consequently, the evening was spent in a turmoil of sorting and eliminating, and remembering lost treasures. Eventually, we went to bed somewhere near midnight, all three of us pretty exhausted. The next morning was hectic; there was a frightful rush to get food ready for the journey, and Helen, after seeing the 'Portable Porter' wheels attached to my case, decided that she also needed some so that we could save on tipping the porters at the station. Sure enough, we soon got into the taxi and set off amid a mixture of gaiety and trepidation.

We found the train with little difficulty and then went to a nearby pharmacy to purchase our last minute needs, one of which was insect powder. Helen asked the assistant if it was all right to take Kwells that were two years old and she replied, 'I don't think they advise it for children.' Whereupon Helen said, 'But I'm not a child,' before realising that the assistant thought she wanted to give them to her two year-old child!

We finally boarded the train and found that some people did not take up their seats in the carriage next to ours, so we were able to move in there and share it with two girls from Thame who were on their way to St Raphael. The journey passed in delightful camaraderie.

We did not have much luck with Helen's Portable Porter. As soon as we got out at Newhaven, the wheels fell off her case, but despite this setback we were two of the first on the boat and we did our trick of getting our seats and then getting our landing tickets before everyone else had the same idea.

A dapper Frenchman admired our Portable Porters and took the address of the manufacturer, and then a herd of guider cadets with a gaggle of intense and responsible looking dames appeared and kept us amused for much of the crossing, which was perfectly calm, despite our fears. We ate some sandwiches and felt no unpleasant motion in the boat or in our stomachs. We landed safely on French soil and bumped our little wheels over the railway lines to the train, but could not find our coach and asked a porter who, before we had time to realise it, whisked our luggage from us and tore off down the train, so we didn't save a tip in the end.

We had nice corner seats in this train and the two and a half hours to Paris went quite quickly. On arrival, we got on the Métro, getting hotter and hotter as we walked from one station to the other, in tunnels and up and down flights of stairs. We had to change at the *République*[34] and then finally reached the *Gare d'Austerlitz* in the early evening.

Parking our luggage, we went off to the station restaurant where we, of course, sat at a table reserved for someone else. However, after much gabble on behalf of the waiter, he moved us to the middle of the room and served us very quickly with a meal consisting of soup, two boiled eggs each and new potatoes in a pink sauce, and a large banana. We had red wine and black coffee, and feeling much revived after our repast, went to collect

34 A station of the Paris Métro.

our luggage. Pulling it happily along to the train, we found our third-class corner seats in a carriage already occupied by a French family consisting of a husband, wife, grown-up son and a third man, and a large and imposing Dutch lady and her rather younger looking husband. She had grey hair piled into a high bun and was wearing a handmade knitted, long-sleeved grey wool frock, a little yellow straw boater and white shoes. When we arrived, she was sewing buttons onto a matching grey cardigan that she must have finished on the earlier part of the journey. Our suitcases with their wheels caused a little disturbance as fitting them onto the rack was rather difficult, but all was soon well and we set off in the pouring rain.

Gradually, we all settled for the night. The French family surrounded themselves with innumerable bottles of wine—some of which had to be mixed together—amid much loud chatter, then two of the men put on new rubber-soled canvas shoes. We put on our slippers, while the Dutch lady—who was already asleep—continued to sit bolt upright, her mouth dropping open as she slept. Her husband lent across the carriage and put his arms on her knees and his head on his arms. The light was put out, the blinds pulled down, all air was eliminated and we all started to snore. I had indigestion, but otherwise all was well. Suddenly, in the early hours of the morning, the whole carriage leapt to life, as if by arrangement. The light went on and the French family produced a small pillowcase filled with bread and began a large meal; the Dutch lady produced rolls and pâté from her hag's bag, so we followed suit, but somehow we could not make ourselves start on the bacon and egg pie, so it continued to sit on the rack and we finished the sandwiches.

In due course, the light was put out again and we settled down again, but sleep was more spasmodic, so at six o'clock, Helen and I got up to have a look at the day and we were amazed at the scenes in the next carriages. One side had a real Henry Moore[35] group with bodies and arms looped and spread all over each other in fantastic positions; the other side was a family with about four children, one of them slung in a hammock between the racks.

---

35 Henry Spencer Moore OM CH was a British artist and sculptor who was best known for his abstract monumental bronzes. The subjects were usually abstractions of the human figure that are pierced or contain hollow voids.

We had breakfast after we had seen Carcasonne. Then came Narbonne and the lovely run through the Palestine-like country around Perpignan, and so down to Cerbere. Here, they came down the train for passports and we were then shunted through a tunnel with no lights in the train or in the tunnel (for a reason I wonder?) into Portbou. Here, chaos broke out. We all had to get out of the train and were lined up at a certain spot on the platform and told to wait. We then moved forward into a solid jam by the door into Customs. After about half an hour, we made our way in. The number of forms we had to complete, the number of pigeon holes we had to visit, and the number of stamps put on us and our luggage was quite fantastic. Our luggage had to be opened before the Customs officials would come near us and then a blasé young man thrust his hands into my suitcase and pinched and pulled at the parcel containing my espadrilles. Hot and bothered, we went to the next room where we had to see a man who gave us a form in exchange for our ticket and then to another who gave us an ordinary ticket in exchange for that form.

At last we boarded the train again only to find our seats occupied, and one of them without even a reserved label on it. Having been told how the public in France think nothing of pulling the reserved tickets off seats and feeling that it was a bit hard that we shouldn't have our second-class seats when we had at last reached that stage of the journey, we consulted an official who told us in voluble Spanish that those were our seats and left us to get on with it. We stood and looked on while the inmates of the carriage had a heated discussion and eventually, feeling distinctly embarrassed, we sat down in two seats, only to find ourselves next to the worst possible type of young English girl in a lace hat. Helen said she felt me freeze, and I did too! Fortunately, there was a nice vivacious Dutch girl sitting opposite me, travelling with two young men, and a charming señor who sat in the opposite corner of the carriage and who spoke good French.

At last we tackled the bacon and egg pie, feeling that this grand second-class carriage, with the valances around the seats, was not quite the right place for picnicking. We could see the brilliant sunshine and the strong wind outside as we started off across our small area of Spain, feeling thrilled and excited. We passed through Girona with its cathedral and lovely old houses on the riverside, and then to Caldes de Malavella where we descended from the train in a cloud of dust into the arms of two surprised porters. They were much amused, as they could speak nothing but Catalan Spanish, and we, only smatterings of Castilian! Fortunately, we found one man in the booking office who could speak a little

French and we learned from him that the bus would be leaving in an hour and a half and not at the time on our schedule. We only had fifty pesetas with which to tip the porters, so had to get change, which Helen succeeded in doing. First the porters put us and our luggage in the full sun outside the station, explaining that although that was the bus parked close by, it was not permitted to enter it (because the driver was asleep inside, I wonder?). We made them understand that we did not want to stand there for an hour and a half, and asked if our luggage could be left in the station. Once again, with much smiling, we all trailed off and having left the cases inside the booking hall, the porters were most anxious that we should go with them and drink in the only other building nearby, a café just opposite, to which everyone was heading until the arrival of the next train. We thought better of it and decided to walk up the long straight road edged with trees to the village. We were pleased that we did as we found that the trees held the loveliest birds, singing just like nightingales, and Caldes itself was a charming little place in the middle of nowhere with wet sandy, unmade roads and the loveliest flowers. All the way from the frontier, the flowers had been beautiful and the picture made with their stunning colours depicted against the greens of the Cyprus trees, olives, and vines, and then, behind it all, the snow-capped Pyrenees, made one feel like they were in a different world.

Having looked at the collection of houses making up Caldes, I suddenly realised that I didn't have the folder with all our hotel coupons and our return tickets. I checked with Helen only to find that she didn't have the folder either. Knowing that we had shown it to the porters and to the man at the station, I felt hot and cold alternately. Boosting ourselves up with the reports that Spanish people were scrupulously honest, we hurried back to the station—two rather silent and forlorn looking travellers—only to find the folder sitting happily on top of our suitcases in the station with only a solitary traveller roaming around. We did a slight reorganisation of the contents of the rucksack and hag's bag and then went and sat on a porter's truck in the shade outside the station to wait for the bus.

In due course, we gathered up our luggage and stood near the bus. The driver of a ramshackle taxi—whose services we had refused upon our arrival and who appeared to bear us no malice—came over and talked to us in a mixture of French and Spanish. Helen's home-concocted phrase book and my dictionary came out and we discussed a varied collection of subjects: nightingales, exhibits at the Ashmolean, places to see, and of course, the Spanish for many different words.

Soon we were allowed to board the bus, along with another man. Our luggage was hurled on top and I remembered too late that I had not locked my case after opening it at Customs. Starting on our way, my interest was taken by the overweight bus driver and his driving skills. The steering wheel of the bus looked as though it was hardly fixed to the bus, but was in a long slit of about two or three feet in length, thus giving the wheel plenty of room for sideways movement. We rattled and crashed along the so-called road for a good many miles, and I saw (in my mind's eye) my case flying open and its contents scattering on the track behind us, unbeknownst to anyone. We continued on up perilous inclines (for the bus—we weren't at all sure if it would make it) and passed more lovely flowers: pale lemon hawkweed, little white roses and brilliant blue anchusa. There were also palm trees, tamarisk in flower, trees like white laburnum, and I think we saw some lemon trees. It was a lovely drive; we saw the coast with its brilliant blue sea and white sand, and then the wooded country and the undulating farmland with corn growing, and in places, the hay cut.

We arrived at Palafrugell at about six o'clock; a clean little town with cream-coloured houses and rough roads of the same colour. We started down the street pulling our suitcases behind us on their little wheels, not knowing where the hotel was until a nice man who spoke French—he was the local chemist—took pity on us and said he would show us the way. He stopped at his shop to tell his wife what he was doing and on we went. Arriving at the hotel, he rushed inside and asked one of the maids to assist us, but she could only speak Spanish. After a lengthy conversation with her, involving much gesticulating, he explained to us that the manager of the hotel would be in shortly and that he would be able to assist us. The smiling maid showed us up to a nice little room, which was clean and very simple, with a tiled floor and a balcony overlooking a small side street. There was cold running water and the tap was so placed that it flowed over the soap. We tried to ask her for a bathtub and were shown a shower first and then a double-bedded room with bath behind a curtain, so as it was all a little involved, we returned to our room to await the arrival of Señor.

The Palafrugell coastline.

He soon appeared, the maid knocking at our door while he stood a little distance down the passage. He was young and smiling, and when we explained what we were after, he told the maid that we wanted a *baño general*[36]. He then showed us into a vast bathroom with a mauve bath and basin, a bright orange and yellow floor with a black pattern, green tiles around the walls with relief figures of large bosomed females carrying pitchers on their shoulders, and red, yellow and green glass windows and door. The maid was sent for two enormous bath towels, which were hung over the rails on either side of the basin and all was set, but the water was practically stone cold!

After having reduced our room to a state of chaos and disorder with dripping travelling clothes, washed in Lux and cold water, draped about the place, we retired to bed to await the evening meal which, we were told, was to be served at nine o'clock. Wondering at the lateness of the meal, it was explained that it was the custom in Spain to have a light continental breakfast, followed by a large lunch at around two o'clock—this constituted the main meal of the day, tapas (similar to appetizers) after their early evening stroll and then a large dinner at nine o'clock. Being unused to this timetable, our stomachs were soon grumbling, so we decided to eat a little more bacon and egg pie to stave off the hunger pangs and then lay listening to the babble of Spanish in the street as the townspeople took their evening walk.

Just before our meal, we went down to be greeted by Señor who helped us fill in all the registration forms and then planned our four-day visit for us! He produced a large book with very bad photos of the surrounding countryside and all three of us went into the restaurant, poring over the pages. Having decided the next day's activities would involve breakfast in bed and a lazy morning followed by a walk in the early evening, we settled down to an excellent meal consisting of a bowl of soup, fish beautifully grilled in oil and piping hot, followed by peaches and petits fours, and a bottle of red wine. By this time it was half past nine and Señor told us that he had someone at the desk who spoke English, so we were taken to meet a wonderful old man of about seventy who spoke English with a ghastly accent (he said he learnt English in New York). He, too, laid down the law as to how we were to spend our days and when we persuaded him that we preferred walking instead of travelling by taxi, he said, 'Flat heeled shoes, none of these high heels. No flip-flap, flip-flap.'

---

36 Bath.

He then proceeded to demonstrate by waving his hands up and down. Then he asked—or so we thought—if we knew of Tutankhamen. We said, 'Yes,' to which he quickly responded, slapping me jovially on the arm at intervals, 'His wife lives here,' pointing at one of the many headlands along the coast. This reduced me to giggles, although I knew he must not see my mirth. Matters became worse when he went on to say that the head of the British Zone of Germany visited the 'maison' a lot during last winter in his '4,000 litre' car which was well-known in Palafrugell. We were then told of an English author who lived in the town and who was a member of 'The Labourist Party' and so could presumably have returned to England in comfort (one gathered that it was pretty hot for the conservatives!), but alas, this was not possible because he had two wives! After greatly diverting us with a bit more of his conversation, the old boy then went home to fetch us an old prospectus for the district and returned with apologies for the delay due to the fact that his daughter made him put on a thicker coat.

By the end of these proceedings, we were absolutely exhausted. We felt, despite his rather amusing but often unintelligible conversation, that his knowledge of the area was extensive and the places he described to us as *necesario*[37] to visit we were very keen to discover. This, coupled with his somewhat assertive nature, made us think that we should not dare face him again unless we had done exactly what he had told us to do!

Eventually getting away as it was nearing eleven o'clock, we bid each gentleman goodnight, with Señor promising to arrange for us to have breakfast in bed at nine o'clock the next morning.

We awoke to a glorious morning and breakfast arrived, in true Spanish style, at half past nine. We lazed away until late morning when we managed to stagger downstairs. Having said lengthy good mornings to Señor, we went out for a walk and wandered past the cork factory (the main industry of the town), up into some lovely olive groves and wild scrubland covered with masses of mauve and white guelder rose. It was hot, but a nice breeze kept us cool.

We intended to rest after our large lunch, but our room was still being cleaned, so we went for a stroll and met the chemist who had taken us to the hotel. He escorted us into his darkened shop (the shops shut between one and four o'clock in Spain for siesta) and

---

37 Necessary.

showed us some wonderful old Pitmans English Grammar books. He then took us into his dispensary at the back of the shop where he showed us his English wares and then presented us with a bottle of Ponds extract, for which we insisted on paying ten pesetas. His wife then appeared, a dear lady dressed in black, with greying hair pulled back into a bun. I made some polite remark about the photo of their daughter and we proceeded to converse in halting Spanish, and rather better French, for quite some time. It was surprising how much we could do even without knowing much of the language. Finally, the chemist poured eau de cologne into our hands to sample, and kissing our hands in Spanish fashion, he bade us *adiós*.

Still feeling rather affected by our bottle of wine at lunch, we walked slowly back to the hotel and to our beds and sank into a deep sleep, awaking refreshed in the cool of the late afternoon. Following the directions given by the old man of the night before, we set out for Llafranc and Callela, a pleasant walk along a dusty road through farmland with picturesque views of the surrounding hills and the banks ablaze of red poppies. Every now and then, there were the straight rows of four or five trees which were very characteristic of Spain.

The countryside was ablaze with red poppies.

At Llafranc, we bought an iced drink—it was supposed to be lemonade, but the lemon was not evident—in a spotlessly clean hotel on the beach, while a girl of about ten in a black frock sat on the staircase and stared at us through the wrought iron banisters. We then carried out the old man's instructions and found a dream of a path up above the sea going out to the point. The small fir trees were full of birds that resembled nightingales (the hotel proprietor and the taxi driver at Caldes were very firm in saying that they were not nightingales but a special Catalan bird) and the ground was a mass of small yellow broom and big clumps of white flowers that looked rather like gypsophila at a distance. There was honeysuckle too, growing low on the ground, a sea variety with a lovely scent. A very grand house on the point showed a wonderful garden of cacti of every sort, in particular, a creeping species with pretty pink and white flowers.

We retraced our steps back to the little bay of Llafranc and indulged in a delicious cool paddle, and then we moved on around the southern side of the bay and found another delightful path. This brought us to a most magnificent residence with palm trees and masses of geraniums in full bloom, and its own flagstaff and sea water bathing pool below the cliff. Upon viewing this beautiful home, we immediately thought of our assertive tour guide of the night before and suspected that this must be where Tutankhamen's wife lived, but we couldn't be quite certain! We continued on our stroll and found ourselves in Calella, a dream of a seaside fishing village, with old houses right down on the beach and groups of bronzed men sitting on their haunches on the sand attending to their nets or boats. Some of the boats had two or even three enormous lamps—very much like the ones that hang out over the street on a long arm in London—used to attract the fish.

Back at the hotel, we found it was nearing nine o'clock and two hungry damsels took their places in the dining-room. There was a couple already there when we arrived, and then during the meal about half a dozen men came in. They rushed in through the door with a terrific clatter, tore down the long room, washed their hands at a basin in one corner and then hurried to the wireless and put it on before making their way to a table. After listening to this program for a short time, someone else went up and changed it to another; this time it was dance music of a decidedly ancient variety. Later, during our meal Señor came to our table to chat and learned that I worked at the BBC. He then asked if I would I like to find my station on the wireless. Having assured him I was on holiday from radio, he then asked if I would like the wireless turned off.

We had a wonderful meal, learning the names for everything we ate from the waitress who could only speak Catalan Spanish. Soon, four handsome Spaniards came and sat at the next table to ours and one of them in particular, stared at us. When we at last got up to go, he asked, 'Aren't you going to stay and dance?' We rather wished we could as they were ever so handsome and charming, but we really felt rather exhausted, so we chatted for a bit about the coast and how we should get to Fornells tomorrow and then we left them with much bowing and smiles.

Another lovely day dawned and our breakfast arrived in the same belated fashion as the day before. It took us rather a long time to get up and organise ourselves and the room, and we didn't arrive downstairs until nearly eleven o'clock. We then had a chat with Señor, who took us over the road to show us the post box in a stationer's shop. By this time, a little fair-haired maid returned with the fruit and we were given two paper carrier bags, with 'Hotel Nuevo' in large letters on the outside, filled with food, knives, beakers for the large bottle of wine sticking out of one and dimity blue napkins. With the rucksack already weighing a ton and carrying items for bathing and painting, books and numerous other items, including the remains of the bacon and egg pie, we set off with an adiós from Señor and the interested stares of various kitchen staff.

It was a lovely road to Fornells, first winding through lush countryside and then climbing up between wooded hills on one side and a sheer drop down the hillside on the other. The sun was hot, but for most of the way there was a pleasant breeze. We passed a little procession of a dog, followed by a mule pulling a small farm cart with latticed sides and a rope floor, and lying in the bottom, rather as though in a hammock, was a man having a siesta while his mule gently pulled him home. Again, the place was a mass of lovely flowers and the roadside was almost white with guelder roses.

We had lunch on the edge of a track looking down at Fornells, and beyond, a lovely little cove called Aigua Blava which attracted us for our bathe. What a lunch! We had great slabs of bread with a whole omelette and ham inside and then another vast sandwich with a slab of cold meat and the bread saturated with a tomato-based sauce. With that, we had the wine and two bananas and an orange each.

Aigua Blava Bay.

With our full stomachs and the heat affecting us, it wasn't long before we had stretched out under a large leafed tree to enjoy a short siesta. Enjoying the wonderful breeze coming off the sea, I lay dozing until I became aware of a tickling sensation on my leg. Believing it to be a leaf fallen from the tree, I reached down to remove it—slightly annoyed at being disturbed—only to find something considerably different. Jumping to my feet, I shook my skirt vigorously, at the same time kicking my legs out in all different directions in an effort to remove the offending object. Helen, looking rather amused, bid me to come to a standstill, when she then pulled a very thin little caterpillar from my skirt. I'm sure she wished she had brought a camera.

My sleepiness now gone, we wandered down through olive groves and more vast cacti to Fornells, a rather small place with large and sumptuous looking villas, belonging, we were told later by Señor, to famous doctors and eye specialists from Madrid. There was no promenade here, but little coves with pine covered rocks all around, and the sea unbelievably blue and green and so clear, that as we wound our way through the trees around to Aigua Blava, we could look right down through the water to the sand and seaweed.

We had two delightful bathes and had to be very strong minded about sitting too long in the sun. I lay with a cardigan around my shoulders and my knickers over my thighs—a pretty sight to see! We ate the meat out of the remaining sandwich from our lunch and sampled our long-hauled bacon and egg pie, but decided it was a little 'muy puy' ('muy puy' was our pet phrase at the time—*muy* meaning 'very' in Spanish and *puy* being our own make-up meaning 'middling'). I was on the point of parcelling it all up when a thin and wistful hound appeared unexpectedly and ate the lot.

We started the long climb back up the hills and found a sandy patch which, though very steep, did cut off a large loop of road. We collected some more wild flowers and Helen got a nice root of freesia, and then we climbed up the hill holding our skirts up around our waists and looking very unladylike, but it was nice and cool so what did it matter? We turned off onto the road to Begur and found it very hot and dusty, but again there was a short cut through the trees and also some heavenly views away over wooded hills.

Begur itself was not very prepossessing at first sight, but nearer to it became a charming old town clustered around a hill upon which stood the grey stone-ruins of a castle. We saw a tree with oranges on it and the buildings were all very Eastern looking with arches, balconies, palm trees and red tiled roofs. We went into the church that was lovely and very simple. The east end looked as though it might have been damaged in the Civil War and was all boarded up. The Stations of the Cross were in ivory relief, and again, their simplicity was pleasing. We asked two men the way back to Palafrugell and our efforts resulted in much giggling and drawing of maps, but we understood them and they were so polite and so handsome.

The town of Begur.

On the way home, a car passed us filled with what we thought were rather stuffy looking English people, but they returned later and the man in front looked quite pleasant. I suddenly felt I must say 'Hello,' to which he replied, 'Hello' too. Helen was, I think, quite horrified at my sudden display of 'English behaviour', but it just had to be. We then pursued a path across the fields and followed behind an old man with his flock of black goats, definitely muy puy, but rather charming.

Our last day in Palafrugell turned out to be a very leisurely day. We ordered breakfast for half past eight and for once it was punctual, so we were ready to set forth at ten o'clock. We were a bit delayed, first in the postcard shop opposite the hotel where the assistant was most friendly and chatty, and then at the wool shop where I bought some grey mending wool for my socks and where the old lady chatted away in a mixture of Spanish and French. At last we got away and we ambled out to Montras where Helen completed a sketch of the church and surrounding countryside, while I wrote a letter sitting on a gorse bush. We returned for a lunch of delicious hors d'oeuvres, *canaletos*[38] (my favourite dish), meat and vegetables and caramel custard; during the meal we learned numbers and vocabulary in Spanish.

We then set out for Tamariu. It was a lovely walk, once more along a dusty road cut out of the rock above the sea. On the road down to the little bay, we came upon a very poor family with four children living in a tent (of sorts) on the grass verge under the cliff face. Mother and father were scouring a waste heap of old tins on the hillside below the road, while the eldest child kept an eye on the younger children.

38 Batter rolls.

Tamariu was a delightful place with an open valley and a dear little beach with lots of fishing boats. We paddled and then drank fresh orange juice and Vichy water at a café on the shore. A Belgian party came and sat nearby and it was amusing hearing another tongue being spoken rather haltingly and carefully for the benefit of the Spanish fisherman who was to take them out fishing the next day.

The walk back up the hill in the cool of the evening was a joy, and when we were within earshot of the refuse heap, we could hear the poor family still hunting about. Helen said that perhaps if they looked long enough they'd find a pressure cooker. When the family came into sight, we found that the little boy was salvaging with his father, while two women were sitting by the tent, one boiling something in a saucepan and the other feeding her baby, quite unconcerned at our arrival. They were all dirty, but looked quite content.

As we tramped through a field near the outskirts of the village, Helen sat down, took our her drawing materials, and completed a very charming little sketch of the village and surrounds as a memento of our visit to this lovely district; it wasn't often that we justified the carrying of our drawing materials on these outings.

Arriving back in the village, we went to say *adiós* to the chemist as he had been so kind to us upon our arrival, but found only his wife as he was away in Barcelona. We shook hands and left messages for her husband.

The following morning we were up early to catch the bus to our next stop, Girona. We bade fond farewells to Señor, who handed me a foolscap envelope bulging with brochures on his hotel for our friends, and we took ourselves to the bus station. We boarded the bus to find it filled with some lovely country folk with whom we enjoyed conversing, but we all bumped and swerved and heaved along the badly-made road, and as I had spent the night previous feeling bilious, I was soon appreciating the benefits of those blessed with a stomach of iron.

Passing the time until the movement would stop, I sat quietly in my seat and took in the landscape. As the *Festival de la Recopilación Christi*[39] was being celebrated across the whole of Spain for the next week, Flassa—a town situated on the road to Girona—was decorated with blue and white paper flowers hung in looped garlands all along the roadside, and with large white paper doves on the houses and trees. It surely was a sight to see.

39 Festival of Corpus Christi (Body of Christ); a religious feast day.

We arrived at Girona mid morning and were thrilled with the town. We met an ardent young man at the bus stop who was learning English and he was most insistent that he escort us to the train station, where he worked. Walking along, he was most astonished to see our suitcases trailing along behind on their Portable Porters, and asked halting questions in pidgin-English about their origin. Reaching the station, he showed us where to put our luggage and we then thanked him for his courtesy and mentioned that we now intended to visit the cathedral. He was quite keen to come with us, but we avoided this as we felt pidgin-English was a bit much for any length of time.

The cathedral met all our expectations; a massive, yet very simple building with lovely glass. A service was being held and we stood at the west door quite entranced by the proportions and the simplicity-cum-grandeur of it all. As we came down a cobbled stepped street from the cathedral, we met about half a dozen of those gross-headed characters seen in processions in the south. The first one gave me two lovely yellow rosebuds and the second and third asked for some *calderilla*[40]. It was a wonderful setting and we felt that we were very lucky to have chosen this one day to visit Girona.

Girona Cathedral.

Back at the station, everything seemed to be shut and we sat on a wooden bench and ate our lunch, or at least Helen did. I picked rather delicately at mine. Then, suddenly the station appeared to come to life—siesta now being over—and we found that we had to queue for our tickets for the trip from Girona to Caldes.

Five minutes before the train was due, our pidgin-English young man appeared and we presented him with a threepenny bit as a souvenir. The young man said he hoped to visit England next year, but that the Spanish Government were not at all anxious to grant passports for people to travel outside their own country.

We travelled to Barcelona in a carriage with a very excited young man just back from a business tour covering, it seemed, almost the whole world, and he and the three other men

40 Small change.

gabbled away the whole time. At one time, when they were talking about England, one of them saw Helen all ears and asked if she understood, so she hastily assured them that she only understood a very little.

At Barcelona, we boarded a hotel bus that we shared with a perfectly frightful woman armed with innumerable bags and a camera tripod, and every sentence had about three 'darlings' in it. She was with a squat little lady who was making a fuss about everything; thank goodness we left them at another hotel. We went on to the Hotel Espana where porters and pages snatched all our sordid luggage and swept us into a lift to a third floor room overlooking a wonderful row of slum flats with balconies containing washing, junk, canaries and a Siamese cat asleep on a cushion. The hotel was built on similar lines to the one we stayed in at Perpignan; the rooms opened onto galleries looking down to the roof of the restaurant on the ground floor. It wasn't a particularly hot day, and yet being on the top floor, the room was surprisingly stuffy.

After a little siesta and a change to more respectable clothes for a great metropolis, we joined the crowds in the streets and soon found ourselves in Las Ramblas, one of the famous thoroughfares of Barcelona. There was a tree-lined walk down the centre with one-way traffic on either side. Each side of the centre walk was packed with chairs brought from their owners' homes. In front of the chairs was a row of steel helmeted soldiers with rifles, and behind them, more or less heedless of the odd cars trying to force their way through, the people of Barcelona were strolling up and down, all in their best clothes. We sat down at a café and ordered martinis and potato crisps, and watched the thronging crowd.

The main street of Barcelona: Las Ramblas.

Every window above us was crowded with people, and if the owners did not possess a flag to hang out over the window sill, then the family tablecloth did just as well. Everyone had confetti to throw and rolls of paper streamers to dangle from the windows. The children in the street below made a game of grabbing the ends of the streamers before tearing off down the street, their hands full of 'spoil'.

Soon the great procession came into sight headed by two vast effigies of presumably, King Ferdinand and Queen Isobella, the latter holding a posy of roses in her hands. They swerved and pivoted about as they almost lurched down the street, followed by an interminable column of clergy, choir boys carrying candles, laymen and boys with their ribbons of office around their necks. Each parish was represented and each group was headed by its own colour-bearer. I believe that the procession took the best part of two hours to pass, and after having sat for about an hour watching the crowds more than the actual procession, we decided to go and explore some of the nearby streets.

All the surrounding small streets were filled with ambling families; little girls in white frocks with coloured cardigans and ribbons in their hair to match their cardigans, white shoes and socks; some also wore white gloves. The little boys were in very old-fashioned suits, some of them with Eton collars and large bow ties. We wandered around for a considerable time and as usual, got lost, but eventually we found ourselves back in Las Ramblas—though we did not know in which direction we should find our hotel—just in time to see the end of the procession. It was rather a wonderful sight to see the Holy Sacrament pass. Everyone knelt, the women covering their heads with their mantillas and the men (even the soldiers lining the route) removing their hats or helmets. For less than a minute, a complete hush fell over the crowd, and then as quickly as it had fallen, it was lifted and the streamers and the shrieking and laughing went on as before.

The next day arrived, a very hot day. We had many good intentions, but most of them were lost in a lust for shop gazing. Whenever we put our noses into any shop, we entered into a long and involved conversation with the assistants, who insisted on our sitting down and having a 'nice chat'. The result was that we reached the cathedral after it had closed and only made it to the museum in Las Ramblas in the morning. However, the museum was well worth the visit; it was beautifully set out in carpeted rooms with magnificent chandeliers. We were practically the only visitors and each room had an attendant looking both bored and hot—poor things!

Las Ramblas had taken on its usual look; during the week, instead of chairs, the centre pathway had become the scene of masses of flower stalls on the one side and vendors selling birds on the other. We loved the flower stalls ablaze with colour from great masses of roses, cornflowers and geraniums. Girls were making enormous wreaths, and as well as the cut flowers, there were pot plants, seeds and quantities of cacti of all sorts. The birds—

pigeons, budgerigars and canaries—on the opposite side were fascinating, but rather sad locked up in their cages. We also came upon tiny kittens, tortoises of all sorts and sizes and white mice. We were much amused at one sight: a row of what looked like telephone kiosks, each containing a man and a typewriter who would execute your work for you in express time. Some of them were tapping away at great speed while the 'customer' stood outside with his head in at the open door. We went into the food market and were intrigued by the beautiful way they arranged their fish, both in the boxes and also on large round trays with basket work edging and covered with cabbage leaves.

The dining-room at the hotel gave us endless pleasure with its cosmopolitan mixture of clients and—thank goodness—a reasonable sparsity of English. We enjoyed a wonderful meal accompanied by red wine, in lovely surrounds, and with good company and feeling mellow we decided to put our Spanish to the test with the intention of visiting the theatre after dinner to see a revue.

Strolling to the theatre, Helen went into an antique shop, and having wandered around, she picked over a dish of old coins and chose a handful for one of her Ashmolean friends. She then looked at a large oil painting in the corner and said it was nice and that it must be old. She was assured that it was very old and that it was for sale for 4,000 pesetas. She asked if she could take down the particulars of it for interest as she worked in a museum in Oxford, whereupon the señora went into ecstasies of delight and promised that she would take it off its wooden frame and roll it, in order to make its transport easier. The idea of Helen struggling along with her suitcase, albeit with Portable Porters attached, rucksack, handbag, and rolled masterpiece caused us much amusement throughout a large part of the evening.

The revue was wonderful; plenty of music and dancing by beautiful girls. We had front row seats at the amphitheatre for five pesetas each. It didn't finish until one o'clock in the morning, and when we came out, a nearby bumper car track was still in full swing. A wonderful elderly couple—she with white hair and he in a grey felt hat—were unable to get their car going and they were bounced and banged all over the place by the other more experienced drivers. The attendant came to their rescue, but still they stayed firmly stuck across the route of the oncoming traffic until suddenly one of the passing drivers snatched the man's hat and put it on his own head, and as if by a miracle their car started to move and away they went just as the bell rang and the session ended.

Barcelona was certainly an interesting place. Walking back to our hotel in the early hours of the morning through narrow streets filled, for the most part, with rather murky looking shops, we passed old women who were selling baskets of bread from their chairs placed on the pavement. We also found that some of the food shops were still open, or shop staff getting ready for the next day's trade.

The next morning proved to be very hectic. We visited the cathedral and two other churches, a museum, various patios including one containing what we thought was a celebrated vine—500 years in age—and another with a fountain with half an eggshell bouncing on the crest of the cascade of water. We finished the morning with a visit to the Zoological Gardens. From there we caught a taxi, and I think we both felt that we had seldom enjoyed a taxi so much; it wasn't a great distance back to the hotel, but our feet would have found it far further.

In the evening, we went out to the Wembley[41] of Barcelona: a very typical exhibition site with a wide drive lined with flag poles and flower beds. At the far end one came upon a vast flight of steps that lead up to what was once a wonderful palace, but which was now a museum. Needless to say, it was closed when we got there. It had wonderful views of Barcelona and the surrounding country.

Having decided to visit Mallorca for a few days, we had an early dinner and took a taxi down to the harbour and boarded a beautiful three-masted barque—the vessel that was to take us on our journey. After settling ourselves in our cabin, we enjoyed standing on the deck to watch the rowdy Spanish crowd who had turned up in full force to see the boat off. It was dark by the time we sailed, and the lights of the Barcelona waterfront was an impressive sight as we slipped out. There was quite a strong wind, and it was none too warm, so we decided to make it an early night as we were planning to get up at six o'clock to be sure of seeing the first sight of Mallorca. We had a cosy little cabin, shared with a Spanish lady and her grown-up daughter; the former in an amazing black brassiere and swathed in what appeared to be an orange bed robe.

It was quite a choppy crossing compared, I think, with the usual sea, and although we were all right, thanks perhaps to Kwells, there seemed to be a good deal of noise going on around us throughout the night. Stupidly, we did not put on the fan in the cabin, but

---

41 Wembley Stadium in England is one of the world's most famous football stadiums.

had the door open through which little air seemed to come; I was unbearably hot and found the noise of the engines very irritating. However, I think I slept more than I realised, but whenever I woke up I felt glad that I was lying down and that by so doing I was pretty confident that my large and luscious dinner would remain with me.

Early next morning, a head appeared from the bunk above and Helen's smiling face said, 'I think we'd better stay where we are while all these men are hoofing their cookies, don't you?' To which, needless to say, I heartily agreed. So we dozed on, feeling horribly dry-throated from the Kwells, until seven o'clock when we thought we must have nearly docked. Getting up, we made our way on deck to find that we were sailing just off the coast of Mallorca; the sun was not yet out but it was quite warm all the same.

After docking at the quayside, which took considerable time, we found that a small car from the Hotel Mallorca had been sent to pick us up from the dock, together with an Oliver's tour group of about ten. The tour group were all gabbling away to the local agent. We decided that we would never all fit into the car, so we thought we would be independent and go by taxi, and we reached the hotel well in front of the others.

The Hotel Mallorca was a sumptuous place and we had a lovely room with a balcony and a view of the sea. It was a corner room, and so as well as having French windows, we also had a window on the other wall looking out over the hills behind the hotel.

Breakfast was on our minds, so we went down to the hotel's magnificent dining-room with windows on three sides and a view over the bay. We then unpacked and thought that a little snooze wouldn't be amiss. Some time later, feeling much more awake, we took ourselves to the little English church we had seen a notice about in the reception hall.

Palma Bay.

We were welcomed with open arms by the Chaplain, Reverend Coleman and his wife. They told us that they had only been there for three weeks, but that they hoped to build up interest in the church which was an old store room behind a private house, about a ten minute walk from the hotel. The room was very suitable, since it had three narrow pillars down the centre and had been very well furnished, together with a very pleasant reredos. Mrs Coleman played the harmonium which had the most awful agonising wheeze; it really made more noise than the notes she was playing. Besides ourselves, there were about half a dozen regulars who were, I think, residents of Palma.

We walked back to the hotel and down vast quantities of stairs to the rocky beach. Here we found a bar with tables and chairs at the water's edge, so ordered a delicious sherry aperitif and a vast lunch and then, with great lethargy, proceeded along the coast to the southwest. We found a charming little cove for a bathe, but it was already occupied by a mother, father, granny and four little girls, the eldest about twelve and the youngest about eighteen months. It was very much a homely scene, and the fact that we had descended on them at what might have been considered to be an inopportune moment as far as the two youngest children were concerned, did not seem to bother them at all. Suffice it to say that the expression on the face of the baby when she was finally 'back in circulation' was the best example of, 'I am a clever girl' that I think I have ever seen. However, what with one thing and another, their final departure seemed to be very long and drawn out and so we decided to move on to find another bathing place which was not quite so inhabited. Unfortunately, by this time the sun had gone down, but we had a nice bathe nevertheless, although we had to navigate a belt of seaweed at the water's edge before we could luxuriate in the warm water.

The rocky beach.

We then took the tram back from the terminus at Cas Catala. It was awfully thrilling to know that we were further south than we had ever been before. The weather was so wonderful that after dinner, one could sit out on the terrace in the dark watching the twinkling lights of Palma across the water without feeling the least little bit chilly.

The following morning saw us take the tram into town, a very colourful metropolis with palm trees, roses and bougainvillea in profusion. We went first to visit the cathedral, and then to the travel agent's office to organise our return trip to Barcelona. We soon were made to understand that there was no boat on a Sunday. Helen took her courage in both hands and suggested flying. We left the agent to explore possibilities, with a promise that he would leave a message at the hotel during the afternoon.

As usual, our beds called to us after our large lunch, and it was wonderful how easily one slipped into the habits of the country. Helen made tea after we woke; she had a little fire of her own on the floor, tiled so that there was no damage except a nasty smell and black smuts flying around. We finished the crystallized fruit we had bought in Barcelona and then set out for our main walk of the day.

We found a lovely track through the wooded hillside with lovely views of the distant hills and occasional glimpses of the deep blue sea and white houses of Palma. We worked our way around on footpaths through a perfect wood with our old friend the mock nightingale singing away and came out on the top of the hill upon which stood a castle. It had obviously been restored and we were a bit scathing of this aspect, but it turned out to be quite lovely with its inner open-air courtyard, a well in the centre, and a gallery all around with earthenware pots of red and pink geraniums on the parapet. We climbed the sixty-five steps to the top of the tower where we had a wonderful view of the surrounding country and coast looking its best in the evening light. Each window in the castle made a frame for an enchanting little panorama of blue sea, white houses, green trees, and blue hills in the distance.

Back at the hotel, dinner was, as usual, delicious, and we watched with interest the faces of the Oliver's tour group when confronted with globe artichokes, which they proceeded to carve with a knife and fork. We then sat out on the terrace and watched the boat leave (the same one we had come on) until half past nine when we then set out by tram for a folk dancing festival, although we were not quite sure where we were going.

Seeing two large effigies of dancers flanking the entrance to the Town Hall as we passed, we alighted from the tram and walked back to investigate, but the commissionaire standing at the door seemed very vague and just pointed up the street, so we walked for quite a long way but without any sign of the festival. Eventually, we asked another man near where there appeared to be a certain amount of fuss. He pointed at a bus on the opposite side of the road, called to the conductor and told us to get in quickly. Well, it already had its doors bulging but we endeavoured to get on, together with four other men who leapt on as the bus moved off. There we were, two English women on a bus full of smiling Spaniards, tearing off out of the town as fast as it would go, and we not knowing in the least where we were heading. The glamorous men around us were all smiles and chat, and for one peseta each, we eventually disgorged ourselves onto the road outside the bull ring. There was a milling throng of chattering people, but one of the gallant men from the bus took us to the ticket office and then escorted us to the entrance inside the arena before bowing his farewell.

It was an impressive sight; a vast open-air arena with rows of lights suspended from the sides to the centre and a concentration of light on a platform straight in front of us backed with four white ionic pillars in a row. I think there were many thousands of people there, and I could swear that every now and then I got a strong whiff of bull.

The program started with two pieces by the Mallorca Philharmonic Orchestra, but these were scarcely audible against the general noise of the crowd. Then came the dancing, and this was really thrilling. First a team from Spain—Palma—with castanets clapping and feet and skirts swirling; then Belgium, led by a lovely flag with a gold lion on a black ground which was waved slowly back and forth in front of the audience. Their dancing was very good, well timed and accurate, but completely lacking in sparkle compared with the Palma team. We couldn't help feeling that their dances would never finish as each figure was repeated many times. Then came another Spanish team—Salamanca. Again, their dance was full of life and with castanets and arms swirling in the air.

By this time, it was after midnight and only the end of the first part, with four teams still to dance in the second half. As neither of us were dressed for outdoor entertainment in the middle of the night, and being dubious about our means of transport home, we decided to leave and come again another night. Outside, we found a row of trams, but none of them were going to move until the end of the performance, so we started to walk, aware that we did not know the way. However, we soon picked up a taxi with a most friendly and charming driver who took us right back to the hotel at the opposite end of the town for a few pesetas.

The following morning we again went to see the travel agent, not having received the promised message regarding our return to Barcelona. Finding that they would not know whether we had seats on the plane until the afternoon (more promises of telephone messages), we consoled ourselves with a martini before going to catch the train to Sóller. Enjoying our drink, we were addressed by a lady we called, 'Mrs Madrid' and her friend, and they regaled us with lurid stories of the bull fight they went to see; we decided that we would not spoil our holiday with such unpleasant sights. The result of all this was that we nearly missed the train because we talked too long, but fortunately, after a few minor mishaps, we finally fell into our third-class coach, filled to almost overflowing with bundles and babies.

The train was a real country affair with open platforms at each end of the coach and wooden seats in our part; first class had the grandest upholstery, more like sofas and armchairs. It was a splendid hour's run, initially through olive groves and bright orange soil, and then through vast tunnels and along the edge of the mountainside. We came upon Sóller below us on the left, went through a tunnel, and miraculously found it on our right. From the station, we took a train to the coast, the route running through orange groves with trees laden with ripening fruit. When we arrived at the port—a lovely little bay—the sun was up, but it was quite chilly with a strong wind blowing; we both felt a bit glum in our cotton frocks and cardigans.

The folk dancers of the night before were all visiting Sóller, and in their national costumes, they were a colourful sight to see. They had formed little groups outside some of the cafés and were dancing and teaching each other different steps, their picnic lunches lying nearby. As we walked by, we noticed the Scottish team teaching the Germans, with bagpipes and accordions working overtime.

Proceeding up a cliff road cut out of the rock above the sea, the clouds rolled away, the sun came out and everything was wonderful again. In fact, it was an absolutely perfect afternoon with the sea the deepest blue one can imagine. Below us, many of the dancers were out in boats, singing their national songs, and also, as we walked up the lovely road, we came upon groups either sitting by the roadside or wandering down towards the bay, their arms full of bunches of wild flowers, and again, singing happily together.

We sat in the sun on a rocky perch above the road and ate our oranges, thoroughly enjoying the lovely area, and then we climbed down to the rocks below and were having a lovely bathe when suddenly three bronzed Spaniards appeared from behind the rocks. I don't know who was the most surprised: the men finding two laughing and splashing white-bodied girls in austere woollen costumes (a good thing they couldn't see the holes from afar), or the two girls, surprised in what they thought was a nice private spot. Quickly mastering their surprise, and quite unabashed, the men discarded their clothes, donned bathing trunks and plunged into the water, diving from a nearby rock. Obviously this was their spot and we were the trespassers. We came out and sat on the rock with our vests draped about our shoulders (we had brought no towels with us), but the handsome men showed no signs of going, and in fact, they came nearer and nearer until eventually they came out of the water and sat themselves down on a rock a few yards away. How were we to get dressed? We decided to give them quarter of an hour and if they had not gone we decided that we should have to put our frocks over our suits and climb up into the scrub above the road—but there was not much cover up there! In due course, one said, 'Excuse me, you are English?' and it transpired that he had been studying English by book for five months. They gathered around and although he knew very little of the language (I should think we were almost the first English people he had the chance of talking to), we had a short, rather strained conversation and eventually I took a deep breath and explained in a mixture of Spanish, French and gesticulations that we must get dressed and go and catch the train. At once and all smiles, they discreetly went off a very little way and sat with their backs to us.

A rocky cove in Sóller.

Arriving back at the hotel, we had a sherry before dinner and talked to the Oliver's tour agent who admitted he had never taken the train to Sóller, although he could write all about it. No wonder some guide books were useless!

After dinner, we took ourselves off to the theatre having first tried to wake ourselves up with some black coffee. It was a poor show and we nodded away through most of it. We came out well after midnight and went to the café opposite to have a drink, still feeling pretty soporific. Here, we became embroiled with a dashing naval officer who spoke excellent English, learned during a visit to Oxford. Within fifteen minutes we were on a first name basis, and he had guessed our ages by looking at our hands. He had a harmless friend with him called Juan, who was in the Merchant Navy and therefore not in uniform. Emile, the officer, was in a white uniform with blue tabs and gold braid. He tried to persuade us to see some Spanish dancing at a nightclub with them, but when we declined graciously, he called us un-British and said that we must, 'Remember that I have an anchor here!' hitting his chest hard as he spoke.

Realising the time, we made hurried excuses and ran across the road to catch the last tram amid cries of 'You won't catch it.' We did—but so did they! When we got off at the bottom of the funicular tunnel, we carried on a rather loud and ribald conversation with Emile accusing us of being frightened. I replied, saying that I wasn't afraid of him and that, being British, I was quite able to look after myself. Finally, we got away by promising that we would prove that we were British by meeting him at the swimming club the next morning at eleven o'clock. At half past two in the morning, we finally climbed the steps to the hotel with cries of 'That's a challenge,' echoing up the tunnel.

The next morning, with still no message being forthcoming from the travel agent, we once again ambled down to his office in the town to find, to our amazement, that we had two seats booked on the plane leaving on Sunday evening. The only snag now was that we had still not received our seat reservations for the return journey home, promised by post from Barcelona.

While we were in town, we decided to have a shop crawl around the local little places. We found a lovely indoor market with fish stalls muddled up with clothes and bread. The noise was deafening and the general air of bustle was great fun. We also visited a small tourist shop where the large señorita spoke some English. She was a real saleswoman because we began by buying and paying for one postcard, and in the end bought two baskets, one child's handbag and two plastic collapsible travelling medicine cups. She even offered to have a pair of leather sandals made for Helen in a couple of days and insisted on her trying practically all the shoes in the shop, but in the end Helen managed to get away with only a pair of espadrilles, which was what she really wanted. When we finally left, the señorita was actually pushing us out, commenting as she did so: 'Go before you spend all your money!'

We arrived at the swimming club twenty minutes later than our promised time, but there was no sign of our señor or his frogmen who he said would be practising there, so somewhat relieved and yet disappointed that we were not to be entertained that evening, we returned to the hotel for lunch. After that, we took the tram again to Cas Catala and had a wonderful five mile walk through the wooded hills inland and passed a fascinating castle with no sign of human life, but plenty of animals. We decided to come back here on the following day.

After our dinner that night, our south-country neighbours in the dining-room commented on our 'sparkling eyes'. Spain was certainly an amorous place!

The day dawned—another beautiful day. We set out at ten o'clock sharp with our lunch in a brown paper carrier bag and we took the tram to Genova where we climbed up the hillside, the route often edged with large patches of lavender. We continued in this way until we rejoined the path that had led us to the castle on the previous day.

The place was really most intriguing. There still seemed to be very little sign of life other than the animals, its land was fenced off with wire, and stone water courses were built along the hillside, resembling terraces. We suddenly came upon a strange underground tunnel and a cave, all rather hidden and mysterious, that we thought might have been built during the Civil War. Not being dressed for exploring dark, damp tunnels and caves, we went back up into the open to investigate the castle itself. It was also rather strange; the larger part of the castle was in ruins, some of which had been buried under the vigorously growing ground cover, but there was an enormous red archway standing alone at the side of the building, the top covered with a mass of green foliage. A nearby path, covered with honeysuckle—the smell was glorious—drew us down to discover a little bay where we sat and ate our lunch, every bit of it, as we were so hungry.

After a siesta, we walked on along a lovely coastal path with meadows of wild flowers on our right and on our left, the sea so blue and clear, you could see the sea bed. Pine trees were growing on the cliff edge right down to the sand, their black cones contrasted against the emerald green and deep blue of the water. Suddenly we saw a gem of a little bay, too small to be called that really, with the sun pouring down on the clear water, a view out across to a wide-open piece of country, and what looked like a lovely large sandy beach. Come what may, we knew that we must find our way down for a bathe, so scrambling over the rocks, we reached the water, and in next to no time, two pink bodies were wallowing discreetly under the shadow of the cliffs.

After some time, the general loveliness of the whole setting became too much for us, and caring nothing at all about the path above us, we swam out into the full sun and cavorted around with the utmost abandon. The water was incredibly buoyant and it was almost impossible to float because one's feet just shot up and out of the water. It was a perfect bathe; an absolutely ideal place with a gentle slope for swimming. We so much enjoyed our adventurous dip that I wondered why bathing dresses were ever invented.

Clothing ourself again in the privacy of the nearby bushes, we continued along this lovely path until we came to the sandy beach we had seen from the cove—Palma Nova by name; it really was a lovely stretch of sand. At the far end, there was a little headland covered with pines and thick bushes, and at the point where we came in, there was a small pine copse and a grand café/bar with a row of bathing boxes beside it. The only occupants were a common-voiced English woman and her two small children, and a French couple situated at the far end with their car radio on. It looked so inviting that I must say, I did wish that I had my bathing dress with me. We decided to paddle instead and then had a lovely lemonade at the café.

We started for home around five o'clock and trudged along the hard high road, hoping we might get a lift, but the only offer was the pillion of a man's motor bicycle. As neither of us had ever ridden a pillion before, we really felt that the two of us behind a reckless Spanish driver would be too perilous along the winding road back to Palma.

When we arrived back to our castle turning, we decided to abandon any hope of a lift and leave the tarmac road, with the result that we had a lovely homeward trek along the hillside in the evening light. As Helen wisely remarked, 'One doesn't feel one's feet when one has to think a bit where one is putting them!'

The tram came fairly quickly and we arrived back at the hotel a couple of hours later to change into our winter woollies, ready to attend the folk dancing at the stadium again. We then went and had a sherry before dinner. Our waiter, who was very keen on his English, came to me with a little book in which he had written very carefully, 'small hake'. This was apparently his dictionary translation of the most delectable fish we had just eaten. I pronounced it for him and he then wrote 'smol jek' underneath and went off to the sideboard where he bent over his little book, presumably learning a new dish to tell the next English party who asked what fish they were eating.

After watching a boat leave while sitting on the veranda, we prepared ourselves for our outing and were just leaving the room when I chanced to look at the program and saw that, as this was its last day, a special session was to be held, commencing at half past five. Feeling dejected and rather silly in our skirts and woollies on a lovely warm evening, we took a little turn around the block and went early to bed.

We went into the town after breakfast the next morning and collected our air tickets, cashed another cheque, and then walked back along the waterfront looking at a lovely old hall with a castellated exterior—Lonja de Palma[42]—which was built in the fifteenth century. There was a very attentive guide who gave us a catalogue of pictures to look at and insisted on trailing around with us, talking volubly all the time. The pictures were a weird mixture and the numbering didn't attempt to follow on in any way. He was most anxious that we should buy a card displaying one of the pictures and rushed across the hall to us, forsaking some newcomers, when he thought we were about to go. He took out a large handkerchief and flicked the dust off the top of a wooden bench before displaying his precious cards.

We walked down a lovely boulevard lined with palm trees and stalls selling the most ghastly common jewellery, plastic belts and other wares. On the waterfront itself, there was a cattle market with some charming foals with their mothers and a sweet looking donkey whose young had enormous ears. They were all sheltered from the sun by a long strip of the Spanish colours (red, yellow and red) and had printed notices on the front of their stalls with their names, antecedents and their owners' addresses. As usual, the time slipped by and it was noon before we were back at the hotel in our bathing things and down on the beach. We lay in the sun on a large flat slab of rock and watched a number of sailing boats, looking very lovely on that brilliant day.

Lunch was again a marvellous meal—what meal wasn't? The entrée resembled a dry risotto with mussels and pieces of meat in it. We spent the evening botanizing between Genova and Castillo de Bellver, mostly in the lovely woods around the castle because we felt we must have something to show for Helen's licence from the Ministry of Agriculture and Fisheries. The ground was very hard and the pen knife and the stalks broke more often than not, however, we collected a bundle of various species for transport home.

Dinner lived up to our expectations for the last time and we had delicious soup, omelette with globe artichokes, meat and fried potatoes, a wonderful French pastry and fruit. We had a long confabulation with a rather charming couple that had just arrived. They had a great sense of humour and told us of having their shoes soled by a shoe-shine man in Barcelona without either of them realising what was being done.

42 Palma Market; a beautiful civil building built by Guillermo de Segarra.

Early the next morning, we ambled down to the church service in the old store room, thinking we had plenty of time, only to find that Reverend Coleman had already started. Afterwards we deposited all our unwanted belongings onto him; frivolous Penguin books to lighten his collection of theological tomes, some sugar and tea, Helen's notepaper and the remains of a packet of Lux. He and his wife seemed duly grateful, although I must say, it looked a funny collection to be handing over just after a communion service.

After breakfast, we hustled down to the beach, determined to enjoy it to the full. Although the wind was strong and the sky was overcast, we found a patch where it was quite warm and disported ourselves with pleasure. The sea was quite rough, and after our bathe, I found I was covered all over in oil and muck; apparently the wind was blowing the harbour refuse our way. No wonder there seemed to be few people braving the water that morning! We decided not to bathe again, and after a talk with a gloriously common couple who had only just arrived and were not thinking very highly of the place—there being no 'nice sands'[43] on their doorstep—we walked back to our beloved bar and sat quaffing wine and Manzanillo olives while watching the myriad of small craft out on the bay. The sun came out and it was superbly hot; we felt very mellow and sad, especially when we thought that our tickets were valid for two whole months. We then joined the couple from the previous night and talked to them for quite some time, discovering that we had acquaintances in common. What a small world!

After lunch and a flurry of disorganised packing, we were eventually ready to leave. We paid the hotel supplement (which seemed very cheap), bid the wonderful hotel staff *adiós*, and were taken down in the funicular for the last time. At the bottom, the page heaved our suitcases (which seemed almost as big as he was) out and we climbed into a taxi accompanied by the Jack Hulbert[44]-like toothless hotel courier who, to our amazement, paid for the taxi on behalf of the hotel. Dragging our luggage on their Portable Porters into the air station, we were told that our luggage was too heavy (of course), but that the excess was only two kilograms and would cost us eleven pesetas. After this, we were whisked off to the bus and away from the miserable weeping issuing from three little girls bidding their papa goodbye.

---

43 Pronounced 'nāse sānds'.

44 A British actor from the 1930s.

At the airport, we had to open our cases for the police which caused us some disturbance as the cases were so full; however, we managed to shut them again after much sighing, heavy breathing and assistance from a good-looking Spaniard. We then went and stood on the airport steps for a considerable time. Helen said that the plane looked rather like the Meccano ones her brother had built as a boy, and made other similar remarks designed to bolster her morale; she was slightly nervous as she had never flown before. We soon boarded our plane for Barcelona after the deafening roar of its engine testing had finished, and found that, unfortunately, our seats overlooked one of the wings, so our view was somewhat restricted.

We were off the ground before we knew it and Helen's eyes began to sparkle as she saw the blue hills in the evening light. It only took us forty-five minutes and we touched down as easily as we took off. So ended Helen's first much-dreaded flight, but for her it ended all too soon, and she continued to marvel for some time about the speed and ease of the whole affair.

Barcelona from the air.

The airport bus took us into the city where we caught a taxi to the Hotel Imperial. Upon arrival, it seemed that the hotel full of common English girls in large parties, but we were fortunate enough to obtain a room away from them. Our room contained a double and a single bed, and being the largest, I was of course delegated the double bed. The room also boasted a vast wardrobe, a rocking-chair, an upright chair and a table and hot and cold running water, so one could not complain. A smiling chambermaid appeared and, bowing and smiling, and escorted us to the toilet in a most regal way.

Our evening meal was simple in the extreme after our accustomed fare, but we tucked it away happily, and after a short stroll up Las Ramblas, we went to bed with the knowledge that our travel agent had for once, come up to scratch and left a message with the proprietor asking us to call about our seat reservations, which had not been done in Mallorca.

We seemed fated in Barcelona—well, as far as animals were concerned. First, it was the Siamese cat behind the Hotel Espana who sang to his lady-love most lustily the first night.

This time, it was a rooster in a coop on the flat roof of the next door house; it was situated in a central well between the buildings, its early morning crowing echoed in a most disturbing manner.

Laying in bed after our early awakening, we heard a group of awful English girls leave at half past seven amid much ado. Deciding to get up instead of waiting for breakfast in bed, we ate in the dining-room—rather cold coffee in a wine glass and rolls without butter or jam. It was very stodgy.

We had a wonderful shop afterwards, especially in a new grocer's where we soon had three smiling men in white coats waiting on our small fancies. They offered every conceivable kind of comestible and finally packed our order up into two wonderful parcels with a cardboard plate as a base.

A narrow street in Barcelona.

Our bill at the hotel—quite in keeping with the general simplicity of what we had experienced elsewhere in Spain—was paid. Counting our remaining notes with care, we took a taxi to the station and found ourselves in a carriage with two of the English tour group girls who had very 'refined' voices, and a nice French trio consisting of father, pretty young daughter and the father's male friend. The daughter was being seen off by lots of glamorous Spaniards and she had an enormous bunch of pink carnations and a cellophane box of roses.

It was a pleasant run back to the frontier but the Spanish Customs were done on the train between Girona and Portbou, and of course, I was the one chosen to open my case as the representative of the whole carriage. At Cerbere, we all alighted again, this time for the French Customs, and Helen and I got through in express time. We then nonchalantly walked across the line, our cases on their wheels trolleying behind us, in front of a puffing engine and landed opposite our third-class coach.

Our carriage contained one rather weedy-looking, silent young man and a reserved seat. Soon, a fair, tall young man emerged with a suitcase, a large rucksack and a guitar in a case. He made a terrific to do about stowing his baggage and we offered advice in our best

French. The weedy young man still remained silent. Suddenly, he came to life and spoke excellent English. He spoke of his Flemish nationality, and besides English, spoke French, German, Italian and Spanish. The fair young man was Swedish and could only speak a very little English, but a most amusing conversation ensued in a mixture of French, English and Spanish, with a bit of German thrown in when all else failed.

At Port-Vendres, a French family consisting of a mother dressed in black with her hair scraped back into a bun, her married daughter, and a little girl of about eight, entered our carriage. A very lively discussion soon started, first by the Swede who said that all the clothes he was wearing had been made in Spain in three days. Then the weedy man and Madame started on a vivacious discourse about poverty in Spain compared with elsewhere. Meanwhile, the Swede solemnly unpacked and repacked his rucksack, quite unmoved by the conversation around him which he couldn't understand anyway. Madame took out a lovely black apron, which she spread on her lap, before starting some knitting, and the solemn little girl was given a doll to keep her amused. They were travelling to Toulouse.

We went to have dinner and sat at a table with a dapper little Frenchman who, I think, understood English, but wasn't going to be drawn into conversation (he suffered, poor man, and took a white powder in water before his meal), and an amusing little Yorkshire man who had spent a week in Barcelona and only had 500 francs, some pesetas and a pound left, so didn't dare have anything to drink. He asked vaguely if Versailles was a museum when Helen suggested he should visit it during his day in Paris tomorrow. He seemed to have enjoyed his stay at quite a grand hotel in Barcelona and was planning a visit to Italy next year. On the other side of the car was a bronzed family of husband, wife and two grown up daughters. They said they knew we had been to Mallorca, like them, because of our tan. Needless to say, they had, according to them, stayed at the best hotel on the island and the only walking they had done was from the taxi to the hotel door and back during their four week stay. I couldn't help but wonder just how much of the actual country this sort of person really saw.

Dinner complete, we went back to our carriage to find that a soldier had joined us. The little French girl, doll discarded, sat gazing out the window and I, in a rash moment, decided to give her my squeaky balloon (a gift from the tourist shop in Mallorca). She squeaked away happily for about half an hour but slowly the carriage sank into repose, except for Madame knitting and Helen and I scribbling in our diaries.

We had rather a disturbed night; I suppose because we were no longer dog-tired and in need of sleep, we just could not get settled. I offered my corner to the mother of the little girl when the latter showed signs of wishing to sleep, but after having been gently moved to the seat, the child woke up and hardly occupied the seat at all.

They got out at Toulouse and a large jovial Frenchman got in—his only fault being a tendency to make loud, succulent spitting noises at frequent intervals. A soldier also got in and took the seat next to mine. Settling himself into his seat, he decided to take off his shoes and the whole carriage found, to our consternation, that he had very ripe Camembert-smelling feet. From time to time, I opened the door a little when the smell became rather pungent, but he would awaken, lean across me, and shut it again. It was amazing how one's nostrils became acclimatised as the atmosphere thickened.

We tried to make ourselves as comfortable as possible; Helen had managed to keep all callers out of the seat adjacent, and so we rested our feet up on the space. I found myself grasping the soldier's hot hand when I went to put mine on the seat between us, but Helen had his woolly black head on her shoulder, and the tall Swedish boy's feet and legs kept appearing in the oddest places—out from behind the back of his neighbour or up from under a mass of legs between him and us.

At around a quarter past five, the blinds went up and everyone became very much awake. During a long discussion in French between the French-speaking travellers, the Swedish boy took down the rucksack again and carefully unrolled a vast pair of woollen pants (also bought in Spain, I wondered?) from which he extracted a two foot high glass bottle made in the shape of a Spaniard in national costume and containing Anis[45]. He sat gazing at the figure until he could attract the others attention, and then having received their admiration, he offered Anis all around, served in a metal cup. Later in the morning, we thought he was going to play his guitar when someone from the group produced some lovely sentimental song tunes, but unfortunately, no. At this point we decided that breakfast called and so set forth. The sights in the compartments en route were rich indeed.

After breakfast, and until we got to Paris, a most exhausting conversation went on in French between us and the 'spitty' man. He worked in the tourist trade and wanted us to visit Orléans on 8th May the following year (the Festival of St Joan of Arc) and he would

45 A liqueur flavoured from a distillation of anise seeds.

'show us all'. He said he might come to the Festival of Britain and we all exchanged business addresses, but I said to Helen that I'd be a trifle horrified if he turned up at the BBC looking 'as grubby as he does now!' However, he was extremely helpful in Paris and carried our little bags for us.

We took the station bus over to the Gare Saint-Lazare[46] and Helen rushed off in search of nylon menders while I watched the Scottish folk dance team. They were joining the train after a day in Paris, dancing an eightsome on the station to everyone's pleasure.

We crossed in the *Londres* and did all our usual tricks. The wind was very cold and we couldn't get a rug, but we went into the bow and sat in the sun and kept fairly warm. The sky and sea seemed so pale, but nevertheless we got our usual thrill at seeing the white cliffs of Beachy Head and Dover. We noticed a young man standing with an American girl who was obviously enraptured with her first view of England. The young man however, was making some rather derogatory remarks about our country, but fortunately, that did not deter her from her theory that England was a most wonderful country with its history and traditions.

The white chalk cliffs of Dover.

We sailed through Customs as the officials were so overcome with Helen's Ministry of Agriculture licence that nothing else mattered.

Newhaven seemed to be small and quiet after the bustle of the foreign channel ports, but we had the bagpipes to send us off again and a lovely view of a burly piper through the communicating passage, who while standing, was leaning against the doorway, one leg crossed over the other, playing away as the train left Newhaven Harbour.

---

46 The busiest railway station in Paris.

Arriving in London, we found that my flat mate Molly was there to meet us. Quickly relieving us of all our many bags—two suitcases with Portable Porters still attached, a bulging rucksack, a hag's bag, and two baskets—we caught a taxi without any difficulty, despite Molly's protestations and whisperings that the fares had gone up again since we had been away.

So ended another wonderful holiday, made perfect by the fact that the sun shone the whole time and it was hot. The itinerary was also just right, without too much rushing from place to place and always packing and unpacking. I was sure that it wouldn't be long before we were on the road again with our suitcases being dragged along behind on those wonderful Portable Porters.

Basel
SWITZERLAND
Lucerne
Berne
Thun
Brienz
Interlaken
Wilderswil
Grindelwald
Wengen
Lauterbrunnen
Kleine Scheidegg
Mürren

Oh, the People One Meets!

1952: Switzerland

A short time after my return from Spain, the chaplain at the Royal Chapel of St Peter ad Vincula in the Tower of London where I attended service every Sunday, introduced me to Jane, a Sister Tutor at the London Hospital. Jane came from a large family living in Maybole, a small town situated in Ayrshire in the southwest of Scotland, and we found that we had much in common and quickly developed a firm friendship.

Jane delighted in people and travelling gave her plenty of opportunity to make new friends—something we both enjoyed—so after hearing about my early travels in Switzerland and recently in France and Spain, she was very keen to show me the Switzerland she knew. So, after booking our trip and giving my flat mate Molly a copy of our itinerary, I again held true to what was becoming a trademark of my journeys—I left home with very little money on which to survive.

Jane and I left London from Victoria Station on a very hot and thundery June afternoon. We had booked our holiday with Hotel Plan, and the representative was very evident on the day of our departure, organising the group and hustling everyone onto the train and into carriages.

At Folkestone, we were almost the first through Customs and onto the boat (well up to my cross-channel standards) where Jane quickly ran into an acquaintance. She seemed to have friends in every corner of the British Isles and they even followed her away from these shores. Jane and I had often spoken about the people one met upon one's travels and had decided that it was all good fun—the good, the bad (and even the very annoying!)

By this time, the sun was out and it was a perfect June day; the sea was calm, the water blue-green and a haze over the white cliffs. The boat wasn't very full, so we didn't bother about getting deck-chairs, and soon after we left, we had tea in a very pleasant lounge in the bow with windows all around and prettily decorated with folk-weave curtains and red and green linoleum on the floor. Tea consisted of new rolls, masses of butter and raspberry jam, and slab cake. A happy couple from suburbia came and sat at our table and as I was in the process of pouring tea for everyone, I noticed a burning sensation coming from my fingers. Quickly pouring into the last cup, I was now feeling quite desperate to put the teapot down, but the couple, not realising my dilemma, had put their butter in the space temporarily vacated by the teapot on the crowded table, leaving me with no place to put it. Jane came to my aid and removed one of the cake plates.

The crossing to Calais seemed to be over very quickly; the sea was calm until we were nearing the French coast when there was a very slight swell caused, I think, by a threatening thunderstorm. We both got the usual thrill at seeing all the French sights—the sailors with red pompoms on their berets, the wooden carts and even the dogs look different. As we came alongside the Customs shed, which was still looking very new and white, it was strange to leave the noise and bustle of the quay and cross to the port side and find complete silence and inactivity, save for two dredgers sliding silently past us to their berths further up the harbour.

After moving through Customs, we walked across to the train and passed a round, blonde female wearing a strawberry pink frock with white spots, a large white necklace, earrings and bracelet, and canvas shoes with woollen flowers embroidered on them. She carried a kettle and displayed a very earnest expression on her face. She was obviously in search of water to which an official soon directed her. Jane and I just looked at each other as she passed by and the words 'the people one meets' kept running through my head as I inwardly hoped that she was not to be one of our companions for the journey.

We found our carriage already occupied by a pleasant looking man, and a large woman all hung about with yellow beads, earrings and bracelet and wearing a brown frock with yellow spots. Her hair was pulled back from her face into a yellow crochet hat and she stared at us as we deposited our various bags on the rack and sat down to recover from the heat. Then, who should arrive but 'Pink Frock', carrying her kettle! This was stowed under the seat and it was quickly apparent that both dames were Irish. Jane and I hastily left the carriage for the cool of the platform before becoming too much embroiled, since a loan of our thermos flask tops had already been demanded for use when the tea-making was to commence. There was still some time before our scheduled time of departure, so we were able to take a little exercise up and down the platform for about twenty minutes. I always loved this first return to French soil when travelling on the Continent, and watching people gave me endless pleasure.

In due course—and with the usual French whistles and hysterical shrieks—we left Calais and started on our long journey to Wengen. The pleasant looking man in our compartment was joined by his wife, a very sweet looking soul, who was apparently not a good traveller. Between the man and the Irish women was a young man who sat and read, not joining in the usual exchanges of 'Where are you going?' The Irish women were bound for Italy and regaled us with anecdotes of their trips to every conceivable corner of the Continent. After this, they both took out their rosaries, and while Pink Frock stared out of the window while her friend in the brown frock stared hard at us while her mouth moved at great speed as she recited the rosary. At intervals she nodded off to sleep, but all the time the fingers were still turning the beads.

Supper was served at eight o'clock with everyone but the young man, laying out their fare. As he had nothing but some cake with him, he was offered something from all of us in turn, which he happily accepted. Then thoughts turned to settling for the night; 'Brown Frock' put on some sock slippers, similar to those being worn by Jane, and then took off her yellow crochet hat to reveal very dull, straight grey hair. From her capacious handbag, she produced some bits of old stocking, and taking her side bits of hair, twisted them around the stocking, giving a horn effect on each side. A pot of cream was the next treasure taken out of the bag and dabs were put on her nose and cheeks. Unfortunately, the light in the compartment would only dim very slightly and the window, like so many on French trains, would not stay open, so we had to have the corridor door open with more light pouring in. Jane and I blew up our little orange air cushions and settled down to a rather fitful sleep; I think we were too tired to get really comfortable. At one point, Brown Frock had the uncontrollable urge to loosen her corsets, and having tried unsuccessfully to do so through her frock, finally stood up and lifted her frock on one side and almost visibly expanded as the iron girders were released. Pink Frock was rather embarrassed by this unladylike behaviour when she thought that we had seen what was afoot. She then firmly put her head on Brown Frock's shoulder—despite a certain amount of remonstration—and they both fell into a deep sleep from which they awoke a couple of hours later. Pink Frock, now wide eyed, said to Brown Frock, 'Did ye lose consciousness at all?' to which Brown Frock nodded her head in the affirmative and then promptly dropped off again. Some time later, she suddenly woke herself up with a tremendous grunt-cum-snore, and Jane, who had her head on my shoulder, nearly jumped to the ceiling of the carriage. I then got the giggles. Oh, the people one meets!

At two o'clock, everyone came to life and took a little sustenance. Pink Frock proved to be a trifle 'high' when she mounted the seat beside us to get down her hag's bag in which we spied a goodly bottle of whisky—but oh dear!—we were not to be blessed with much sleep that night because soon after our light meal, the sight of the first streaks of dawn was too much for both the ladies and they spent some time exclaiming at the glory of this particular time of the day—a pleasure that the rest of us failed to appreciate at that hour. In the meantime, I had lent my cushion to the pleasant man's wife, and she being thoroughly disturbed, got up and went into the corridor to stretch her legs, whereupon Pink Frock unhesitatingly moved over to the vacated seat and settled herself down comfortably, making full use of my cushion as well.

We reached Basel at six o'clock feeling decidedly sleepy. While leaving our entire luggage on the platform, we noticed Pink Frock's hag's bag with an ominous trickle of liquid running from it. Fearing it might be the whisky, we thought we'd better warn her. Moving inside to the buffet and the room reserved for Hotel Plan travellers, we located her and told her of our observation. After a moment's consternation, she decided it was only water—presumably from the kettle that hadn't produced the promised early morning cup of tea.

After breakfast, we took a short stroll outside the station in the hope of seeing the Rhine, but on enquiry, found that we were walking in the wrong direction and that it was too far away. The Hotel Plan courier advised us to catch an earlier train to Lucerne than was advertised and so we gathered up our bags, and having found the train, settled ourselves into a nice compartment that we hoped to have to ourselves. However, just before the train left, two English girls arrived, quite breathless from rushing down the platform with their entire luggage, having been in the wrong section of the train.

We passed through some very lovely agricultural country, but neither Jane nor I could help falling asleep, so we missed quite a bit of that journey. We revived considerably as a result of a good sleep, but the last part of our rest was somewhat disturbed by the arrival of a very loud girl who was very kindly disposed to the other two in her keenness to help them with their respective journeys.

Arriving in Lucerne in the middle of the morning we found it to be a lovely day so we decided to leave most of our luggage at the station, taking just one bag with the remains of our food for lunch. We strolled along by the lakeside, past some rather clever floating reserves for ducks and swans. They were square pens with little platforms on which there were small dog kennel-like houses, and then a wide square of water with—a few inches below the surface—a duck boarding. There were some birds from Australia, from China and some that looked like our old friend, the English swan. Beyond the pens, we came to a fascinating old wooden bridge with paintings on each side of the rafters, and further on, a delightful street market with the stalls backing onto the waterside and laden with flowers and fruit of every colour. The stallholders were typically Swiss—women in black with coloured pinafores, and young girls with clear complexions and their hair coiled over their heads. All were smiles and there was a general air of early morning bustle.

On the opposite side of the narrow street was an arched colonnade with a fish market and stalls with many rather scraggy chickens. Up behind the waterfront we found some glorious narrow cobbled streets, all over-hung with rows of coloured flags bearing emblems of bears, birds and other strange devices—a most festive sight. Here we found a comestibles shop with a smiling girl in a white overall who sold us an enormous bottle of Gilbey's Gin, ready for our clandestine bedroom drinking. How we managed to squeeze it into our already bulging bags, I don't know, but we did.

It started to rain then, so we hurried back to the wooden bridge and sat on one of the seats at the top of the flight of steps leading onto the bridge, well under the cover of the wooden roof. The rain streamed down and the inhabitants of Lucerne and their tourist visitors crowded onto the bridge with us. They were amusing to watch—elderly women dressed in black from head to foot, middle-aged residents in very smart mackintoshes and delightful children in their long white socks and brightly-coloured mackintoshes. The procession of small chattering boys and girls, accompanied by a nun, who stampeded over the bridge when the rain was still pouring down, was especially memorable. The children all carried large white balloons on sticks with a slogan in black painted on them. There were also of course, the usual gangs of chatty English discussing the food at their respective hotels.

The rain went on and on and finally we decided we could bear the pangs of hunger no longer and must, regardless of etiquette, eat our lunch. Out came the remains of our sandwiches, which had survived the ordeal of the night remarkably well, and with food inside us and the rain stopped, we packed up and left the bridge with the continuous stream of shoppers, passing back and forth. We turned right, away from the market, towards the lakeside with its boulevard lined with trees and the little jetty where boats could be hired. Just off the boulevard, its twin spires a landmark for many miles around, was the Cathedral of St Leodegar, its stonework, and that of its close neighbours, an attractive warm beige that gave a clean new appearance. We approached by way of a broad flight of steps and observed the long open cloisters beyond the grass on both the north and south sides of the cathedral. Upon closer examination, we saw that the cloister walls had been painted white and were covered with memorial tablets.

Lucerne Lake and the twin needle towers of the Cathedral of St Leodegar.

The inside of the cathedral was not as ornate as some continental Catholic churches, but was decorated with garlands made of evergreens, and young trees stood between the pillars stretching the length of the nave. Up in the sanctuary, five small boys were being taught to serve at Mass, but the whole affair appeared to be rather a joke to the boys, for when their lesson was over, they came down into the body of the cathedral giggling away, even when they turned to genuflect.

Walking back towards the station, with the summit of Pilatus almost able to be seen through the persistent cloud hanging over it, we decided that a drink was essential, so we sat under the stone arches of a very attractive café facing the lake. Jane asked for coffee in a glass (being the cheapest alternative), but to our consternation, we were brought a jug and cups. However, our thirst was such that even Jane's recollection of the cost, remembered from a previous holiday in Switzerland, did not spoil our enjoyment of that coffee, which ran to nearly three cups each. The bill—oh joy!—was less than expected, so this café was stowed away in our memories for future occasions when we might find ourselves in Lucerne.

What with the sun, our sightseeing, and the hot coffee, we were absolutely overcome with sleep by this time, and so with quarter of an hour to spare, we crossed the road and sat down on a seat facing the lake and slept. After our refreshing nap, we then trotted back to the station, collected our baggage and found the train to Interlaken.

As we were walking up the train, we met the pleasant man of our earlier journey and he told us where to find his wife, who was situated further up the train. So we joined her in a most luxurious observation car with armchairs upholstered in red and fawn, which could be moved about according to one's fancy. Both sides of the carriage were glass, and I supposed the carriage had accommodation for about two to three dozen people. The washing facilities were spotlessly clean and complete with soap and paper towels, so we were able to have a really good, refreshing wash and brush-up before settling down to enjoy the trip over the Brunig Pass to our destination.

We left in the early afternoon and it was the most wonderful run, despite another overpowering urge to sleep which got the better of us at intervals. I think it was partly due to the sun that was now very hot and streaming into the coach. The meadows were a mass of flowers of every colour—such vivid colours too—and the views back down the valley were quite unbelievable. It seemed impossible to realise that the day before we had been in London and now we were in a fairyland.

The coach was by no means full and behind us sat an American couple, the man in inevitable green mica eyeshades, presenting a humorous spectacle from the rear with the white band stretched across his shiny, burnt bald head. He had numerous weird gadgets that he peered through at intervals, and a camera with colour film with which his wife insisted that he photograph the meadows from the moving train in order to get the mixed colours of the flowers. It must have been an absolutely super deluxe camera if those photos were to come out!

Up we went to the summit, with slightly popping ears, and down the other side to Meiringen where we halted briefly. We were fascinated to see that the guard did not use a flag to indicate to the driver when all was clear to move on. Instead he used a round white disc on the end of a stick, the disc having a different coloured diagonal stripe on either side.

We were soon down in the Aare Valley, the lovely Lake Brienz shimmering in the afternoon sun and the towering blue snow-capped mountains on either side. Brienz itself was the woodcarving centre of the Oberland and the popularity of the trade was apparent by the number of chalets displaying the beautiful carvings on their exteriors. The train skirted the south side of the lake, past little clusters of chalets, their wooden walls chocolate against the blue-green water and their window boxes full of scarlet geraniums. We viewed a stone jetty where little boys were fishing and a small sailing boat was out for a trip.

Lake Brienz.

We reached Interlaken Ost in the middle of the afternoon and were met by a Hotel Plan courier and a very charming hostess who said our train to Lauterbrunnen was waiting on the opposite side of the platform. Now we were to leave behind us the influence of the big Swiss railways with their efficiency and organisation and move onto the friendly atmosphere of the small mountain railways. Jane's excitement really reached its height as she began to point out the familiar landmarks of the country she loved so much, a love that I know she was so anxious that I should share, and yet had a tiny fear that I might be disappointed.

So began the most thrilling ascent up to Lauterbrunnen. I was still pretty sleepy, but the beauty of it all left me quite speechless. Leaving the outskirts of Interlaken behind, we skirted the banks of the Lutschine River, foaming white over its bouldered river bed with woods and flowers everywhere. Just before we reached Zweilutsehinen, the two rivers—the black from the Grindelwald Valley and the white from Lauterbrunnen—met in a swirling milky torrent, and from then on the track climbed through glorious woods with views down through the trees to the white Lutschine, hundreds of feet below us, until we reached Lauterbrunnen, a nice little village on an open plain in the valley. Here we changed trains yet again.

Lauterbrunnen village.

Winding our way up the steep side of the valley, climbing higher and ever higher through the woods and mountains, this part of our journey then took us through a tunnel and surprisingly brought us out with the valley on the opposite side of the train and here we quite suddenly got our first view of Jungfrau. I had no idea it would look like that—it was so vast and majestic in its pure white glory, with only the smallest cloud on the summit, and I felt that I was indeed lucky to have a clear day for my initial sighting of the famous peak.

At about half past four, we arrived at the little station of Wengen. A row of about a dozen peak-capped porters stood in a line on the sloping approach to the little platform and we soon picked out Emile from the Alpenruhe Hotel. With a smiling greeting, he took all our sordid little bags, and directing us to walk on to the hotel, he went off to collect our registered luggage.

In brilliant sunshine, we walked up the hill and through the delightful little village dotted with a few shops, and the houses with gardens full of flowers and strawberries. Leaving the main part of the village behind, we climbed a steep little hill until we saw our hotel just above us, standing out against a background of blue sky and pine trees, facing the mighty Jungfrau, the Grosshorn and the Breithorn mountains. In front of the hotel was a little raised garden with mulberry trees giving shade to comfortable deck-chairs, and red and white tables and chairs. The bank bordering onto the road was laid out in three layers of pansies—yellow, purple and mixed—their size and colour surpassing all but prize specimens in England.

The entrance to the hotel opened into a cheerful and very comfortable lounge with lovely views of the valley, and the young receptionist, who spoke a little English, met us in the absence of the proprietor and his wife. She smilingly took us up to the third floor and I'm sure you can imagine our thrill when we found we had a room with a balcony overlooking the mountains containing a window box full of pink geraniums. Both Emile and the receptionist stood by smiling while we ran to the window and exclaimed at the view, the pleasant room and the joy of being in Switzerland.

We were soon unpacked, washed and very much ready for our meal—and what a meal it was too! We both managed to do it justice, although we did not quite clear our plates. The dining-room was not full and the people seemed nice. They were mostly Swiss, with a few English and one American lady, but that first night we decided not to tarry long and were soon off to bed after watching a lovely sunset which turned the rocky face of the Männlichen range to a delicate pink.

We woke the next morning to a brilliant day and a clear view of Jungfrau was reflected in the glass of our open French casement windows. This made us very lazy because if we placed the sash in just the right position, we could see the weather without leaving our beds! Finally rising to a late breakfast of fresh rolls, croissants, cherry jam and coffee in the garden overlooking the valley to Jungfrau, we later attended the little English church for Service; a charming little whitewashed building with a brown-tiled roof. Inside was plain and restful with the words 'I Will Lift up Mine Eyes unto the Hills' inscribed over the arch at the entrance to the Sanctuary. We sat by an open window with a view of Jungfrau and joined what was already quite a good congregation. A small choir occupied the front pews on the opposite side—a lovely group of middle-aged and elderly English women in large straw hats with bows and bunches of flowers. The care of the music was entrusted to two dear souls who tried hard, but gave no assistance to our singing efforts. The chaplain, an Australian, was very sincere and preached an extremely good sermon. After Service we spoke with him for a while and then he sent us on our way with a very friendly, 'Have a good holiday, girls.'

After lunch, we lay in the garden on deck-chairs with footrests and nice yellow garden mattresses for a short while and then we decided to break ourselves in with a gentle walk up to the Leiterhorn. Stopping at a viewing area that stated that it was over 4,000 feet above sea level and 2,000 feet above the Lauterbrunnen valley, we stood on a platform on the very edge of a sheer rock face to see the wonderful views of the valley.

While sitting on one of the comfortable seats provided so frequently by the *Kurverein*[47] and admiring the view from the Leiterhorn, we were joined by an elderly German couple. Despite the fact that their French was not fluent, we managed to have a little conversation with them and we admired her posy of flowers. On our way up, we had found our first Swiss gentians, the little star variety which was really so much more attractive than the large specimen, and so we were able to give her a couple for her collection. While sitting, a woman with her hair coiled over her head and wearing a gentian blue dress and large white apron, accompanied by two children carrying bunches of alpen rose, came past us singing. They stopped and spoke to the German couple and then continued through the woods, their singing floating back to us as we sat listening, entranced.

Gentians.

Making our way back to the hotel, we arrived back in time to partake in a wonderful dinner in the hotel's dining-room. Later, while relaxing in the lounge before going up to bed for an early night, we found the American lady of the previous night looking rather lonely. Starting up a conversation with her, she told us all about her family and that she was hoping her newly acquired daughter-in-law would be joining her at the end of the week when she would start some excursions.

The following day, we were blessed with another lovely morning and taking a packed lunch, we took the train down to Lauterbrunnen and then the funicular railway up the opposite side of the valley to Grutschalp. We had lunch close by the little station—two doorstep sandwiches with enough cold meat of varying sorts to feed two or three people, a huge triangle of cheese, a packet of biscuits, an orange and an apple. It was a good thing we

47 Electors; a body of German princes with whom rested the election of the German King, from the 13th to the beginning of the 19th century.

had not gone further, since it began to rain before we had finished and we gladly took shelter in the station during a heavy and rather cold shower. Clearing quickly, the sun shone on us for a wonderful walk along to Mürren, with magnificent views of the Eiger, Mönch and Jungfrau. The path was easy; we walked through some lovely woods and then out into open pastures where we came upon some cows with their lovely bells jangling away as they moved. We saw hardly anyone else, except at one point where we passed a very old peasant couple cutting wood.

View of the Eiger from Mürren.

Reaching Mürren as it started raining again, we walked fairly briskly down the little village street to fill our kettle at a trough with sparkling mountain water running out of a pipe. We then returned along the path above the railway line towards Grutschalp until we found a most convenient seat at the top of the bank sheltered by thick fir trees. Now reasonably protected for the rain which had become quite heavy, we got out our tea-making things, including the milk we had bought at a little shop in Wengen, and were soon refreshing ourselves with cups of Earl Grey China tea.

We had decided to walk back to Lauterbrunnen and realised that we had a long and steep descent before us and not too long to do it, so we set off at a good pace. The path was good and clear, but very steep and it zigzagged through lovely pine woods and over rushing streams, but we really had no time to admire it. We arrived down at Lauterbrunnen rather tired, only to find that the next train was not until seven o'clock which meant that we should be late for dinner.

We both awoke the next morning to find that we were quite sore from our efforts on the previous day, so decided on a more leisurely pace for this day's activities. Walking down to the village to get some maps—a stroll we both enjoyed—we then returned and were thoroughly domestic; washing our hair and mending, while sitting on the veranda in the sun.

Deciding to have an aperitif before lunch, we agreed that we could think of no better way to enjoy a drink than sitting, as we did, out on the little wooden balcony that abutted the dining-room. The view was magnificent; the snowy white mountains created the most beautiful backdrop for the clustered brown roof tops of the chalets and the green of the meadows of Wengen, together with mulberry trees and the flower boxes filled with pink geraniums in the hotel's garden. All the petty annoyances of everyday life at home seemed so very, very far away and so unimportant.

After a superb meal, we caught the train to Wengernalp, and in brilliant hot sunshine, walked up a glorious broad path to Kleine Scheidegg with the giants Eiger, Mönch and Jungfrau towering above. We were forced to stop every few minutes to admire their immense beauty and listen to the sound of the glacial streams cascading down from their icefields. From this path, the north face of the Eiger was a most impressive sight, just as if someone had taken a knife and sliced off the side. Our first view of it showed a small, wispy cloud, caught in a hollow just below the summit, but as we reached Kleine Scheidegg, even this vanished and left the whole wall of peaks clear against a deep blue sky, with the two pure white conical peaks of Jungfrau looking like pyramids of castor sugar. As we walked up this comparatively gentle sloping path, we viewed lovely pasture covered with a mass of flowers of every kind and colour. Below the path, sloping down to the valley between the mountains and us, large patches of globe flowers made brilliant yellow patterns amongst the green.

Eiger, Monoch, and Jungfrau from the trail to Kleine Scheidegg.

Just before we reached Kleine Scheidegg with its station and large hotel, we had a peep of the Wetterhorn as the summit came into view between the group of buildings and the Eigergletscher. Here, on the slopes, we picked a bunch of gentians where they were growing profusely together with wild pansies. It was an unforgettable sight for me, since I had only once before found the large gentians and had never seen them growing in such profusion; here one could almost say with honesty that the ground was blue with them.

From just beyond the little station, we had the most superb view of the Grindelwald Valley with the Faulhorn range away in the distance. Covered by a blue haze, the Wetterhorn and the Shreckhorn were standing sentinel over the valley's wide green expanse of field, with the wood stretching down from where we stood to the village of Grindelwald itself.

Leaving all this beauty behind us, we retraced our steps a short way, and then with typical English pragmatism, sat down by the side of the path and brewed our tea. The people coming down the path all seemed to know that we were English—little kettle on tripod, rucksacks and cardigans surrounding us, happily drinking our delicious tea from china cups—and greeted us accordingly.

By the time we reached Wengernalp, it was becoming overcast and chilly, but we stopped a few minutes to watch for any avalanches that might come rushing down from Jungfrau with an eerie crack as the snow and ice broke away from the mountainside. Undaunted, we started off to walk what was sign posted as a one and a quarter hour walk down to Wengen. Soon we came up with a group of three beautifully made-up English girls, one of whom commented that she was glad to meet some English people. Another of the group then remarked that she hoped it wouldn't rain before they got down because she didn't want to get her hair wet. Walking a little way with them, Jane and I found that we had to stop fairly early to put on cardigans, and by the time we were once again organised, the girls, much to our disappointment, were well out of sight. We later agreed that one of the many joys of this holiday, we believed, was that one's natural complexion was quite sufficient when out walking, and that for the most part, powder compacts and lipsticks were an unnecessary addition to one's baggage!

Continuing on our way, we enjoyed the walk through the woods and meadows, and past our first patch of snow which we were both childish enough to walk in. Every now and again we had a lovely view of the valley below, but all around were heavy thunderclouds and it got darker and darker. Although Wengen looked no distance away, it was deceptive and we knew we still had quite a distance to go. Luckily, we reached a disused wood shed before the rain became really heavy; under the eaves was a convenient bench where we sat completely sheltered while the heavens opened. Fortunately, it only lasted about twenty minutes and then there was a lovely rainbow and brilliant sunshine once more and out we came like hens from a hen house and scuttled for home, arriving just in time for dinner.

While we were seated in the dining-room, the American lady whom we had by now nicknamed 'Mrs America', asked us if we liked 'thriller-dillers' which she had to explain was her name for mystery stories. Apparently, she had some that had kept her reading until the early hours of the morning, so later we offered her our Agatha Christie books, which she accepted gratefully. We were a little perplexed by her unusual way of speaking, especially when we announced we were going to bed. She then asked, 'What? Are you going to your hay? I think I'll come too.'

There was no sign of Mrs America at breakfast the next morning, so we were happy to know that Agatha Christie must have written an acceptable thriller-diller, although we were a little disappointed not to find her there. We had hoped that we might be able to further our acquaintance with her, especially as the thick mountain mist seen from the dining-room windows gave every impression that the weather was only going to become worse. There would be no excursions for us today.

Back in our room we found it to be was quite chilly, but a nice electric radiator near our armchairs kept us pleasantly warm as we read, knitted, and chatted. After a particularly large lunch, we determined on some exercise so we ventured into Wengen in search of a shop that could supply us with some orange squash to go with our gin (we had exhausted the bottle we brought with us!)

The first shop only produced the fizzy variety, but we were most impressed by the fact that the young girl who served us understood when I used the word 'fizzy' to Jane. Finally, we bought a bottle of lemon syrup from a white-coated man in a shop selling every kind of wine. He was most anxious that we should have raspberry syrup as it seemed to be popular with his customers, but we did not like to explain the reason why we preferred the lemon.

Dinner was well up to standard. Every meal seemed too short because everything was so good; we started with soup and then partook of some omelette. While eating, a nice little hot plate, warmed by two night lights, was put on the table and our plates were placed on top of the hotplate, ready for the next course. When we had these put in front of us, they were then replaced on the hot plate by a large dish of chicken, served with potatoes and green vegetables. Despite the large helpings, a maid always came and asked if we had had sufficient. Then finally, a delicious sweet—meringue chantilly—and to accompany our meal, we had white wine.

The next day was definitely a more promising day, and though still cloudy, we decided to be optimistic and take lunch up to Männlichen in the hope of seeing the beautiful flowers mentioned to us by one of the dining-room maids.

We caught the mid-morning train to Wengernalp, sharing a compartment with a party of Americans who had whirring movie cameras in front of our noses most of the way. They were very thrilled with all they saw, and Jane was a most excellent guide to them, pointing out landmarks and flowers for which they were most grateful.

Arriving at Wegernalp, we quickly found the path that lead to Männlichen. Striding briskly along its winding track we viewed the flowers away in the distance and as we approached, we saw them to be just as lovely as we had hoped—beautiful gentians, forget-me-nots, and large wild pansies, making a carpet of yellow and white intermingled with patches of blue. We both felt it was the best display of alpine flowers we had seen anywhere.

Moving on past the village of Männlichen, we found a beautiful view of the countryside. Sitting on the very edge of the Lauterbrunnen face, looking down towards Interlaken and Lake Thun, with Wengen at our feet (literally so, when I dangled mine over the edge much to Jane's perturbation) it looked like a child's miniature village.

The sun was so hot, the grass so soft and the view so lovely that it was hard to drag ourselves away, but we knew we had a long walk back to the hotel as we did not propose to try the very steep way down the side of Männlichen to Wengen. We were lucky, as the sun went in soon after we had started back and some heavy clouds loomed, but it did not rain and we enjoyed every minute of the walk. We had our usual greeting with all nationalities, and on the way passed an observation post where we were entertained by a Swiss male choir as they stood on a raised platform near a café, looking down towards the Grindelwald valley. It was a lovely scene and so typical of the Swiss who seem to enjoy impromptu singing.

At this point on the homeward journey, we met two English lads with large backpacks, looking very tired. They had walked up from Grindelwald and were heading for Lauterbrunnen. We put them on the right path and their faces brightened considerably when we said it was all downhill. One of them, we suspected, had a blister and Jane's calling as a nurse

Lake Thun.

made her wish we had our plasters with us, but when she saw them join up with two young Swiss boys, she felt happier.

We stopped on the way down from Wengernalp for a short rest and while sitting on a pile of wood, a tall, well-built woman carrying a neatly rolled umbrella with a modern frill, came up the path accompanied by a small, petite grey-haired lady in a skirt and blouse. The younger woman greeted us in English and started a most animated monologue during which we learned that her name was Frau Sandreuter, she was Swiss, lived at Basel, that her husband had died seven years ago, that she was holidaying in a chalet situated just beyond our hotel that had been lent to her by a friend, exactly how they fed themselves and what they were proposing to do the next day if the weather was good. She then went on to say that she understood we still had food rationing in England and that we must eat all we could while in Switzerland 'leaving nothing on the plate'. As she said this, she made a large circular movement with her arm as if clearing the dish herself. Then, rising to continue on her way, she expressed the hope that she would see us again and told us to look out for her passing the hotel in the morning with a shawl over her head, or in the afternoon in her Florentine hat.

Her companion stood a little apart all this time, uttering not a word, but had a sweet smile on her face. With that, they both walked briskly up the path with great long strides. My eyes twinkling, I murmured quietly to Jane, 'The people one meets!' but we hoped we might get an invitation to see over her chalet just the same.

Entering the dining-room in time for dinner, we were soon pounced upon by our friend, Mrs America. She greatly entertained us throughout the meal and ended by inviting us to visit her in California, saying also that she was in the meat business and had two or three ranches in Mexico. Our eyes sparkled; she really meant this and we meant to accept since she was a lonely soul with a large, empty house. When I said we didn't know her name, she said, 'Everyone calls me Pam, but my name is really Virginia G. Studivant.' She was most amusing and had us in fits of laughter over her way of saying things, for example: 'I sure must get rid of some of this lard,' meaning we believed, that she must lose some weight, and 'Gee, did you ever see anything quite like the toilet paper in Switzerland—why it's just like taking up the linoleum!'

Before going to bed, all three of us went to her room where we looked at an American guidebook on Britain and the Continent, and we underlined the hotels we thought most suitable for her in London. She gave Jane some peach cream for her sunburnt nose and we came away with three thriller-dillers.

A really glorious day arrived without a cloud in the sky. Reflected in the glass of our French window, we saw the rosy sunrise on Jungfrau, but were both too sleepy to get up and look at the real version—what it was to be lazy! The birds in the early morning were wonderful and the cuckoo was still very talkative, especially early in the morning and evening, and could be heard even right up at the foot of Jungfrau.

We had breakfast in the garden, sitting in the sun, and then went off to church. The congregation was not as large as the week before and this made singing hard work, but this time we were helped by a very good organist. We sat by the window with a lovely view of Jungfrau; what more could one want to make one realise how much we had to be grateful for?

Lunch was terrific with celery soup, delicious young asparagus and tornadoes with potatoes and cauliflower. The potatoes were cut into perfect balls of equal size and fried, and the cauliflower had grated cheese on top. This was followed by a goodly helping of strawberries and cream; the cream was fresh and thick—absolutely too delicious for words.

With our cups full to overflowing, we settled ourselves in the deck-chairs in the hotel garden and enjoyed the sights of the populous going to and fro up the little road as they took the air on this lovely hot Sunday afternoon. We had hoped that Mrs America might join us on her return from Jungfraujoch, but there was no sign of her, so we had tea and biscuits at four o'clock and then walked down to Wengen, enjoying the lovely evening. It turned out that Mrs America was stuck with three rather dull English visitors that night, so we went to bed fairly early, having watched a near-rosy sunset.

We rose with the lark the next morning intent on going up Jungfrau, but by the time we had breakfasted, it was not looking so good and so we did a very hurried change of gear, from extra coats and woollies to mackintoshes, and caught the morning train down to Lauterbrunnen, changed and then travelled on to Zweilutschinen, changed again and so up the other valley to Grindelwald. It was possible to go by the Wengen railway via Kleine Scheidegg, but it cost far more and our meagre allowance would not run to this sort of luxury.

On arrival at Grindelwald, we walked up the main street, a pretty little place, but not to be compared with Wengen on account of its cars and general air of tourism. There was even a horse-drawn taxi at the station ready to take one up to the first *bahn*[48] at the opposite end of the village. We took this and reached the start of the chairlift just as it started to rain.

This mode of travel was something quite new to me and I was fascinated. The chairs were in pairs with an awning above and hanging from a cable. The arrival and departure platform was rather like the start of a fairground bumper car sideshow; the chairs were pushed around by the attendants who brought out extra ones from a siding as required. Due to the weather, a mackintosh blind was fixed down one side of the pair of chairs and we were provided with heavy wool-lined burberries that the attendant wrapped around us before fastening us in with a bar across our fronts. He then punched our tickets, stepped back to the wall and pulled a lever down. With a bump, we shot out through a doorway and up over a field; the rain had temporarily stopped and the sun was peeping out. The initial rush as we left the station came as a slight shock, but after this there was little feeling of movement, except a slight dropping sensation when we crossed a supporting pylon. We sailed over the fir trees, thick with cones hanging like Christmas decorations, and across the fields which were a mass of glorious flowers, all with very little sound.

There were three stations en route and at each, our tickets were punched, the handle pulled, and off we shot, as it were, into space. Each time the attendant seemed amused by our squeals as we left the shelter of the platform. At the second station, a hailstorm hit us and the attendant told us we could get out and wait until it cleared. He showed us where to

---

48 Way; road.

look to get a good view of the valley and after about five minutes, he tucked us back in our mackintoshes and sent us off with a smile and a wave.

At the top, it was cold and still raining with low clouds overhead, so we went into a delightful chalet restaurant where there was a buzz of cheery talk to a background of vibrant Swiss music. There were families sitting down to a full dinner, and at the next table, hikers with their bags of sandwiches spread out on the folk-weave cloth. We had glasses of coffee and our own sandwiches. No one seemed to mind how long we sat or when we paid, and a large black stove in the centre of the room, its chimney going straight up through the roof, made the room beautifully warm and inviting.

When we eventually left the warmth of the restaurant, it was raining again, so we decided not to venture out into the wet environment, but to take the chairlift back down again. Luckily for us, the sun came out and we had a magnificent view all around, although our beloved giants were still quite enshrouded in mist.

Back in Grindelwald village, we fell to the temptation of half a kilo of strawberries. They were enormous, some about the size of a large plum. We boarded the train half an hour early and wolfed down all the strawberries there and then, being so very hungry and the strawberries being so very delicious. It was extremely fortunate we did as we were late for dinner yet again, due this time to the returning Wengen train. It appeared that it was a part of its daily routine to deliver bundles of hay to the surrounding chalets. Halfway up the hillside, the train suddenly stopped and the guard alighted. With the aid of a pitchfork, he then filled the flat open truck that was attached to the front of the train with bundles of hay which had been gathered into large net bags and stacked by the side of the track. As you would imagine, all of this took some time but we then proceeded on our way, only to stop again just before we reached Wengen itself. Here the guard, helped by two others who were waiting for our arrival, unloaded the bundles and prepared to carry them off to their chalet stores.

After a hurried dinner, we again passed a pleasant evening in Mrs America's company; she kindly offered us coffee, gave us her highly amusing assessment of Agatha Christie's famous thrill-diller, *Murder on the Orient Express,* and then, after being told that we were hopeful of visiting Jungfraujoch on the following day, organised to meet us upon our return to Kleine Scheidegg where we were to have tea in one of the hotels.

The next day looked promising, although there was some cloud, but we decided to risk Jungfraujoch, travelling via the morning train. We gathered together every warm garment we possessed, despite the brilliant sunshine, and off we went. We had become so accustomed to travelling third class that we automatically squeezed into an already full third-class compartment as far as Kleine Scheidegg where we had to change trains. Remembering in time to board a select second-class carriage, we found the other occupants were a young girl from Grimsby, and a South African couple whom we initially thought were a bit stuffy, but turned out to be quite the opposite, handing chocolates around and the husband talking very knowledgeably about South African politics. We felt justly proud when they said that of all the cities they had visited during their tour of the Continent, none of then could compare with London for cleanliness, the friendly people, and as a place where you got good value for your money, even if prices were high. They were cutting short their time in Switzerland in order to return for a last look at London.

We started a steep climb towards Eiger as soon as we left Kleine Scheidegg and when we reached Eigergletscher Station there was quite a lot of snow. Soon after this, we entered the tunnel and our first stop was to look out of a window at the rocky face of Eiger looking towards Grindelwald and Lake Thun far below us. The sun was well out by now and in the distance there was a lovely blue haze, giving the impression of warmth. However, we were not to be deceived and were very glad of our coats when we left the train.

Once on our way again, we scrambled into our additional garments; I wore a blouse and trousers, sleeveless pullover, cardigan buttoned to the neck, wind-jacket, coat, a thick scarf on my head and woolly gloves. The others were far less warmly clad and we felt very sorry for them with their thin shoes and bare legs.

Our next stop in the tunnel was to look through a large plate-glass window in the face of Mönch, this time looking over the Eismeer Glacier (about 10,400 feet). Here, we had a wonderful view of this vast expanse of white snow and ice which was contrasted by a number of largish black birds suddenly coming into view and circling around .

We reached Jungfraujoch, and on leaving the little station platform, found ourselves in a large hall which was beautifully heated and had a souvenir shop, post office and restaurant leading from it. Straight in front of us, as we came through the swing-doors, were two large windows looking out onto a small terrace, and beyond, an expanse of brilliant snow and the Aletsch Glacier stretching away to the south. On each side were peaks of all shapes and sizes, and of course, snow covered. From the terrace, we looked right down onto the glacier and some unpleasant-looking crevasses. The rock face next to the terrace was covered with

Aletsch Glacier.

large icicles, and while we were there, the sun melted one and it fell with a loud crack. Up here there were more of the black birds seen at Eismeer Station and a strong wind was making landing difficult for them. We threw them some bread and they folded their wings right back so that they looked rather like heraldic birds, and in this way they managed to land on the snow, although even then it was not always possible for them to get down to where we had thrown the bread.

Back in the hall, there was a lot of bustle and noise, with people of all nationalities writing postcards, eating sandwiches, talking and moving in and out and around and about. We went into the restaurant where we ordered some coffee—and was it good! We sat at the same table with a little lady from the hotel, but as she only spoke a little French, conversation was not easy. We were also joined by the lovely South African couple who had been in our compartment on the train ride between Wengen and Kleine Scheidegg.

Warmed and refreshed, we set off down a vast tunnel at the end of which we turned a corner. There before us was an archway of ice, almost blue in the sun, and through the arch, a view of the glacier and its overlooking peaks. The path rose up a short incline which people without nails in their shoes seemed to find very perilous. On the left, a wall of frozen snow of about five foot high, and on the right, a sheer drop to the glacier and some nasty looking crevasses, so it was small wonder that brave hearts failed when feet began to slither and slide.

Over the little rise, we came down into the sun to shelter from the wind, so we were able to sit on wooden seats in the snow, take off our scarves and feel quite warm. Dark glasses were most necessary in this vast expanse of snow and moisturiser was plastered on faces against the burning glare of the sun on the snow.

The long tunnel seemed very dark after the glare of the snow but once our eyes became accustomed to it, we took the lift up to the observatory. Words just cannot describe the view from this beautifully heated platform, surrounded on all sides by glass, and we both felt we could have remained there indefinitely. The South African couple were up with us and the man told us where to stand on the outside platform in order to avoid the bitter wind. He also kindly showed us his map and pointed out the various less well-known peaks visible on each side of the glacier. Being up at this height, it really seemed hard to believe that the little white houses far below were really quite busy hotels and Wengernalp Station.

We came down from the observatory in the middle of the afternoon and found there was no train back to Kleine Scheidegg until later, so we sat in the waiting hall and watched the people, which was an endless amusement. We boarded the train in good time and found it nice and warm, but we unwittingly put ourselves in an end carriage with the only door to the coach. People continually clambered in and left the door open and even our fierce looks and candid remarks made no difference.

We reached Kleine Scheidegg, and there waiting for us as planned, was Mrs America, looking immaculate in a grey frock and cardigan, but rather cold since we were an hour later than we had expected. We, in contrast were very hot and dishevelled with all our clothes, but notwithstanding, she escorted us into the very smart lounge of the hotel for tea.

Summoning a passing waitress, she announced that she wanted a 'high ball' and that we would have tea and cakes. Of course, the waitress was completely nonplussed by the mention of a high ball and had to be enlightened on its ingredients—a double whisky, water and ice. Jane and I had a delicious pot of tea and a creamy pastry each while we heard all about how she had broken her leg, and that she always carried a complete dispensary around with her whenever she travelled. Technical discussion then ensued and dear Jane, being a nurse, offered to give her 'a shot of liver' with the surgery to open just before bedtime.

We took the train back to Wengen and on the way up to our hotel from the station, Mrs America suddenly stopped outside a shop and said, 'I guess I'll just go in here for a minute and you'd better come too because I want to buy you some candies. Now go ahead. I don't eat them, so choose what you want.' I was so overcome that I was speechless, but Jane, also overcome, regained her manners more quickly and suggested a mixture of the luscious chocolates on show. We came out carrying one kilogram of the most delectable candies we ever saw, and whenever we thanked her she said, 'Gee, you must be nuts!'

Back at the hotel, Jane made preparations for 'the shot' and boiled the water for sterilizing in our kettle upstairs and carried it down to Mrs America in her first-floor room. (What a useful adjunct a kettle can be when one is on holiday!) Mrs America once again offered us coffee before the surgery.

On the following day, we decided to take it a little more easy as the Jungfraujoch trip had been quite tiring and also Mrs America was 'picking up her sticks' in the morning and going on to Berne. Wanting to say good-bye, we tapped on her door at half past ten to find her a little bemused; she was still in her dressing-gown and surrounded by cases, clothes, and pots and bottles of every size and shape. Jane, seeing her distress, did wonders helping her as I shovelled boxes of medicines into a large hag's bag, followed by her toothbrush and powder quickly placed into a plastic bag, together with various other oddments. Her clothes and luggage were all magnificent and her undies like fairy gossamer!

At last, Emile took her luggage—at eleven o'clock as planned—all of which she insisted on registering, including the medicine chest. Immaculately clad in a black suit, suede shoes, pale yellow blouse and gloves, and a very Parisian hat in teasle straw, we escorted her down to the station.

In the afternoon our feet were drawn to our beloved Wengernalp and we sat in the meadow below the Kleine Scheidegg path, basking in the sun and gazing happily at our beloved mountains. We had the usual excellent dinner, followed by the pleasure of a rosy sunset on Jungfrau. The colours were superb; the pink glow of the sunset on the snow against the soft blue of the evening sky. Down in the valley below us, someone was playing a horn, a rather lovely soft, lilting tune. We both felt the loss of Mrs America.

We rose later in the morning and breakfasted in the garden, deciding to go to Schynige Platte. It was a perfect day and we set off to catch the train. On leaving the booking office, my hand was suddenly grasped by a woman in dark glasses and I realised it was our Swiss friend, Frau Sandreuter from Basel whom we met in the woods on the Wengernalp path. She seemed delighted to see us and was accompanied by the same smiling lady who turned out to be her sister; we all boarded the Lauterbrunnen train. They were going to Grindelwald and this produced a song from Frau Sandreuter, who had a lovely singing voice and sang with a broad smile on her face, gesticulating and tapping Jane on her arm at intervals. They left the train at Zweilutschinen and Frau Sandreuter stood outside our carriage window, still singing to us. She was an interesting woman who spoke seven languages, and invited us to visit her in Basel to see her home that she said was largely furnished by Heals and Liberty[49] and was very English, her saloon being Queen Anne.

We went on to Wilderswil where we changed to a little train that was to take us up to Schynige Platte. It was of the cattle-truck variety with striped awnings, which on this occasion were rolled up and not in use. The coach was full of singing youths in Swiss souvenir forage caps and dark glasses, and two very English dames; one a bespectacled spinster, angular and unbending, and the other—her companion and cousin—a dear old lady, very deaf and wearing several dimity silk scarves, a blouse and gloves in navy blue and white. We sat on the narrow wooden seats, our knees almost touching those of the people opposite. The spinster was very intent on seeing the flowers, but appeared to have little idea of how to preserve all the specimens she proposed collecting. She was not at all impressed by the stupendous scenery.

On arrival at the little station, we hurried away from the crowds and climbed to the top of a little rocky point with a cairn. From here the view was quite indescribable; the whole range of the Bernese Alps lay before us, clear against a blue sky except for an occasional piece of white cottonwool cloud, which added to the beauty. Working from the left we could see the Wetterhorn, Schrekhorn and Finsterrahorn with their very lovely peaks just peeping out from the shoulder of Eiger, Mönch, Jungfrau, Grosshorn, Breithorn and Tchingelhorn. Below, the two valleys of Grindelwald and Lauterbrunnen, their rivers shining like white ribbon as they wound their way through woods and meadows. Looking the other way, we could see Lake Thun, Nissen and the Kandersteg Valley. It was terribly hot, but we felt we must eat our lunch looking at this tremendous scene, so we perched on the hillside, while below us, near the hotel, parties of children sat in groups singing.

Few people seemed to make the effort to reach our vantage point, until the spinster lady from the train was seen to be bearing down upon us with a scarf full of flowers. And do you think we could get rid of her? Oh no! We had to identify some of her plants and then we heard all about her cousin and how she was too old to be much of a companion. She then went on to complain about the food and that she had not eaten her packed lunch, saying it was unimaginative. Her dear old cousin hobbled along to say she was going for a little walk and received a rather unenthusiastic offer of companionship from the spinster.

---

49 English department stores.

The cousin responded with: 'Oh no dear, you rest,' and rest she did—with us! Jane said she sensed my boredom, and so when the opportunity came, we got away and went and sat on the grass below the station, having a last loving look at our mountains from this perfect viewpoint.

Later, we took the train back to Wilderswil only to find the poor old cousin waiting in the full heat of the sun in the hope of catching a bus. She had left the spinster looking for gentians. How anyone could leave her alone like this was incomprehensible to us both.

We had just missed a train due to a misdirection by a station official, so we went across the road to the hotel and drank glasses of delicious tea while watching the locals bring in cartloads of hay; one particularly delightful sight was of a man pulling a cart along and being helped by what appeared to be his young son and his black and white collie dog.

After dinner, as we were relaxing in the lounge, Frau Sandreuter came in to give us her visiting card and told us that she proposed to return now to her chalet and 'bathe myself in water, first hot and then cold here and here,' patting her front as she spoke. She then told us that she would 'put on dabs of—what do you call it?—odo-ro-no? Here and here.' We of course were nearly convulsed with laughter realising that she meant to put deodorant under her arms, but it was all quite a serious matter to her, because as she said, she was most particular about such things. She obviously enjoyed chatting to us, as it took quite a lot of encouragement from us to finally get her home to her ablutions and allow us to go to bed.

Another lovely day dawned, clear and bright, and we realised sadly that this was to be our last day in Wengen before staring our journey home. We decided to spend the morning lazing in the garden, but Frau Sandreuter arrived and very kindly invited us to walk with her up to her friend's chalet where she was staying. To our delight, she invited us in on the understanding that we sat in the salon while she made her bed. The salon was very pretty with big French windows that opened up onto a balcony and net curtains that were looped back with little strips of frilled net—a present from her, she said, to her friend the owner. She had made forty-four of them.

Taking us on a tour of the chalet, we found that it was spotless and had everything one could wish for including a nice bathroom with a shower, hand basin and two electric water heaters. Frau Sandreuter's bedroom had windows looking towards the mountains, two very comfortable beds covered with folk-weave bedspreads, nice plain furniture in light wood which seemed to fit in exactly and two lovely little bedside lamps with pleated shades in the same kind of small flower pattern material as the curtains. Then there was a little room looking out to the forest and a small double spare room with its own little breakfast room leading out of it; this would just have suited us nicely. The chalet also possessed a very modern kitchen with an electric cooker and an Aga[50]-type stove, built-in cupboards, shining pots and pans and a zinc-lined sink and draining board. She then took us up to see the flat above, which was self-contained and occupied temporarily by a nice Swiss family who seemed only too pleased that we should be shown over it.

The tour now over, she said good-bye and told us that she would come and collect us in the evening and take us for a walk around the outskirts of the village. Sure enough, she arrived just as we were all collected in the garden watching a perfect Jungfrau sunset. A horn player was playing a wonderful tune and Frau Sandreuter explained that it was a Swiss folk song, the words being something along the lines of 'Turn your eyes from the valleys to the foothills and from the foothills to snow-capped peaks'. The song was repeated until the rosy glow faded from the peak—altogether a most memorable experience.

The walk we took with Frau Sandreuter was a most attractive one, made especially so when the colouring was so lovely and a new noon was shining above the opposite side of the Lauterbrunnen Valley. She gave us a lesson in pronunciation and was most amused at our efforts. It was such a perfect night that we both rather wished we could have been left in peace and quiet to take it all in, but nevertheless, it was very kind of Frau Sandreuter to show us this delightful path which led around the village, through the woods and out onto the Hunnenfluh path. It took us a long time because she would keep stopping to press home a point and we kept thinking of our packing to be done that night. At last we were able to say goodbye, with a promise to visit when we next we came to Switzerland.

We woke feeling very sad. We had our breakfast in the garden and then took a short walk down to the village for a last look around. The hotel very kindly gave us a hot lunch and after the meal we gave the head maid a small tip; she seemed quite overwhelmed and beamed at us. Frau Giger, the proprietor of the hotel, came out into the garden to see us off and dear Emile took all our cases off to the station—after having tied a piece of strong string around Jane's case, it being so full—registered our luggage for us, and then having stowed

50 A gas stove which would burn unattended for twenty-four hours.

our hand luggage into the train, he stood on the platform and waited to wave his cap in farewell as we left; how charming the Swiss were in every way!

We were now back to travelling second class and so were able to give ourselves plenty of space and air on this very hot day. Having left Interlaken, we skirted Lake Thun, which looked simply wonderful; the water blue and so clear that we longed to leap from the train and plunge into it. The gardens by the lakeside were a mass of roses and every now and then we passed a café with its coloured umbrellas vivid against the blue of the water. Jane excitedly pointed out Oberhofen, where she had stayed on a previous visit.

On arrival in Berne, we deposited our bags in the Left-Luggage area, donned sunglasses and set out to make the most of our two and a half hour visit.

The city of Berne.

Jane was a wonderful guide and I marvelled at her memory, for she had only paid a couple of fairly brief visits to the town before and yet she seemed to know, without any hesitation, in which direction she wanted to take me. The cobbled streets were quite fascinating; there were picturesque fountains placed down the centre of the street with each base planted with red geraniums and the central column topped by wonderful painted figures of women and warriors, their colours shining in the sun. On each side, the streets were lined by arcades of lovely stonework where one could walk in the shade and admire the very beautiful shops. These arcades seemed very full of people, and after the peace and quiet of our dear Wengen, the heat and bustle proved rather exhausting. The shops were very grand and their window-dressing most attractive, the sweet shops in particular having the most wonderful designs and figures made out of chocolate.

We took a bus down as far as the bear pit, not for the purpose of seeing the world-famous bears of Berne, but in order to get a view of the streets and also to reach the river and the old part of the town. Everything was fascinating in these streets and if one could drag one's gaze away from the arcades and fountains to look upwards, the tall houses themselves were lovely with their colour-washed walls, their little wrought-iron balconies and their window boxes stuffed with flowers. Some of them had delightful carved gargoyles under the eaves. We gave the bears a quick look, but the odour was rather strong and so we quickly turned our attention to the lovely wide bridge over the river. The view here of old Berne was superb; squalid-looking houses, their walls lapped by the river and rows of washing hanging from small window to small window. The scene reminded me rather of the houses at Girona in Spain; the architecture was of course very different, but they both had the same very vivid tomato-red tiles and light brown brick walls. Squalid though they undoubtedly were, they certainly had charm.

It was now time to think about the tea we had promised ourselves before we continued our journey to Basel. As we approached the famous Zytglogge[51] standing above the crossway of the town, we realised there was a small crowd of people gathered and that it was just coming up to four o'clock, so we were lucky enough to see the whole cycle from five minutes to the hour when a number of little figures came out and circled round and round, to the little man coming and striking the hour itself.

The Zytglogge tower in the old town.

Jane then led me to a delightful tea shop where we had two cups of tea each, a cream cake covered with nuts and two strawberry tarts with cream. This really made us feel good and we were able to sit for some time and watch the inhabitants of Berne as they came, choosing their cakes and sitting down to enjoy them.

Our journey to Basel was uneventful and we arrived to find our next train was due to leave at thee o'clock.

51 A clock tower that has a display of mechanical figures which are set in motion four minutes before every hour on the clock's east face. Zytglogge is also famous for its astronomical clock from the 16th century.

There were masses of luggage with Hotel Plan labels outside the buffet, but no sign of a courier, so we added our bags to the general pile and went off to spend our remaining money. We bought two bananas, which were very expensive, and a bottle of white wine. The white-coated woman behind the counter of the wine stall seemed to be a bit offhand at first, but turned up trumps in the end and offered to open the bottle and put a cork in for us.

On our return to our luggage, we found the Hotel Plan courier who told us the train was in and we could go to it if we liked. So, we gathered up our cases and we went off through Customs—who were not in the least interested in us—and out onto the station. Here we found a mass of people all herded together like sheep, patiently waiting to get through the barrier. Suddenly, I recognised the back views of the people standing just in front of me as the pleasant man and his sweet wife from the journey out. They both seemed to be so pleased to see us, saying they had been enquiring about us on the train from Lucerne and wondering what had happened to us. They suggested that we should try and get into a carriage together on the way back. Not long after this, we suddenly saw the two Irish females too—Pink Frock and Brown Frock. We exchanged greetings, but we did not invite them to join us!

Managing to obtain a carriage with our newly found travelling companions, we settled down to enjoy a cosy chat. Soon, we were all feeling pretty hungry and so started to prepare our supper, but here we seemed to be dogged with bad luck. Our companions had to break open the lock of one of their cases before they could get at their food, and we found that we had left our store of eggs, cheese, nuts and chocolate behind in the table drawer of our room. However, we had nice fresh croissants, fruit, and the remains of an orange cake, together with some coffee, so we were quite all right. During this time, we did a certain amount of exchanging of experiences and we learnt that our companions had been staying at Wilderswil in the railway hotel where we had had such a good glass of tea while watching a cart being pulled along by a man, his small son and his black and white collie dog.

We arrived at Ostend at about eight o'clock the following morning and found that Customs was not open and the Hotel Plan courier not very helpful with information about where we could obtain breakfast. Slightly annoyed at this poor example of customer service, we took our place in the queue for Customs. Happily, it wasn't too long before we were allowed through, although at this point we had to say good-bye to our companions who were travelling on to another destination.

Boarding our boat to Dover, we procured deck-chairs in third-class (the first-class was all under cover and we both preferred the good sea air) and then decided on a wash before breakfast. Taking our hag's bag containing our bathroom things with us, we found a beautifully clean bathroom on the port side of the boat where we had a good scrub and tidy, and then, feeling terrifically refreshed, went off in search of the lounge.

While we were eating, we could see people pouring along the quay to the boat and we were thankful that we came on board straightaway without getting breakfast first, since it was obvious that the boat was going to be very full indeed. Back on deck, this was at once all too obvious, since the deck was already about three or four rows deep in chairs and it was quite a problem getting to our places against the rail. Suddenly realising that I had left our hag's bag, with our bathroom things in it, in the restaurant. Jane, very nobly, insisted on going to find it; she had quite a chase but ended by having a lovely chat with the Purser, so perhaps it was worth it!

It was a perfect day of brilliant sunshine and a blue sea with hardly a ripple. We passed the time very pleasantly by reviewing our holiday; the very beautiful places we had visited, the great kindnesses we had received, and the many people we had met, and our thoughts naturally turned to Mrs America, Frau Sandreuter and many others. Smilingly, I turned to Jane and said, 'Oh, the people one meets!'

CANADA
Lake Louise
Johnstone Canyon
Banff
Vancouver
Calgary
Quebec
Montreal
Ottawa
Toronto
Niagara
New York
THE UNITED STATES
OF AMERICA
Salt Lake City
Colorado Springs
New Orleans
Miami
Nassau

With Oh So Little

1953–1954: Canada and the East Coast of the United States

In 1953, Helen and her mother planned to visit Helen's brother John in British Columbia. This put travel ideas into my head yet again, and I toyed with the thought of going to Canada 'for just one year.' The necessity of having to resign from my job at the BBC caused me some qualms, but I knew that the time was right for me to move on. I approached Jane with the proposal of going to Quebec City and she unhesitantly accepted my invitation. So we made our plans, organised our bookings and then investigated how much money we would be able to take with us.

Finance was still tight in post-war England and the authorities only allowed us twenty pounds each, but this was to be halved as Jane had admitted to going to a post as Sister Tutor at one of the hospitals and had been instructed to return her twenty pounds at the end of the first month. Accordingly, we started life in our new environment with only ten pounds each.

It was 14th April 1953; a red letter day indeed. Jane arrived at our flat in South Kensington burdened with a mammoth amount of luggage, and then we all—Jane, Molly and I—left by taxi for Euston Station, travelling by way of Langham Place so that I could have a last look at the window of my BBC office—Room 504, The Langham Hotel. With a spray of lilies-of-the-valley pinned to my coat (a gift from my two year-old godson), I felt a little apprehensive about our big adventure, but I kept telling myself, 'You are only going for a year and then you will be home again, picking up the threads of your life where you put them down.'

Finally, the sight of the platform with piles of luggage all smothered, like our own, in Canadian Pacific labels and the sight of our reception committee—our dear families and friends—got me excited. We stood chatting, but the time seemed to fly by and soon the loudspeakers proclaimed, 'All aboard for the *Empress of Scotland*' and so, with farewells all around, we left London on the biggest adventure of our lives. But the goodbyes were by no means over. As we approached Hatch End, the train conveniently slowed down and we were able to call goodbye to Jane's sister and young nephew as they stood, two strangely emotional figures, on the far end of the district line platform. This was the moment when hankies ceased to flutter from the windows and were put to other use.

We reached Liverpool in due course to find it looking very industrious with its mass of sheds and warehouses, and as the train chugged along I had glimpses of the canals through stone archways, and of horses pulling cartloads of sacks along cobbled streets.

Alighting from the train, we were hurried over to the Customs area, and then having had our luggage checked, we handed in our ration books and felt rather like displaced persons with no homeland. Next, we were bustled onto the quay to be confronted with our massive ship—the *Empress of Scotland*—which was to be our home and the centre of our life for a week. Boarding through a gangway, we descended into the rabbit warren of passages to find our cabin and the final stage of our memorable farewell—the dressing table in our cabin was scarcely visible under a mass of flowers, greetings and telegrams.

The Empress of Scotland.

We sailed during dinner, and after a view of the twinkling lights of Birkenhead, we went to bed and slept the sleep of the just, despite the unfamiliar sounds and surroundings.

Our first day on board was typical of all we had been told. Passengers appeared to quickly settle down to the routine of ship life and this was to a background of Scottish hills and calm water, for we had sailed up the coast during the night and anchored in the Clyde off Greenock. It was a mild, damp day and the morning was spent writing letters and postcards and watching the tugs and river craft. The steamer bringing passengers and luggage out from Greenock also brought a piper who was later seen pacing the first-class promenade deck and playing all the well-known Scottish airs. During the early afternoon, the steamer, carrying waving friends and with pipes skirling, drew away, circled the *Empress* and then made for Princes Pier. Almost at the same moment, we moved downstream and the sun came out to give us a glorious view of the hills, still with some snow on them. What a picture to carry away with us.

Before reaching Arran, a Clyde pilot boat came out and it was amazing to see her tossing up and down while our 26,000 tons remained almost motionless. The pilot came on board by way of a rope ladder, and with sirens exchanging farewells, the pilot boat sailed away, leaving us feeling so detached from the last few bustling weeks of preparation. Not far ahead lay the Atlantic Ocean and a week with no concerns or pressures. We did not know what future lay in store for us, but for the time being, it was out of our control so we decided to relax and make to most of this carefree time.

It really is amazing how one manages to put away more and more food without taking very much exercise. We sat on deck all day, every day, sometimes in brilliant sunshine, sometimes under a grey sky, and on the last day, in snow, but always under rugs and thick coats, with a hardworking steward to tuck in our toes and keep us warm with mid-morning bouillon and afternoon tea.

There were a great many children on board; little Peter going out to join his father, Bryony who loved to play deck tennis, and particularly James, Roger and nineteen month old Elizabeth. They came from Scotland, and if you asked five year old Roger where he was going, he would say, 'To Edmonton, Alberta, where it's always very cold.'

Our first sight of land came on Sunday. Snow and sleet had been falling sufficiently heavily for a sailor to be out sweeping the decks; the ship's siren wailed at intervals and through the blizzard we saw a line of snow-covered land—a grey, bleak, cold and most uninviting Canada.

On Monday night, the Canadian and the US immigration officers came on board. The Americans especially, were most charming, wishing us luck and telling us all they knew about Quebec and how to set about visiting the States from there. We were told to be ready to disembark early the next morning, so with rather large butterflies in our tummies, we went to bed.

Amongst the telegrams and flowers we received at Liverpool were letters from the Church of England Port Chaplain wishing us bon voyage and saying he was notifying the chaplain in Quebec of the date of our arrival and enclosing badges to be worn on landing so that we could be singled out. As we finished breakfast, together with the only other two tourist passengers disembarking at Quebec, we were handed a note from the chaplain's representative saying that he was waiting for us at the Purser's Office, and to our surprise, we found that he had come to help us through the landing formalities and then drive us in his car to the hospital where Jane was to work. We were most impressed by the interest shown by the churches since we also received a letter from the Presbyterian minister, welcoming us to Quebec and offering any help we might need.

A cold, grey day with light snow, and trees without a sign of spring, greeted us as we left the Customs sheds and climbed the steep road leading up to the Plains of Abraham.

Our welcome at the hospital was most warm. I was to be their guest until Jane and I found accommodation in the city and the Matron told us that we were to feel free to do exactly as we liked, and that Jane was not to hurry on duty. Later in the day, one of the nurses who was off duty took us down town to buy Jane's uniform and the Secretary of the hospital offered me a position, but warned me that the pay was poor in comparison with what I should probably get outside, unless I was fluent in French.

We had arrived on the Tuesday, but did not start work until the following Monday, when we also moved to temporary accommodation in the town. During that first week, I obtained a stenographer's post with the Canadian General Electric Company at forty pounds a week; we found a room with a very kind woman who provided us with an electric hotplate, despite a no cooking rule in her house; we heard around the hospital of a delightful furnished apartment that was available for the summer months; the Matron took us to an impressive St George's Day Service in the cathedral; and by the Friday, we were able to watch the *Empress* sail by on her way home without any feeling of homesickness.

Our ship (as we'd grown to call her) was at that time the flagship of the Canadian Pacific line, and after her stop at Quebec, she had continued her journey to Montreal, and then three days later, she commenced her return voyage back to Scotland. A few days after our arrival we went down to watch her grand procession.

A cold wind was blowing, and although it was late April, there had been a light fall of snow earlier in the day. We stood looking down at the Old Town and at the ferries that provided a fifteen minute service between Quebec City and the town of Levis, situated on the opposite bank. A ferry left from each side at the same time. They were funny tub-shaped boats and their combined routes almost formed a perfect circle. A very talkative man told us that 'she'—the *Empress*—would dock at about in about an half an hour's time, so we decided to come back later.

We returned to find our friend sheltering from the cold wind against a wall of the elevator—or *ascenseur* as it's called—which travels up and down to Lower Town. 'She'll be a bit late. More like eight o'clock,' he said. It was practically dark by this time. Across the river and way down as far as we could see, lights twinkled along the water's edge and up the sloping hills behind Levis. The ferries seemed to be running almost continually, making a cheerful ball of light that reflected in the rippling water. Our friend, who admitted he seldom missed seeing one of the big passenger liners pass, drew our attention to the tender, which would be taking passengers out to the ship. Before long, it drew away from the quay below us and set off upstream, steaming quickly around the corner out of our sight.

About a quarter of an hour later came a sight of a lifetime. With lights ablaze along her whole length and with the tender nosing alongside her port side, the *Empress* slipped into view—and 'slipped' was the only way to describe it, for she appeared to be making no movement in the water. We could see the lights of the two dining saloons and could picture the scene in the tourist one (we wondered who was sitting at our table and how they were feeling about their trip). The ship never entirely stopped to pick up her passengers, but they were transferred from the tender while she moved slowly downstream. When she was opposite us, the tender drew away and then across the stretch of water between us came three siren blasts from the tender, followed by the familiar deep, muffled tone of the liner in reply. That farewell somehow defined better than anything the difference in these two ships; one small, fussy, busy, urgently hurrying to and fro with its cargo of passengers, its voice rather loud and bossy, almost as if it suffered from an inferiority complex. The other was majestic, a huge floating hotel whose life went on, day in and day out, voyage after voyage. A ship who had reached the peak of her career and didn't need to lift her voice to be heard.

The farewell over, her deck lights went out and she was quickly out of sight behind the Island of Orleans and the south bank. We said *au revoir* to our friend and walked quickly back along the wooden structure known as Dufferin Terrace.

We came to know Dufferin Terrace well during our time in Quebec and it was a wonderful place; its appearance and character forever changing depending on the season. The structure itself was similar to a seaside pier, but instead of jutting out into the sea, it was built along the top of a high cliff. On one side stood the Château Frontenac, a massive red stone building with a central tower and a number of smaller turrets all around. On the other side stood a white balustrade that, at intervals, bulged out into covered shelters with seats. In between were lamp standards, each with three large white lamps. Two hundred feet below was Lower Town, a narrow strip of land densely packed with old houses, and beyond this conglomeration of roof tops, was the St Lawrence River.

Dufferin Terrace with the Château Frontenac in the background.

A few weeks later, we had another view of the Terrace. Dining at the Château Frontenac, we were given a table with a window overlooking one end of the Terrace. The flags fluttered from their poles outside, and away in the distance the rolling Laurentian Mountains were wrapped in a pale blue haze. Gradually, as dusk deepened, the pale blue turned to deep purple and the lights of numerous little farm houses on the Island of Orleans downstream began to twinkle through the mist. After a sumptuous dinner, we walked across the hotel garden to the Terrace. There was a sea of faces looking up to the bandstand, perched up on a shoulder of the cliff, where a high school band was playing; the boys all wore white suits, white capes lined with red, and red berets. Later, there was dancing on the terrace and a firework display on top of the cliff in celebration of Her Majesty Queen Elizabeth's Coronation Day.

It had been a splendid day. We woke bright and early, eagerly waiting to hear that phrase from the BBC radio announcer—'This is London'. Expecting to hear news of the coronation, we were instead amazed and thrilled to hear the announcement of the conquest of Mt Everest by the New Zealander Edmund Hillary. Both Jane and I were so excited by this momentous achievement that we kept saying, 'Everest conquered! I don't believe it!'

Soon the broadcast returned to the most important event: the Coronation. Speaking from Trafalgar Square, the BBC's Raymond Baxter told of grey skies and rain, and how the crowds were lining the streets, hoping to catch a glimpse of the Queen as she made her way to Westminster Abbey in the golden state coach. I don't think we missed a word from the commentators until the end of the Abbey service; the reception was so good, that with the exception of some of the music, the broadcast might have been coming from the studios of CJQC, the Quebec English station.

We scrambled through our breakfast and hurried off to the cathedral for morning service to be taken by the Archbishop of Quebec. A large congregation had gathered and the service followed the pattern of the Westminster Abbey service—a noble tribute to the Queen. Outside on the steps, the talk was all the same: 'Did you hear?' 'Wasn't it wonderful?' and 'I'm off home to listen to my radio again.'

We returned to London via the radio in time to hear of the golden coach leaving behind the roar of the crowds and entering the comparative peace of the inner quadrangle of the Palace. Then our voices mingled with the rest as we chanted, 'We want the Queen! We want the Queen!' and then later, at four o'clock, we were again listening avidly as Sir Winston Churchill introduced the Queen. Strange to think that it was nearly the end of her arduous day, while we had several hours more in which to celebrate her crowning.

Our memories of Coronation Day 1953 were first and foremost, the most memorable radio broadcast and the immense effort of the BBC Outside Broadcast team including of course, Audrey Russell[52] and those from the Commonwealth and Empire. How did the radio announcer in the Abbey Annexe recognise, without a falter, all the famous people, most of whom he'd probably never seen before? They brought tears to our eyes as we listened to their description of the crowds and the streets of London—not tears of sorrow or even homesickness, but of excitement and thrill as we pictured the streets we loved. And for me especially was the added appreciation of the quality of the broadcast, due to my first-hand

---

52 The BBC's first female news reporter and in 1944 she became the first female accredited war correspondent.

knowledge of the planning and testing, the crises and all the thousand and one details that would have gone into its making. That was the chief memory. Second, was the dining-room of the Château Frontenac with its panelled walls and twelve branched chandeliers, the gold cover of the menu with the picture of the Queen and the special dinner consisting of dishes with English names (why Harrogate Trifle I wonder?). This, together with the magnificent firework display and dancing on Dufferin Terrace until the early hours of the morning, capped off an exceptional day that would always hold a special place in the hearts for two oh-so-British subjects of Queen Elizabeth II.

The Coronation Day menu from the Château Frontenac.

Dufferin Terrace was always a wonderful place to meet people from all over the world, especially during the summer when there was a tremendous influx of tourists, particularly from the United States. Every night, crowds strolled up and down and it was really quite a fashion parade. Many visitors took rides in nearby *calèches*[53], their drivers only too willing to take them on a leisurely tour of the city with its fine wall, old buildings and the ramparts and cannon overlooking the docks. For those who were energetic, tennis was played at night on open-air courts lit by huge arc lights, and for those whose appetites were keen, there were drug stores open until late at night where you could sit up at the counter and eat hamburgers, hot dogs, French fries or toasted sandwiches.

Our weekends, during this time of blue skies and warm summer breezes, were spent by mountain lakes, on river boats, or at seaside resorts down the St Lawrence River. This wonderful river held a great fascination for us and there was always something to watch: a liner on her way up to Montreal or back to England; the fussy, ferry boats that plied between Quebec itself and the township of Levis, or just the ever-changing colours of the river and the distant hills. Living beside it made us want to explore it further, so that summer, Jane and I decided to take a cruise along its regions.

53 A light, two wheeled carriage drawn by a single horse, with a folding hood and seats for two passengers with another for the driver on the splashboard.

A calèche.

We left the quay early on a beautiful sunny morning by river boat. It was a delight to be on the deck, feeling the warm breeze and seeing the sun glisten on the water as it flowed by on its push to meet the ocean. Soon we were able to distinguish the Island of Orleans or the Île d'Orléans as it is called by French–Canadians. The Island, we were told, was discovered by French explorer and mariner Jacques Cartier in 1535 and had a rich farming history. To the south of the Island was the shipping route, while on the north side, the Island was joined to the mainland by a single span bridge. At this point were the Montmorency Falls, where the Montmorency River joined the St Lawrence. These falls were one hundred feet higher than Niagara, but of course, not so wide and after the winter, they become a raging torrent.

Beyond the Island of Orleans, the width of the St Lawrence grew considerably and on each side we saw much green hilly country. We also passed many small islands with fascinating names like 'Eagle' and 'Hazel', and 'Nut Island' where Champlain[54] first landed on Canadian soil. On the river itself, we saw the occasional cargo ship as it went by—we were cruising much too slowly to keep pace with these impatient vessels—and also many timber boats that had been built especially for trading up and down the St Lawrence between the small timber settlements and Montreal, Quebec and Three Rivers.

Our first port of call was La Malbaie which was situated a distance of eighty-one miles from Quebec. We were told that its name, which means 'bad bay' in French, was given to the region by Champlain, when low tide left his ships aground in the bay. The bay was also known to English-speaking people as 'Murray Bay' after British governor James Murray.

54 Samuel de Champlain (1567–1635) was a French explorer and navigator who mapped much of north-eastern North America and started a settlement in Quebec.

Having lived in Quebec for four months, we had heard tell of La Malbaie as the seaside resort of the St Lawrence; the water was salt and the whole place had a real holiday atmosphere. Tourism in the area was said to date back to 1760, when two Scottish landowners began receiving visitors at their manor. Soon, the region's glorious landscape and its name for hospitality became known, culminating in the building of the beautiful Le Manoir Richelieu in 1899, a beautiful 250 room hotel atop the cliff of Pointe-au-Pic, overlooking the St Lawrence.

Leaving La Malbaie behind us, the water became a most beautiful deep blue, and on our left, the majestic Laurentian Mountains undulated against the clear blue sky as we travelled further down the great St Lawrence until we reached St Siméon.

St Siméon was tiny hamlet grouped around a wooden jetty. It was an important hamlet, though; besides its timber trade, a ferry ran from St Siméon across to Riviere-du-Loup on the south shore carrying both passengers and their cars, and during the summer, it was very busy taking people who were going to spend their holidays on the famous Gaspé coast on the Atlantic.

The next thirty miles was almost like being out in the open sea. The wind whipped up little white horses on the water and suddenly someone called 'Whales!' and pointed ahead to a telltale spout of water. Shortly after this, we turned into the mouth of the Saguenay River. At this point, the cold waters of the Saguenay River flowed into the St Lawrence, creating a wonderful place for whales to feed and breed. Apparently, they had little or no fear of the shipping. In fact, two came right alongside us.

We called at the nearby village of Tadoussac. Established in 1600, it was oldest village in Canada, being France's first mainland trading post after the discovery of the area. We spent some time ashore and decided to take a *calèche* ride, but unlike those in Quebec, they were almost tied together with string and we rattled and bumped up a dirt road, the wheels wobbling in a most precarious manner. It all proved to be rather a hoax, since there was nothing to see which was not within five minutes walk of the quay—a small village made up of some charming old houses, a lake and some surrounding hills.

We left there in the early evening, starting the sixty-three miles up the Saguenay River and soon after leaving Tadoussac, we entered a stretch of water that was literally alive with pure white porpoises; they rose up in the water all around the ship with sometimes as many as eight in a group. The Saguenay reminded us very much of a Norwegian fjord with its walls of rock falling sheer into the water with an occasional tree growing on the tiniest ledge and the river winding among the dark hills so that one couldn't tell whether the next turn was to port or starboard. Whenever there was a small bay and a break in the high hills, there was also a tiny cluster of houses, their lights twinkling in the dusk and their little boats pulled up on a pocket handkerchief-sized beach.

Saguenay Fjord.

About halfway up, we passed Capes Trinity and Eternity, the first named in this way because of its three levels; the top level being 800 feet. At 600 feet stood an immensely high white statue of the Virgin, erected there by a man who had been seriously ill and was sent to the Saguenay district to convalesce. He said that if he recovered he would build a statue in grateful thanks—he lived for another ten years. The ship's searchlight was directed on to what Jane would persist in calling the 'Dame of the Saguenay'[55] and over the ship's PA, a record of a lush tenor voice sang *Ave Maria*. We were ashamed to say that we wanted to giggle while most people stood in hushed wonder.

We reached our destination—the wood pulp town of Bagotville—just before midnight, and from the distance it appeared as if we might have been coming to an exciting little place with a casino as there seemed to be many bright lights and a considerable amount of activity going on. But the chains of light turned out to be the pulp mill working a twenty-four hour day and the activity was due to every inhabitant of Bagotville, both young and old turning out to see the riverboat dock. It really was an amazing sight at this time of night and made one feel rather like a circus turn. I had the urge to turn somersaults all the way up the ramp for their benefit!

As we sailed back to Quebec next morning, I thought about the St Lawrence; she was lovely all the way and it seemed hard to realise that she could have such a different look during the long, cold winter months when all shipping stopped and the great slabs of ice crunched and scraped against each other as they were carried along by the tide. Would we

---

55 *Notre Dame de Saguenay.*

feel cut off, like the people in the seventeenth century, when for about six months of the year, no supplies came, not a cask of wine or a sack of flour, no gunpowder or leather, and not even a letter to tell them what was going on at home in France?

The advancing months soon brought in the autumn and the streets were once more filled with boys and girls with satchels on their backs returning to school after their summer break. The distant Laurentian Mountains were like one huge bushfire with the colour of the Canadian Maples, their brilliant red broken occasionally by the yellow of a silver birch wood. Standing upon Dufferin Terrace in the chill of the autumn evening, Jane and I were lucky enough to see one of the many glorious sunsets. The cliffs across the river were tinged a rosy pink and Château Frontenac, black against the sky, looked like a fairytale castle.

The Château Frontenac at sunset.

The entrance of the cooler weather made us realise that we had been in Quebec City for five months and we had not yet been anywhere else. Soon we were planning our first visit to Montreal.

Leaving from work, I arranged to meet Jane at the station. With our finances now in a much healthier position after working for five months, we had decided to travel first-class with a reserved chair in the parlour car. As we walked along the platform to the carriage, a tall attendant came forward and took our cases. He then showed us into a very pleasant carriage and two comfortable green upholstered chairs that swivelled around either to face the centre of the car or the window. At one end of the carriage was a table with a selection of newspapers, comics and periodicals, all in leather covers like those in a doctor's waiting room, and further on there was a nice sized drawing room. At the other end, was the ladies' restroom which, besides the usual facilities, had a boudoir with comfortable chairs, mirrors, and free facial tissues were even provided. The attention to the passengers comfort was very apparent even to the extent that, just before reaching a station, the attendant walked through the carriage, and if any of his male passengers were about to leave the train, he took their hats away to brush them and then returned them to their owners.

We reached Montreal late in the evening and quickly caught a taxi to the YWCA. Both in Canada and the United States, the young and old stayed at 'The Y'. Jane and I had a room on the sixth floor with a private bathroom, and of course, there was a large modern lift which took us up.

Having only the weekend to view this wonderful city, we decided that we would have to do some of our sightseeing on this first visit by organised tours. So, having booked what sounded to us like a very varied and colourful journey, we started out early the next morning. Boarding the bus in Dominion Square we overheard the bus driver explaining to another passenger that at one time they used to call the buildings in the Square 'skyscrapers', but then the American tourists came, and now they quietly refer to them as 'our tall buildings'.

One of the great sights of Montreal was Mount Royal and West Mount as they appeared to rise almost from the centre of the city itself. These two hills were the best of Montreal with their wooded slopes dotted with beautiful homes, and from the summit of West Mount, there was a splendid view of the city and the St Lawrence River, as it wound away into the distant mist.

That afternoon we crossed the St Lawrence and drove to see an Indian reservation. Reservations had by this time become a commercial business and when we arrived at the pow-wow we found that there were stalls selling moccasins, carved wooden knick-knacks and leather goods. In the centre of the pow-wow was a large barn-like building, the top of the roof decorated with carved wooden animals and birds symbolizing the various lesser tribes (like the Mohawks), which made up the large Iroquois tribe. Inside this building, we were introduced to Big Chief Poking Fire, resplendent in full Canadian–Indian regalia, and his relations and they entertained us with some songs and dancing around a camp fire. Of course, intermarriage and the progress of civilization meant that the villagers we saw had few Indian characteristics, but here and there one did see the sallow skin and high cheekbones of the Indian native.

Well, after this somewhat hectic day, we decided that a good meal was definitely indicated, preceded by an aperitif or two. Finding a wonderful restaurant in the centre of the city that provided an appetizing menu, we ordered our drinks and our meal consisting of French onion soup to be followed by grilled salmon with a green salad and potatoes. Upon our drinks being served to us, we were delighted to find that our cocktails contained swizzle sticks—a popular form of advertisement by hotels and restaurants in Canada. These were plastic, long-handled spoons in various colours, with the emblem of the restaurant at one end and its name written down the handle. You could collect literally hundreds of them during a stay in Canada or America and whenever we saw those paper knives afterwards, we remembered that weekend in Montreal.

On our way to the station via taxi after our dinner, we encountered a traffic jam with, I'm sure, every car's horn blaring. We sat for sometime and watched the time tick by until we came to the realisation that we were not going to make our train back to Quebec City unless we made the rest of the journey on foot. So, after paying the driver and taking our luggage in hand, we raced off in what we thought was the direction of the station. Realising our mistake, we retraced our steps and finally arrived at the station only to find that we had missed our train. Despite this, and the need to travel most of the night by road, it was a very enjoyable weekend.

We were back at work and October passed all too quickly. We had bought our boots, woolly caps and our snuggies[56] in preparation for the winter but the first fall of snow didn't occur until November. This sprinkling did not last for long though and it wasn't until mid December when it started to snow all day and all night; this was the real thing and I was thrilled to see the layers of snow getting thicker and thicker and the landscape changing from brown to white.

With the heavy falls of snow, out came the skates, the toboggans and the ice hockey sticks. Wearing brightly-coloured woollen caps, thick padded jackets with fur collars, and heavy boots, the children skated up and down the streets as soon as school was over, playing ice hockey or making snowballs to throw at each other. The older ones dispersed off to the flooded and frozen over tennis courts to skate under the arc lighting that made the ice glisten. Around and around went the brightly-dressed skaters on the frozen surface to the strains of the ever-popular *Skaters' Waltz*. At weekends, the children were to be seen upon the Plains of Abraham. Even babies took to sledges, strapped firmly on and one day,

---

56 Woollen knickers with legs reaching below the knee which one wears for extra warmth when outdoors

I even saw a mother pushing her young twins in a sledge built just like a small pram but on high runners instead of wheels.

The 7th December was the date scheduled for the last ship to traverse the river before ice made navigation impossible, and by Christmas Day, everywhere was deep in snow. The *calèches* were exchanged for sleighs, the horses' bells tinkling as they trotted along the streets, which were kept reasonably clear by the snow ploughs. The wooden walkway of Dufferin Terrace was no longer visible. Instead, right down the middle and extending to the top of the cliff, was a toboggan run, built out of solid ice on a wooden frame. Instead of people in pretty cottons or the latest fashions, the crowds were rugged up in woollen caps, fur coats and heavy boots or full ski togs. At night, the run was floodlit and the Terrace rang out with the wild screams of happy folk as they shot along on their toboggans, waving to the onlookers as they went by.

As far as the eye could see, the St Lawrence River looked like some huge length of off-white satin ribbon winding between the silent quays and harbour of Quebec City and Levis. For most of the winter, the ferries kept going during daylight as icebreakers kept a narrow channel open for them, but as they moved slowly across, the river froze around them and great pieces of ice cracked against their bows, sometimes rising out of the water only to fall back and break.

I needn't have worried about feeling lonely and cut off from the outside world; our letters by air reached us much as usual and those by sea took perhaps forty-eight hours longer. There seemed to be a more intimate atmosphere in the city when the thick snow had added a softness and quietness to everything.

Our Christmas day was spent attending Service at the cathedral in the morning and then at a friend's house, basking in front of an open fire while we drank egg-nog and exchanged our meagre gifts. Walking through thick snow on our way home we came upon a small boy of about eight or nine, wearing lovely shining skis, but sobbing, with great tears running down his cheeks onto his fur collar. How easy it was to realise the misery, the weariness and the frustration of trying to make those long narrow pieces of wood stay pointing straight in front of you. 'Did Santa Claus bring you those?' we asked, and tearfully he answered, 'Yes.' So we told him how boys in England would envy him because they seldom had snow at Christmas or the chance of learning to ski. 'No-o-o?' he said, in amazement. I don't think he could believe that Christmas could be Christmas without snow. 'You know,' I said 'I expect learning to ski is like learning to ride a bicycle. Do you remember how often you fell off when you first began to ride?' He nodded his head and the tears were drying up fast. 'Well, you'll suddenly find you can get along fine on those beautiful skis,' I said encouragingly, and it must have sounded good too because he turned himself about and very methodically showed us how he could get along, perhaps in rather an unorthodox manner, but still he was going forward and he was still standing upright.

Our greatest excitement came four days after Christmas. Late one evening we heard below our window the sound of tinkling bells. Wrapping ourselves in all our warmest clothes until we felt quite circular, we hurried as best we could down to the entrance of our ten-storey block of flats. There at the door, just like any taxi, was a real, red sleigh, with a low door on both sides and room for two people on each seat. Settling into the conveyance, we noticed a large fur rug hanging over the back; three more were placed around and over us to be certain we were warm. Our driver, a young Canadian named Leslie, wore a fur cap that came well down over his ears, and Nellie, a quiet grey horse, was to pull us over the snow. Nellie, whose only eccentricity was her habit of dragging one hoof along the icy surface of the road was soon ordered to 'Lift your feet, Nellie,' but it made little difference. Off we went, our runners gliding smoothly over the snow with a pleasant swish, swish and the sleigh bells ringing into the lovely, clear, crisp night. In the city itself we travelled mostly on cleared roads, but once we were out towards the country, the snow became deeper. We passed the brilliantly lit ice rinks, and at intervals some lit Christmas trees. Can you imagine the sight? A long straight road lined on each side with snow-covered fir trees, some decorated with a mass of scattered variegated lights, some all blue or red or green, some with the lights

Sleigh riding over snow filled roads.

stretched from top to bottom on straight pieces of wire, others done in symmetrical bands of colour with dark stripes between and some with a star on top flashing on and off. Some large trees, some small, some standing out in the centre of a patch of thick, unbroken snow, others on the steps or even on the balconies of the houses. The scene was the same in every street and every country road where there were homes, or for that matter, buildings of any sort, for even the shops, offices and factories had their trees. The houses themselves often had lit wreaths, a Father Christmas or large red candles on their doors or in their windows. One small house had a life-sized Santa and his reindeer riding along the full length of the flood-lit balcony. Then we were suddenly beyond all the lights and out in a lane running through a small silver birch wood; the snow a soft blue, and gentle white flakes falling on our fur coats and thick rugs. Nellie shook her head, and with words of encouragement from Leslie, trotted briskly along, steam pouring off her back. The snow was piled four or five feet high on each side of the road, sliced straight and cleanly by the snow plough like the side of a block of salt.

Every shop, office and home had a Christmas tree.

As we returned to the lights of the Christmas trees we saw a happy group of boys playing ice hockey on the approach to a private garage which had been allowed to freeze, just like a real rink. They had the goal posts up and the click, click of the puck and the encouraging cries of a couple of staunch onlookers seemed extra loud in the otherwise still snowy night; and so after two hours, Nellie brought us safely home.

I shall always remember Christmas in Quebec. Even the temperatures, sometimes in the minus twenties, didn't damp my enthusiasm. What could be lovelier than my walk to work in the morning? A clear blue sky above, every twig outlined in sparkling white and the crisp crunch, crunch of the packed snow under my feet.

March arrived and the important topic of conversation everywhere was the maple trees. I was told that the trees required hot sunshine during the day and cold nights to make the sap rise. My informant's eyes sparkled and I began to imagine a miniature Niagara Falls flowing from each tree. Everyone wondered if the weather would hold until Saturday and the few pessimists among us pointed out that it was only three days after St Patrick's Day, and muttered something about the storm which always came around this time. We were inclined to laugh at them, but how right they were. On the Saturday morning, we woke up to driving snow and a howling wind. In fact, it was one of the worst blizzards we had seen.

A party of about twenty of us from the factory where I was working as a stenographer, left Quebec City by bus at midday, and in true French–Canadian style, it was a case of song and more song, all the way to Château Richer, a small community down the north shore of the St Lawrence River. It was an admirable way of passing the time because the countryside was completely blotted out by the snow and the wind was blowing drifts against every wall, bank or parked car. We arrived at the Cloutier's farmhouse soon after two o'clock and entered a spotlessly clean home with a large kitchen where the family were grouped around a shining, cream coloured stove. To the right of the door was the front room. Its furniture had been pushed against the wall; there were hand-woven rugs on the floor and in one corner there was an upright piano. At the back of the house, also leading off the kitchen, were two small bedrooms.

'Okay, away we go,' called the young man who had made himself the leader of the party and, innocent of what was before us, we followed him out into the snow. Across the road a steep path, almost hidden by the snow, led up a hill and on top stood a lone figure in a skiing outfit. He waved, called to us, waved again and as we struggled up he called down words of encouragement from time to time. Being relative newcomers to Quebec, we were real greenhorns where such weather was concerned; we were wearing overshoes and nylon stockings while everyone else was warmly clad in full ski clothes but we did not let this dampen our enthusiasm even though the snow was quickly over the top of our boots and our legs stung with the force of the driving wind.

Having struggled to the top of the hill, we found ourselves looking out at what might almost have been the Everest expedition on the lower slopes. The bush was invisible behind a curtain of driving snow and all we could see was a vast expanse of undulating whiteness, with two short black lines curling across the middle, each line composed of four or five people in single file, heads down, woollen caps well over their ears and each one straining against the force of the wind. It was our turn to get across that barren plateau. Speech was almost impossible and our eyebrows and hair quickly became caked with snow. It was only about a quarter of a mile across, but it certainly felt far further that day, and when we reached the shelter of the bush, we realised that the punch had not only been taken out of the wind, but out of us as well; besides the force of the wind, we also had to contend with deep, soft snow into which we could easily sink—and we did, right up to our knees. The last little way through the trees was steep and slippery, but sheltered so we had a chance to catch our breath and look around us.

Scattered throughout the woods were the maple trees, easily discernible because each one had a round tin tied to the trunk. Of course in such a storm, with the temperature well below freezing, the sap was not running and we found only one tree with a thin frozen needle hanging down from the tiny spout which was driven into the trunk. So there was nothing else for it, but to push on, and the sight of a small log cabin with a curl of smoke coming from the chimney was most welcome.

Maple trees with tins for collecting the sweet sap.

When we arrived, the cabin already seemed to be full to overflowing with people who were foot stamping, rubbing numb hands and shaking the snow out of any crease in their clothing. The hut was divided into two; the first half housed two large aluminium vats supported on bricks over a fire and these were filled with steaming brown syrup. In the second half, there was a roaring fire in a large iron stove, but even here, despite the fire and the crush of people, it still struck cold, especially if you happened to catch the draught penetrating through a crack in the wooden walls. Outside the hut, stood a narrow trough on legs about three or four feet high and into this Monsieur Cloutier was shovelling fresh snow. When the syrup in the vats had reached the correct temperature, he brought it out in a small pan and poured it on the top of the snow in the trough. In a second or two it became tacky like sticky toffee, and we were all given small wooden spoons with long handles. With these we scooped up the sugar, twisting it around and around until it was reasonably manageable. To use a Canadian expression, 'Was it ever good,' but it was too sweet to eat a great deal, so we all soon began to be drawn back to the warmth of the hut, where we also literally steamed and sizzled if we got too near the stove! We stayed in that one small room for about an hour and once again we sang French, Irish, English and Canadian songs. If you didn't know the words, you hummed the tune or got around it in any way you liked as long as you joined in.

Around four o'clock, we turned up our coat collars, pulled down our caps and set off down the hill again, but the going was much easier now even though the snow was still being lashed across our track. Dusk was falling and the old French–Canadian style houses and barns looked like buildings in an old print that had lost its colour and sharpness over the years. The trees, farm carts and fences quickly merged into a background of white and we could only imagine the view of the St Lawrence that should have completed the picture. The little white houses appeared uninhabited; their double doors of solid wood were firmly closed and their shutters closed against the cold. The Cloutier home was just as lifeless as the rest from outside, but inside the scene was very different.

Boots of all sizes and shapes already surrounded the large kitchen stove and the two beds in the back rooms were piled with wet coats. Poor Madame Cloutier; I suppose she was used to the mess made by a large party on a day like this. The younger members of the family, two attractive wide-eyed small boys in dark brown breeches and long woollen stockings, sat and watched the comings and goings with obvious interest. I wondered if our party was very different from others, and whether they were old enough to appreciate each one of us as individuals. We were a joyous group and were soon gathered around again singing songs and making merry until supper was ready.

From the outside, this home looked more like a doll's house and gave no hint of its real size. Downstairs in the basement, there was another kitchen and a very large room with a shining range covered with equally shining pots and pans. Long trestle tables covered with white cloths edged this room and in no time at all everyone had clambered over the wooden benches; with food in sight, it certainly did not matter whether your neighbour was French-speaking, English-speaking or bilingual. Certainly, the family did us proud; soup, roast veal with mixed vegetables and mashed potatoes, maple syrup tart, slices of iced cake and tea to drink. Next came the toasts. They were very simple, but completely genuine—'I wish to thank George for organising this delightful party,' 'I propose a second toast to

George,' '...a third toast,' '...a fourth toast,' '...a fifth'—some in English and some in French. George should have known how grateful we were!

A lovely mellow feeling began to take hold of me. The intense cold and the exercise, and now a good meal and the warmth were taking effect. I rather yearned for a nice easy chair beside the fire, but it wasn't time for us to leave yet and the Cloutier family, with incredible speed, cleared away the tables and the room was ours for dancing and merry making until ten o'clock. On the stroke of ten, we struggled once again into our boots and topcoats, now nice and dry and warm. The wind had dropped a little and the snowflakes were falling gently instead of driving down. The sky was clear and the snow looked blue as we came out onto the wooden steps of the house. Away in the distance, we could see the frozen St Lawrence, and beyond, the high ground on the Island of Orleans. We clambered into our heated bus. The French–Canadians, led by George, were still singing.

As we drove away, Madame Cloutier waved from the veranda, and a dim light shone from one of the two upstairs dormer windows, outlining two small pyjama clad figures, still watching those strange people from the city who came and sang and laughed and took possession of their home for six enthralling hours. But as we drove back to Quebec City, we could not help thinking of that family; they must have been tired after caring for us, but no doubt they were busy tidying up in preparation for the next day when they were expecting two more parties. The maple syrup season was short, but for people like the Cloutiers, it certainly meant hard work and long hours.

Towards the end of March, the snow began to melt and everything was very wet and bleak looking, but we'd just finished our first winter in eastern Canada. It had been a wonderful time of thick snow, sunshine and even temperatures in the minus twenties and I wondered why I had been so nervous about winter. There was no sign of spring on the way and the dreary weather was becoming a chore. Discussing our prospects, we planned to take a five week holiday in early May. We were to travel by bus right down the eastern states of America to Miami, then across Florida to the Gulf of Mexico and New Orleans and finally back up through Texas, Colorado and Montana into Canada, in time to start work in the Canadian Rockies for the summer months.

We had written to a number of summer bungalow camps in Banff and Jasper National Parks, seeking employment. We received forms of application from a couple and then came a letter from Walter L. Camp (believe it or not), proprietor of Johnston Canyon Bungalow

Camp. He wrote: 'It would appear that your qualifications are sufficient for cabin girls.' As you can imagine, we were greatly amused to think that a Sister Tutor from the London Hospital and an Administrative Assistant from the BBC should just meet the intelligence required for cleaning bungalows, but naturally we were thrilled to think he was prepared to have us without any further question.

It was a lovely sunny morning and one of our friends arrived to drive us to the bus terminal. We hardly had time for regrets since we were swept so quickly out of Quebec and along the Montreal Highway. We each had a folder containing thirty-seven tickets in one long streamer. Each time one was detached we had quite a sentimental feeling and our spirit of adventure intrigued the bus drivers throughout the trip. We spent the first night in Montreal, visiting both the Neurological Institute and the Montreal General Hospital. On Sunday night, we left by bus for Ottawa, arriving late in the evening. It was a pretty drive with some lovely views of the Ottawa River at sunset.

We were disappointed in Ottawa and felt that much more could have been made of the river below the parliament buildings. We went up the famous Peace Tower and stood behind the vast clock face while the chimes rang out. There was a beautiful War Memorial in the parliament rather like a very miniature Edinburgh Memorial, with the book listing those who lost their lives. The pages are turned so that the same page is open on the same day each year. We attended a session of the Lower House and were fortunate enough both to see the Speaker's Procession and to hear Prime Minister St Laurent speak on the new Quebec tax, a subject that of course, interested us immensely.

We left late that night in pouring rain and reached Toronto early the next morning. It was bright and sunny, but there was a bitterly cold wind blowing off Lake Ontario. What we saw of Toronto did not impress us very much, since it seemed just another large city with pleasant residential districts. As we were there only the one day and were more socially inclined than sightseers, it would be wrong to pass judgement either way.

Handing over another of our bus tickets, we drove the eighty-eight miles to Niagara in two hours the next morning. The lake was like the sea with waves and a pier and then we entered the fruit-growing country known as the Niagara Peninsular, where peaches and grapes were abundant. We were just a little too early for the full glory of the blossom, but there were many splashes of pink and white stretching away into the distance. One of the memories of this part of the trip was the change in the countryside. We had left Quebec where the trees were not yet in bloom and snow still lay in shaded corners, and travelled on to Niagara, where the blossom was out and beds of tulips were everywhere.

Niagara Falls was superb, as one would expect from the pictures. We saw them from the Canadian side only, but most people considered it to be the best view. A very large park covered all the land opposite the Falls, while the American side was mostly industrial.

Niagra Falls from the Canadian side.

From Niagara, we left Canada and entered the United States. We spent the night at Buffalo in New York State and saw our first American television in the bus station. We left Buffalo next morning en route for New York, a distance of four hundred and four miles. Beautiful roads took us through even more beautiful country, especially through the Allegheny and Pocoho Mountains, where we saw woodchucks and I kept murmuring the old tongue twister: 'How much wood would a woodchuck chuck if a woodchuck could chuck wood?'

Our route took us through the states of New York, Pennsylvania, New Jersey and Wyoming County. A vivid memory was the many prosperous looking farms in New York State, the buildings being very Dutch in architectural design. We entered New York by the Skyway, a great road sweeping over the river and the suburbs like a never-ending bridge; and late at night it looked like a double row of stars stretching across the sky in front of us.

We stayed in a large hotel in Times Square near Broadway and our room was on the nineteenth floor. The porters were all very helpful and the one who showed us our room told us to be sure and lock our door at night. The lock was a complicated affair, but we thought we were safe until I was coming out of the bathroom one night in the nude. The door opened quickly and the face of a porter appeared in the doorway. 'Your door is open, madam,' he said, and just as quickly closed the door. Slowly recovering from my embarrassment, I remarked to Jane that the hotel's care and attention to their customers was very impressive.

Shall we ever take to city life again? New York was certainly exhausting even though the numbering of streets made life easier. Our first day was warm and pleasant and we were soon up the one hundred and two floors of the Empire State Building. Unfortunately, visibility was only two miles, but we could just see the big liners in the docks and it was fascinating to watch the traffic far below looking like long rows of coloured beetles or Dinky toys moving very slowly amongst cardboard buildings.

In the afternoon we took a river trip around Manhattan Island and the Statue of Liberty; what a view of the skyscrapers! We couldn't stay in New York and not see a Broadway show, so the first night we went to see *Wonderful Town*, a musical comedy, and the second night to *Anniversary Waltz*, a very amusing, but rather borderline comedy.

Our second day was wet and we spent the morning, shop gazing on Fifth Avenue and peeping into Radio City, an amazing place. In the afternoon, we visited the United Nations headquarters and here, 'amazing' was hardly sufficient. The outside was like a large oblong of corrugated iron standing vertically and precariously on its narrow side. A closer view showed this to be made almost entirely of glass. Inside, the foyer reminded one a little of the Royal Festival Hall[57] entrance, and the many conference and committee rooms—although excessively modern—had something fascinating and intriguing about them.

So ended our brief visit to one of the great capitals of the world; New York to Washington, 228 miles. Washington was a city we would never forget with its beautiful white government buildings, very wide tree-lined streets and feeling of spaciousness. We visited the Capitol, attended both the House of Representatives and the Senate. Oh how different from our stolid Parliament, even when in a lighter frame of mind. We also went through the State Rooms at the White House, which were very lovely, and we took a bus out to Mount Vernon where George Washington had lived. This was a charming spot with a real English walled garden just packed with flowers.

There were two highlights of our visit: the first, standing outside the White House to see President Eisenhower leave for the Capitol. We believed we saw him, but did we? He was so

57 A concert, dance and talks venue within the South Bank Centre in London. The Hall's design is unashamedly Modernist.

surrounded with detectives and was driven away so fast we weren't sure. The second was that we had a television in our bedroom and almost stayed up all night to watch the most awful stuff.

The longest through run of the trip was from Washington to Miami, a total of 1,110 miles in a luxury coach complete with a W. C. and running hot and cold water. Despite this comfort, one old spinster complained because she believed that there was also to be a canteen.

With our streamer of bus tickets quickly reducing, we drove through North Carolina during the evening, South Carolina during the night and Georgia early the following morning, crossing into Florida around eight o'clock. We would never forget the glories of the tropical south: the colour washed houses, palm trees, coconut palms, the brilliant displays of nicotena, hibiscus, bougainvillea and poinsettias and last, but far from least, the vast groves or oranges, lemons and grapefruit. The trees seemed to be laden with fruit and everything was very lush and exotic. The people too were different from the other folk further north. At a North Carolina rest stop, the colour problem hit us for there were the large notices that read: 'Coloured Waiting Room' and 'White Waiting Room', and again the next morning when we changed to a new bus, we found a notice requesting that the African–American people sit at the back of the coach. This segregation continued until we reached Colorado Springs.

All that day we drove through the fantastic state of Florida with its festoons of moss hanging from the trees, and the knowledge that the wide, uncultivated swamps or everglades were the homes of alligators and snakes. Daytona Beach and West Palm Beach—names familiar to us as the homes of motor racing, film stars and millionaires—now became a reality. We arrived in Miami just as darkness was falling and the neon signs and streetlights began to twinkle against a background of palm trees and the still water of Biscayne Bay. Our hotel was an imposing looking building that at one time, we might have called a skyscraper, but to quote one of the Montreal tour guides, it was a 'tall building'. We had a large room with a dressing alcove, private bath and windows overlooking the bay.

Miami and fabulous Miami Beach greeted us with a violent tropical storm. After the storm, the atmosphere was very humid and heavy and so we were pleased to take a boat trip around Biscayne Bay. We passed the homes of many millionaires and saw how Miami Beach and the small islands or 'keys' were built from sand and stone dredged from the

Miami River and the bay. As we came back to the jetty, we saw what looked like wooden pier supports with large carved birds on five of them. As we passed closer alongside, we saw that they were in fact live pelicans standing quite motionless and appearing to watch us with baleful expressions.

In the early evening, we took a bus out to Miami Beach, passing over many bridges linking the small keys one with another. The beach was an amazing conglomeration of lush hotels, each hotel having its own private beach and swimming pool. The beaches were nothing to write home about, since they were merely narrow strips of sloping sand fenced off from its neighbour. The public beach, from the air at any rate, seemed much nicer. We saw this early the next morning as we flew over on our way to Nassau.

Our hotel in Nassau was very modern and luxurious and was built alongside the harbour. Our room, which was on the first floor, had a veranda built out over the water, and as soon as we appeared outside, a chorus of voices greeted us. 'Throw me a penny, missy,' '...a dime, missy,' '...a sixpence.' Looking down, we saw a couple of yachts tied up, and standing on the deck were three or four boys, smiling up at us and calling to attract our attention. Of course, the temptation was too great and down went the coins. The boys all dived together, and then up they came laughing and chattering and started calling again.

While we were watching their antics, we became aware of people watching from the next balcony too. Our neighbours turned out to be five extremely wealthy Americans. They'd all been out fishing for ten days and were staying overnight in Nassau before going back to their homes in Florida. They were entertaining the skipper of the boat and his wife to dinner that night, and they asked us to join the party. We went initially to one of the most famous Nassau clubs. It was most attractively furnished and decorated. The white panelled walls were hung with mirrors and wall lights and the ceiling was a deep blue, studded with stars. After dinner, we went on to a nightclub where calypso dancing went on in the open air all night. We finally got back to the hotel about three o'clock, but it was too hot to stay in bed late in the morning so we were soon out in the main street of Nassau.

It was quite a sizeable town with nice shops, but everything had a wonderfully peaceful, unhurried atmosphere, accentuated perhaps by the natives. The women wore a conglomeration of European clothes; often a shapeless cotton dress with a voluminous jersey on top or skirts and blouses that seemed to give them most strange figures. On their heads, they wore either straw hats decorated with flowers or they carried baskets filled with fruit, vegetables and other market produce. They walked with a strange, slow, rolling gait, possibly something to do with the art of balancing the baskets on their heads. The men wore European dress, smiled broadly and often rode penny farthings.

Alongside the hotel was the market—a glorious sight with its stalls shaded from the hot sun by coloured umbrellas. The major trade of the market, besides fruit, were beads and shells of all kinds. These were made into necklaces, bracelets, earrings, tablemats and different coloured raffia handbags covered with designs in small shells.

Small islands surrounded Nassau, and the most important from the tourist point of view, was Paradise Island, the home of Paradise Beach. The second morning, when we came out of our hotel, we were greeted with a broad grin and 'Charlie's waiting, missy.' Charlie was a young lad of about fifteen, wearing a brightly-coloured shirt hanging out over the top of his khaki shorts and he had the most engaging smile. He led us through the market to the harbour and then out to a small motor launch.

On the way across to Paradise Island, we were entertained by a musician playing a guitar and singing some local folk songs and spirituals. We disembarked onto a small jetty and then a short walk along a shady path with orange lizards running hither and thither brought us out to the far side of the island and to a long beach of pure white sand. At one end was a row of cabanas and under each cabana was a brightly-painted table and four chairs. There was no charge to use this furniture and, as the sun was far too hot to sit in, everyone made good use of them. If you wanted refreshments, white-coated waiters were ready at any time to take your order for sandwiches and drinks. What a lovely life it was, dipping in and out of the sea, and in between times, quenching one's thirst with iced drinks.

Paradise Beach.

It didn't matter at what time we came out of the hotel in the morning, we were always greeted by 'Charlie's waiting, missy.' Certainly, Paradise Beach was so lovely that we accompanied faithful Charlie most days, but once we did miss a day and this was when we went for a cruise on board the *Dry Martini*. To give the vessel her correct description, she was an auxiliary sloop and was owned by an ex-Royal Navy captain. We'd seen an advertisement for Captain Gerry's cruises in the same paper as we'd seen our package tour and it sounded almost too good to be true. The very reasonable cost for the day included lunch and drinks of any sort, except champagne. We sailed around the coast of Nassau and then anchored off a tiny uninhabited island. The water was as clear as crystal and we enjoyed a swim before lunch. Captain Gerry provided a delectable meal, preceded by an aperitif and his promise of 'anything except champagne' was about right.

We loved everything about Nassau, especially the markets—the peaceful, sleepy atmosphere appealed to us. We had to take a parcel to the Post Office, half a mile from the main street and the posting of that parcel took us the best part of an hour.

From Nassau, we went to see friends in central Florida where we experienced true southern hospitality. We had all our meals and in fact, spent all of our three days on the patio under a large grapefruit tree, already bearing masses of fruit due to ripen in October. They also had oranges, bananas, mangoes, limes, lemons and avocados growing in their garden.

From there, we drove through the night and next day to New Orleans, passing through Alabama, Mississippi and Louisiana and skirting the Gulf of Mexico for a number of miles. We found the French quarter of New Orleans quite fascinating, if somewhat smelly—*à la vrai Français!*[58] Actually, the architecture was more Spanish than French and the little paved courtyards with their shrubs in full bloom tucked away behind the houses and seen through wrought iron gateways, were something out of this world.

Our next destination was Colorado Springs. We went through Texas, Oklahoma and New Mexico with their oilfields and ranches, all looking very prosperous. There was something very fascinating about this vast rolling green country with the straight highway cutting through it.

Colorado Springs—where we spent the next three days—introduced us to the Rockies, but how different they were from the Canadian mountains. There was very little snow and dry stream beds everywhere. We were lucky as the season had started two weeks earlier and we were able to go to the summit of Pike's Peak (1,400 feet plus). The view from there was magnificent, but a very cold wind prevented us staying outside the restaurant too long.

58 In true French style!

Our final stop was at Salt Lake City. We had heard the Dean of Quebec preach a sermon on the Mormons and this was a stimulus for our interest. The Mormons (or to give them their correct title, the Church of Christ of Latter Day Saints) were good Christian people in every sense. This was very evident in the city both in the good manners of the people and in the general feeling of happiness that seemed to prevail everywhere. In fact, we were told that the Mormons were in the minority in the city itself, but nevertheless their influence could definitely be felt everywhere. Brigham Young[59] certainly had great foresight when he planned Salt Lake City. It was one of the most beautiful cities we had seen; clean, wide tree-lined streets and masses of roses everywhere. A beautiful capitol on the hill, surrounded by superb gardens, dominated the city, with a background of snow-capped mountains. We toured Temple Square with a very interesting guide and also heard a recital on the world famous organ in the Tabernacle. Inside the Temple was hallowed ground, used only for Mormon baptisms and weddings. With regards to polygamy, the guide said that in the early pioneering days there were so few people that they practised polygamy in order to increase their numbers and only those who could afford to keep their wives and families were allowed by the Church to have more than one wife. In actual fact, only three percent passed the test that the Church imposed. The guide said it was easy to become a Mormon, but it was a very difficult religion to live up to. They all gave a tenth of their income to the Church, hence its prosperity. We got talking to a German woman in a newly-opened pastry shop and she told us that although not a Mormon, she found a bushel of tomatoes and plants for her garden left on her doorstep shortly after her arrival in the city. We had to admit that they certainly had something and as the Dean said, 'We could learn a good deal from them.'

The trip from Utah through Idaho and Montana was just glorious; many miles through the mountains and beside the upper Missouri. We crossed the border at Sweetgrass in a thunderstorm, but nevertheless there was something really comforting about being back in Canada and the sight of many Union Jacks in Alberta gave us a great thrill.

So the final part of our five week trek around the United States came to an end. Catching the Greyhound bus for the last time, we sadly gave up the last of our long streamer of thirty-seven bus tickets for the journey from Calgary to Banff, in order to take up our posts

59 President of The Church of Jesus Christ of Latter-day Saints.

as cabin girls at Johnston Canyon Bungalow Camp. We learned that the bus was the first of the season going beyond Banff and that it would drop us right at the camp.

The day of our arrival at the camp was a cold, bleak day and our summer frocks and straw hats seemed very out of place, so we decided to carry our hats in the hope of locking the part a little more. The drive was delightful, but being a little nervous, we were in no mood to enjoy it to the full and before long we were crossing the small stone bridge over Johnson's Creek and recognising the camp from the photograph on their notepaper.

The driver pulled up opposite a large gravel parking area with a small gas station on the highway, and at the far side, a low wooden building, which we soon learned was the tearoom and kitchen. We must have looked a strange sight as we were left standing with our four suitcases on the edge of this large parking ground. A tall, dark young man came out from the gas station and said, 'Hi', picked up our cases and led the way across the parking ground to the kitchen. Inside, we found five women, three of them sitting and watching a hairdressing session in progress. From an inner room appeared a very expectant mother and everyone greeted us with the usual, 'Hi.' We learned that the young man was the owner's son and the expectant mother was his wife Jackie. The four older women were kitchen staff and there was also a young German girl who spoke little English. We were then told to go up the flight of steps outside the kitchen, between the row of cabins and up to the laundry situated in the centre of the camp.

The laundry was a two-storey building and the top floor consisted of six rooms. We were shown into one of the smallest rooms and left to settle in. It was very small and we wondered how we'd ever get all our belongings into the space. No one thought of offering us any supper and we went to bed pretty cold, hungry and miserable, saying, 'What sort of a place have we landed ourselves in?' Little did we know that it was the last thing on this Earth that any of these people would have allowed had they realised that we had had nothing to eat since noon.

It was snowing most of the next day, and out of kindness we were given the day off, but how much more happier we would have been working. Our warm clothes were awaiting collection at Banff Station, and in desperation we spent most of the day sitting in bed, just going down the hill for meals. Later that evening, we moved to a slightly larger room vacated by two girls who had been sacked and warmed ourselves up by cleaning everything and polishing the floor. This room became home to us for four months. Jane, being a nurse, exclaimed periodically, 'This room, it's frightful!' usually just after I thought I had tided it rather successfully.

On Monday, things looked brighter. The owner's son fetched our luggage and we started on the job. We were each sent off to clean a deluxe cabin with one of the two other cabin girls who were to show us the ropes. After that, we were left to work on our own and were kept pretty busy getting the cabins up to our standard. It still continued to be cold, but our duffle coats helped and we found that once a cabin had been occupied even for one night, it soon lost the damp, icy-cold feeling.

We spent the first three weeks getting the cabins ready, equipping them with standard quantities of china and cutlery, cleaning cupboards, drawers and stoves. Around 1st July, the rest of the staff arrived, numbering thirty odd and the season began with a vengeance. All our cabins were occupied every night, the tearoom had about seven bus loads in every morning and afternoon besides the tourists travelling in their own cars—life was really a bit too hectic at times.

It will always amaze me the way the cooks provided the ample quantities of food and how all the staff managed to find somewhere to sit and eat meals in the comparatively small kitchen. The happy bedlam soon became too much and the management had to stipulate less chatter at meals; imagine about fifteen boys and girls laughing and teasing each other while two or three waitresses tried to make themselves heard with their orders of 'A stack of hots' or 'Hot dogs on two with…' to which the cooks replied, 'Ham sandwich on one up' and rang a bell.

We were given the fifteen deluxe cabins to look after, and with an average of nine checkouts a day, this was quite a big assignment if we were to keep up our standards. These cabins were really more like five-roomed homes, beautifully equipped and furnished. We had beds to make, fires to lay, baths or showers to clean, china and cutlery to check, sweeping and dusting throughout and sometimes floors to wash. To us, our cabins were a great pride, but believe me, an eight-hour day was too short for them, although quite long enough for us. The youngsters flicked around the modern one-room cabins, leaving a trail of dust behind them, but we, in the five-room deluxe bungalows, really put everything we could into making them look nice and with fifteen of them between the two of us, it was some job.

We had some amusing incidents too. For instance, the time we went to drink martinis with a couple from Chicago after a hard day and without any supper. The Canadian vermouth did something to us and we were lucky we could get to our room and beds. Inevitably, word got to the boss and a few days later we found a notice on the cabin door which read:

> *Will tourists please refrain from supplying liquor to Old Country girls at any time.*
> *The Management.*

What a kick they got out of it! Then there was the time we drank some ginger ale we found in a cabin, afterwards discovering that the owners had not, as we thought, checked out. Or when some people took all their luggage away and the Reservation Clerk re-let the cabin thinking they had checked out a day early. She rented it to a family of eight, and as they all ran around in their night attire ready for bed, three nurses (matrons, we believe) arrived home and walked into their cabin, still being in possession of the key. Perhaps that would teach them to leave their luggage behind them another time.

We had a day off a week and how eagerly we planned our trips on these carefree breaks in our cleaning routine. One trip will always stand out: the day when we went to the Columbia icefields.

In the parks, there was no means of transport except by private car or the tourist buses and people working at the various camps and motels during the season could often get a free ride on the buses if the driver had room and was willing to take them. So on this particular day, we were out on the road early—before half past seven—to catch the bus on its way from Banff. Stopping at Lake Louise to pick up more passengers, we then set off north-west. Leaving the Bow Valley far below us, we climbed to the top of Bow Pass, a height of 6,000 feet. On our left were Bow Glacier and Bow Lake, and on this glorious crisp day, the reflections in the water were as clear as the mountains and glaciers themselves. On both sides of us were towering snow-capped peaks with hanging glaciers, looking like icing running over the side of a cake. We passed the Crowfoot Glacier, which was receding at such a rate that its name will one day be a reminder only of its one time shape. Ahead of us was the road stretching as far as the eye could see between two long lines of magnificent peaks, all named after early explorers of the district—Mount Chevron, Mount Patterson, Mount Wilson and Mount Coleman—and we seemed to be on top of the world when we stopped at the North Saskatchewan Lodge, where the whisky-jack birds were flying around everywhere.

Bow Valley.

I had always been fascinated by some of the names to be found in Canada, in particular, names like Saskatchewan, Medicine Hat and Kicking Horse Pass.

Leaving the Saskatchewan River below us, we climbed again and then came out onto an open plateau and to the border between Banff and Jasper National Parks with the superb view of Mount Athabeska—another lovely name. We really were on top of the world here because a small stream beside the road appeared to change its direction of flow. Just around the shoulder, we saw the Athabeska Glacier, like the hem of a white tablecloth hanging down from the icefields. I believe they covered an area of one hundred and thirty square miles. We wondered if they looked like that from the air, and believe it or not, glaciers from those icefields feed rivers that eventually flow into the Pacific, the Atlantic and the Arctic Oceans.

We could see in the distance a row of three or four little crawling, beetle-like creatures traversing the glacier as they made their way toward us. These were the snowmobiles, built like tanks and with skis attached to the front; they were painted in either a bright red, green, yellow or blue. The bus took us right down across the lower moraine and then we had a short, slippery scramble to the starting point for the snowmobiles. Each vehicle took about ten or twelve people, and when we weren't sliding and slithering up the steepest gradient with the engine roaring, we were allowed to stand up so that our head and shoulders were out of the top. In places, the gradient was terribly steep and then a great deal depended on even balance of the machines, so we all had to sit very quiet and still.

The ice was a beautiful blue and the rivulets of water on the surface sparkled like diamonds in the brilliant sunshine. We climbed several hundred feet and then came onto a wide plateau of ice. The snowmobiles stopped in the centre of this plateau and we were allowed to get out and walk around on the ice, which we were told, was about 900 feet thick. Ahead of us was a massive cliff of ice and away over the top, the icefields themselves. Below us, hardly more than a tiny white speck, was our bus against a backdrop of grey moraine; a little further back towards the rocky face of yet another peak, was a patch of green and in the middle, a tiny doll's house. This was the Icefield Chalet; quite a sizeable hotel and restaurant.

It was hard to drag oneself away from this wonderful scene, but the snowmobiles were lining up once again for the return trip. We clambered into ours, which was painted pillar-box red and away we went, sliding and slipping down the steep slope. It was a lovely warm summer's day, but a keen wind was blowing off the ice and it made it so cold that it was quite a joy to get back into the waiting bus and travel back to the camp. As evening came, all eyes were on the watch for the wildlife of the mountains; the bears, moose and elk.

Our snowmobile.

We had left home early in the morning and eleven and half hours later, we were back, sleepy from the strong air on the glacier, but not too tired to make the most of a good evening meal, which had been kept hot for us by our employers.

We were a very happy family at Johnston Canyon Bungalow Camp; Will, Lee, Reservation Jim, Buck, Ina, Edna and many other names would always remind us of those hectic fun weeks. I will particularly remember the midnight picnic by the full moon at the Lost Lake, the camp fire sing songs, and the expedition to the Hole in the Wall when the mosquitoes won the day by noon and we returned sadly home with disfigured faces and legs.

As suddenly as the staff had come on 1st July, so they went on 6th September and Jane and I were once more alone 'up the hill' as it was called. We then became laundresses as well as cabin girls and we thoroughly enjoyed every minute of this new experience. We were lucky with the weather and we washed one hundred and twenty-three white and thirty coloured blankets, besides doing the daily wash. This was usually our morning's work and then we cleaned the cabins in the afternoon. We only had five of our deluxe and six modern cabins open, and except perhaps on a good weekend when they would all be filled, we usually had about four or five occupied on any one night. So now at last we were able to breathe and to enjoy the lovely weather while we hung out the washing.

So ended a wonderful summer; hard work, yes, but rewarded by the many interesting people we met and especially, the kind ones who gave lifts to two English girls, enabling them to see so many of the beautiful spots in the Rockies. Our last view of the Canyon and the camp was early on 1st October. It was almost four months since we had approached the Rockies from the east with snow falling. Next we were to head west to Vancouver and onward to home, and instead of boarding a Greyhound bus, this time we were to travel in a truck with seven wood stoves. We had very little money again!

Going Home—the Long Way

1955–1958: The West Coast of the United States, Hawaii, Fiji, New Zealand, Australia, Hong Kong, Singapore and… Home!

We had left home for one year. It still seemed like yesterday that I was telling myself, on that first day of our journey to Canada, 'You are only going for a year and then you will be home again, picking up the threads of your life where you put them down.' How wrong that comment was proving to be.

We had received a telegram from our friend Virginia (or Mrs America as we had called her during our travels in Switzerland in 1952) requesting that we meet her in San Francisco and then spend the winter with her in southern California. It sounded marvellous, but we really thought that we must go home. Quebec had been wonderful, the east coast of the United States had been fascinating and the Rockies had been spectacular, but now? We were curious about the west coast of course, having heard so much about it from Virginia. Wouldn't it be rather a pity to go back more or less the way we had come?

It was not long before our relations were getting letters which read: 'We've decided to come home via Australia, with a short detour through the west coast of the United States.'

We left Johnston Canyon with seven wood stoves as our travelling companions and a wonderful drive of 437 miles saw us at the interior of British Columbia where we caught the train to Vancouver. From there we crossed on a ferry to Victoria, the capital of the province. I'll never forget that first view of Victoria: it was a beautiful still, soft evening in the autumn and our boat docked almost on the steps of the parliament buildings. Some small yachts in the harbour were reflected in the unruffled water and on each street lamp post hung a basket of red geraniums. It would have made a perfect painting.

The Parliament buildings in Victoria, British Columbia.

Our stay in Victoria was primarily for the purpose of finding employment in order to fund the next part of our journey, so the following day saw me taking a civil service exam before joining the staff of the Superannuation Department of the Provincial Government, while Jane obtained a job working in one of the big hospitals. We also found a very nice furnished flat, situated almost on the seafront, with a lovely view from the kitchen window across the Straits of Juan de Fuca to the Olympic Mountains in the United States. You would hardly credit it, but we saved our fares to Australia in the next four months. The travel bug had certainly attacked fiercely.

Our farewell from Victoria was quite touching. Despite the shortness of our stay, we had made many friends and the week before our departure saw both of us involved in a series of social gatherings. The time went all too quickly and soon we were again packing ourselves up and preparing ourselves for our next trek across the American continent.

Departure day, 2nd February 1955, dawned frosty and misty. Our friend arrived in her car and we sadly drove away from the lovely sea-fronted flat that I shared with Jane. The sun couldn't quite break through the mist in time for us to get a good view of Victoria as we sailed, but nevertheless it was a lovely morning and by the time we got out into the Georgia Strait and opposite South Fairfield, the white houses were shining in the sun and we could pick out our flat quite easily.

We reached Seattle in the mid afternoon. It was a pretty trip; the Olympics just peeping through the mist, the water a soft blue, and when we turned into the Pugit Sound, the hilly coast made the scene reminiscent of Norway. Most of our trip was taken up with reading from the Quebec newspaper we had received the day before. It contained pictures of the wonderful Ice Carnival taking place there, so we were kept busy reading all the local gossip, and strangely enough, an article on my one-time boss at the BBC.

Seattle welcomed us with open arms. We found ourselves to be the only people with an appreciable amount of luggage and the Customs officials were the most charming people, chatting to us about our experiences and finally arranging for a taxi to take our luggage. In fact, we needed two taxis and they whisked us up precipitous hills from the dock to the Greyhound bus station. We had been told by the Customs officials that the bus company would probably charge us for our excess baggage (150 pounds overweight!) so we felt rather guilty when our two trunks were trundled into the baggage room, but we needn't have worried, for no one showed any consternation and we were not asked to pay a cent. Armed with only one small case, we felt decidedly less laden and took no time to stow that case away in a bus station locker and enquire about the way to the shopping centre. We just had time to look around one of the large department stores, marvel at the cheapness of the clothes and wish we had more money to spend, before boarding the bus for our four hour trip to Portland, where we found upon arrival, the hotel nearest the bus station already full! Fortunately, we managed to get into a hotel nearby and tumbled quickly into bed with the alarm clock set for an early rise.

It was raining when we left Portland at seven o'clock the next morning, but it cleared as we approached the coast. What a wonderful drive it was down the Oregon coast; mile upon mile of winding road on top of the cliff, with a new and lovely vista of rugged rocks and huge Pacific rollers at every turn. The sun shone the whole way and we stopped once to look down on Otter Rock and the caves far below us. As evening came, the road became decidedly tortuous for our tummies; 854 curves in 36 miles, rising to 1,715 feet. At this higher elevation, there was snow and it was amazing to realise that we had been in such lovely sunshine all day. We arrived at Crescent City in time to see a really beautiful sunset. Crescent City was built around a large bay, used as a good sheltered harbour and both the bus station and the hotel were on the main esplanade. Our bedroom looked over the bay and so we were soon lulled to sleep that night by the lapping of the water on the beach.

We were off again at half past seven for the more famous part of the route—the Californian Redwoods. They were a magnificent sight with their dark red-brown trunks of gigantic circumference dwarfing the brilliant green ferns and undergrowth as they started their journey up into the sky and out of our sight. Unfortunately, the driver was keeping very strictly to schedule and did not offer to stop so that we might rubber neck up at the terrific height of the trees.

Leaving the Redwoods, we came out into the fruit orchards and grape vines of northern California, spreading through a long valley running between the coastal range and the

Cascade Range of mountains. The light was just departing as we arrived in San Francisco, a wonderful approach along the opposite shore of the bay with the lights of the city sparkling in the water and the Golden Gate Bridge, its chain of lights showing the length and apparent narrowness of the structure.

As we entered the bus station, there was our dear friend Virginia sitting waiting for us as arranged. We all laughed as Virginia walked up to us holding a small American flag and said, 'Well gals, Mrs America is here to meet you as arranged!' Over the preceding years, Jane and I had regularly corresponded with Virginia and we had told her of the pet name we had made up for her when we had met in Switzerland three years earlier. Fondly embracing us both, she then whisked us off in a taxi, explaining apologetically that as the hotel she was staying in was full, she had booked a room for us in the hotel just across the street, in fact, we could see her window from ours.

We went first to the Chancellor Hotel, where we had a most luxurious room, with of course, our own bathroom. A beautiful box of flowers lay on the dressing table with irises, tulips, daffodils and freesias and a card welcoming us to California from the management of the hotel. After a quick wash, we crossed the street to Virginia's accommodation, the Sir Francis Drake Hotel and into the Drake Tavern for dinner. This was a delightful room with panelled walls, wooden nooks around the wall to seat four and colourful check cloths on the tables. After a couple of martinis and some food, we fully refreshed, but decided to make it an early night, although it wasn't very early by the time Virginia had come back to our hotel and had ordered celebratory drinks up in our room—Virginia's daughter had given birth to her second child.

The next morning, as Virigina was somewhat occupied with visiting the hospital, we took ourselves off to the bus station to sort our luggage—we even ended up unpacking one of the cases on the floor of the baggage room with the help of an attendant. Our next errand was to find a firm who would be responsible for collecting our repacked luggage and delivering it to the *Orsova*, the ship that was to carry us to Australia via Hawaii, Fiji, and New Zealand on 18th February. All this achieved, we met Virginia for lunch in the tavern and then went to see Chinatown, which we found quite fascinating. Like all of San Francisco, it was spotlessly clean and the brightly-painted roofs and Chinese signs made a lovely picture against the blue sky. The shops were full of fascinating lures for the tourist with plenty of money, but we could only wander around and gaze at the embroidered slippers, wrought iron pictures, ornamental boxes and all the other wares that we saw and would have dearly liked to have bought.

As San Francisco had been built on a steep hill, we literally clambered up one street and ran down the other, there being no plateau between. They had old-fashioned cable cars on many of the streets which just seemed to add to the city's personality, contrasting with the surrounding modern architecture.

The next day we had our breakfast served in our room and felt like duchesses in our glamorous nylon housecoats, sipping fresh orange juice. We enjoyed to the full the leisure of breakfast in our room and by the time Virginia finally phoned us, it was time to take the cable car over the hill to Fisherman's Wharf where we were meeting a friend of hers for lunch.

The sun was brilliant and the little white yachts and fishing boats packed tightly together looked their best. Virginia took us to a restaurant built right over the water whose speciality was seafood, and we had a most delectable shrimp salad. Virginia's friend Peggy, a most charming and highly intelligent woman, then suggested that she drive us around the city during the afternoon, to which we agreed. She took us to a high hill overlooking the bay and what a splendid view we had from this point. The hills across the bay behind Oakland were almost as blue as the sky, and the white walls and brown roof of the prison of Alcatraz, as it stood on its rock out in the middle of a blue expanse of water, seemed to sparkle in the sun. Down the hill again we drove, through a lovely park skirting the bay, passed the approach to the Golden Gate Bridge and back to Peggy's home for tea. Here we met her mother and four aunts—and what an experience that was! One felt as if one was back in the days of Cranford[60]. Peggy then drove us back to the hotel, stopping on the summit of one steep street for a view of a truly magnificent sunset.

Alcatraz Island and its prison.

60 *Cranford* is a novel written by Elizabeth Gaskell in 1851. The story amusingly describes the lives of the inhabitants (mostly women) of Cranford, a small town in the north-west of England.

The Golden Gate Bridge.

We went out to dinner that night; walking down Powell Street from our hotel to the lovely paved centre of the city—Union Square. Surrounded on all sides by towering buildings that dwarfed the tall date palms placed in rows throughout it, this was San Francisco's central theatre, hotel and shopping district. Pigeons strutted about on the ground amongst the busy people and below our feet was an underground carpark, four floors deep with space for 1,500 cars!

Monday morning saw us out shopping, then consuming an early lunch before taking a Greyhound bus out to San Mateo to visit Virginia's sister-in-law and her English husband. We were to spend the night at Carmel, a few miles from Monterey, and we had hardly seemed to have arrived when it was time for us to depart for the airport to catch our plane at half past five. It was a lovely forty-five minute flight to Monterey with a call at San Jose on the way.

Virginia had chosen this stopover, both to show us Carmel, which was once, very many years ago, the capital of California, and also to see a very dear friend of hers, nicknamed 'Toots'. Meeting us at the airport in her lovely car, Toots soon had us at our hotel—the Pine Inn—where we were kindly greeted by the hotel staff and assisted to check in. The very name of the hotel, 'Pine Inn', was reminiscent of something divorced from the Biltmores, Hiltons, Plazas and Carltons of America and the whole place was equally enchanting. A huge fire blazed in the entrance hall from which a narrow staircase led to the bedrooms. The walls of the corridors were covered with red and white striped paper and hung with old prints. The dark panelling of the bedrooms was shown off to perfection by the light carpets and curtains and two or three lamps, rather than one centre light, but despite this old-world appearance, our room boasted a bathroom of it own!

Having eaten a good dinner, Toots took us for coffee to her own very delightful little cottage home and then she drove us along part of the coast road where the Cyprus trees leaned in the direction of the prevailing wind, black against the white of the Pacific rollers as they crashed on the rocky shore. It was a grand sight as our headlamps brought to life each new piece of shore as we turned a bend in the road.

The next day, 8th February, Toots kindly offered us the use of her car for the morning as she was required at work. So, after a stroll in the sunshine to admire the quaint old-world charm of Carmel's village street with its shops with their bow-fronted windows, bright red and white striped awnings and pointed eaves, we drove over to Monterey to see its Fisherman's Wharf. On leaving the car, we at once heard the hungry barking of the many sea lions, whose grizzly faces were obvious amongst the hundreds of small craft moored within the natural harbour.

This Fisherman's Wharf was less sophisticated than the one in San Francisco, and the small shops seemed to straggle along the edge of the many wooden jetties. We chose a delightful little restaurant at the end of one of these jetties with three sides of glass overlooking the harbour, and here we were served delicious clam chowder—a speciality of this part of the country—fried dabs[61] and white wine.

We had quite a scramble to catch the mid afternoon plane for Los Angeles where we arrived at half past four to find no friend to meet us as Virginia had hoped. After waiting for some time, she decided that we should take a taxi to her sister's home in Hollywood. Shooting along one of the many freeways across the famous Wiltshire Boulevard and into Hollywood, we left the main road, climbed a winding track set in a precipitous hillside and turned into the narrow driveway cut through rock to view a lovely, but unpretentious home. Entering the house, Virginia was told by the manservant that her friend (who was to have picked us up) was in hospital and so had been unable to bring the car up from San Clemente. Virginia's sister Bebe warmly welcomed us and seemed reasonably unperturbed at our sudden unexpected arrival and promptly set to organising beds and directing the cook to provide us with supper.

The next afternoon, Bebe drove us to the station to catch the three o'clock train to San Clemente. The station was across the city and so we took one of the freeways and

61 A type of flatfish that resembles a flounder.

raced along at what seemed like a minimum speed of sixty miles per hour in the heart of the city. My, they drove fast! Bebe said that there were seventy-two miles of these freeways in Los Angeles. I found it an amazing experience to stand on one of the main shopping thoroughfares and look over a bridge to a vast highway far below ground level with about six carriageways and a stream of cars tearing along at what looked like a break-neck speed.

Throughout our one hour train journey, we passed through the largest orange and lemon groves we had ever seen. What a lovely sight the trees made; thick, green balls on short trunks, dotted all over with the bright orange and yellow of the fruit. Our route was all inland through rolling green hills until we were almost at our destination and then the train suddenly came out through a cutting in the hills, practically onto the beach. San Clemente station consisted of one tiny white building housing the booking office, no platform, a single track and then the sand and the ocean. Back a little from the shore, the main highway ran through about half a mile of shops, including a supermarket. The rest of the community consisted of delightful white homes scattered over green grassland, mostly with lovely gardens, a blaze of colour.

Virginia had just recently sold her home at Laguna Beach and was living in what they called a furnished beach home. It was a little all-on-one-floor white house, rather box like from the outside and differing in this way from many of the attractively designed homes in the neighbourhood. The front door led into a very large living room with a light wood floor and unstained wooden bookcases lining the walls. It was comfortably furnished with bamboo furniture and well-upholstered chairs. There were two double bedrooms, a bathroom and a large kitchen. Like the majority of homes in the United States, it was centrally heated and thermostatically controlled, so after our dinner, we returned to a warm room and a super television set. This television was Virginia's real joy and every evening from about six o'clock we were expected to watch plays or boxing. If we stayed in for supper, then the meal was eaten off television tables.

Our next four days were spent sunbathing on the beach. Virginia drove us down at about ten o'clock, together with a large beach umbrella and plenty of reading material. She would then go off and return around noon with hot dogs for lunch. By three o'clock it would be usually getting chilly and by five o'clock it would be dark, after a really superb sunset.

One day, Virginia drove us over to Laguna Beach, a more sophisticated resort north of San Clemente. It had a beautiful bay, large beach hotels and simply wonderful public gardens along the cliff top, just a mass of antirrhinums and sweet Williams. Virginia decided that we should call on one of her friends, but found her out, although the house was open. Quite unperturbed, Virginia took us in, showed us around, offered us a drink and answered the telephone twice. It was a charming old cottage with a garden full of avocados, oranges and lemons from which, Virginia said, the owner made quite a bit of money.

The following day, we went to San Diego. This outing was not only to see the country and say that we had almost been into Mexico, but also to allow us to visit the Department of Inland Revenue and obtain an income tax clearance which was required because we were sailing from an American port. The outing was most enjoyable, with strangely, the visit to Inland Revenue being the highlight. What a time we had. Our expectation, upon entering this official office, was to obtain the required tax clearance and continue with our outing, however, suffice to say that we were there for about twenty minutes, and it was obvious that we were certainly something quite foreign to the row of male clerks who took the opportunity of having some fun at our expense. We enjoyed it too, needless to say.

We left San Clemente by the afternoon train on 17th February. It was sad leaving Virginia and she looked a lonely figure standing beside the track as we started on another long journey. She had very kindly insisted on paying for our return to San Francisco and had reserved a bedroom for us on the *Lark*, which was *the* night train from LA to San Francisco.

We arrived at San Francisco at nine o'clock on the following morning and drove straight to our ship, the *Orsova*. It was a lovely day, but a very strong wind was blowing across the bay. Virginia's friend Peggy and one of her aunts came on board to see us off, bringing a lovely box of chocolates with them. It was grand having someone to show over the ship and it was worth seeing too, this being her maiden voyage on the two-way Pacific crossing.

Unfortunately, the wind was too strong to sail and so we were delayed until four o'clock when a battery of tugs managed to pull us safely away from the quay, and after our sad farewell to San Francisco and the American continent—the grim white walls of Alcatraz, the serrated skyline of the city with its tall white buildings and the Golden Gate Bridge seeming like a strand of brilliant tomato cord stretched over the water—we once again settled down to life on board ship, assisted by the pleasant cabin, the always moving and inspiring church service, the 'daily dozen'[62] around the decks, the sports, the dancing, the films, the concerts and the amazing way one can sit for hours in a deck chair accomplishing next to nothing.

We arrived at Honolulu on the Island of Oahu, the capital city of the Hawaiian Islands and the most isolated land group in the world, being over 2,000 miles from the nearest mainland. The day's excitement started early with the arrival of a launch bringing hula-hula girls and a great many boxes of leis made of real flowers. The dancers sang and played for us and gave every one of the 1,200 passengers a garland of sweet-smelling tropical flowers.

We had booked a day tour, leaving at nine o'clock, so Jane and I—and two newly-made friends—set off in high spirits, despite the rather wet and humid weather. We were each provided with a well-stocked lunch box containing a chicken leg, turkey and ham sandwiches, potato salad, lettuce, olives, celery, spring onions, pickles, a bag of sweet biscuits, two large slices of pineapple, and two chocolate peppermint creams, all served in a box also containing a tin foil plate, cup and paper serviette.

Our coach took us through the centre of Honolulu and then we climbed up through a beautiful residential district with lovely homes and large gardens—just a mass of tropical flowers of every colour—up through tropical bush country to the top of Mount Tantalus, a 2,013 foot peak overlooking the valley, the city, and Diamond Head, a rugged headland beyond Honolulu itself. From there, we drove down to the east coast of the island, passing through villages with fascinating names like Kaneohe, Kaaawa and Hauula. We made a short stop at a shop selling native bead work, basket work and coral of all colours, and at a roadside stall where we were able to buy the most delicious, sweet-tasting bananas. Nearby we found a native selling grass skirts and hats for tourists who liked to dress up and be photographed.

Next, we drove right up through the valley to our next stop, the Mormon Temple. This was a really beautiful building surrounded by the most gorgeous gardens. The layout reminded one rather of pictures of the Taj Mahal, but on a smaller scale—long grass between strips of water, an avenue of tall palms, and in front of the dark green hedges down each side, a red bank of double poinsettias. Beside the ornamental pools down the centre were bushes of

62 The 'daily dozen' consisted of twelve exercises which were designed, both from a scientific and a practical point of view, to give exactly the right amount of exercise to every muscle of the body.

Diamond Head Crater in Honolulu.

the most beautiful-scented honeysuckle. The temple was built on a hill and it certainly had a most delightful setting.

Leaving the temple, we turned inland across the centre of the island through miles of sugar cane country and pineapple groves with their artificial irrigation channels. We stopped at another stall where we each bought two huge slices of pineapple wrapped in greaseproof paper. We all agreed we had never eaten anything quite like it before, the juice pouring out of it at every bite; thank goodness for the paper which acted as a cup.

We returned to the *Orsova*. Our main impression of the day was of the glorious green everywhere and the people, oblivious to the rain, walking about bare footed. Everywhere seemed very prosperous; all the small homesteads in the country had one or more cows tethered in the garden and a large car at the door.

We sailed at midnight from Oahu. More rain streamed down and as we pulled away from the quay, a small band of smiling locals sang to a guitar both the Hawaiian and New Zealand songs of farewell. Slowly, the gap between the side of the *Orsova* and the wet quayside widened and the black water was dotted with circles of flowers as the leis went overboard; they'd done a good day's work around the necks of the passengers and so they were, according to tradition, left to float ashore and signify the owner's return one day to that lovely dream isle. As we watched the lights of Honolulu fade, we still found it hard to believe that we had been lucky enough to visit this small, but world-famous, playground in the Pacific.

We crossed the equator on the evening of 25th February. As it was expected to be very hot in this locality, we had been provided with camp beds to enable us to sleep on deck and avoid the intense heat of our cabins. Fortunately, we never needed to use them as a pleasant breeze reduced the temperature to a reasonably enjoyable environment.

Our daily routine began with a swim before breakfast and the rest of the day was spent in deck-chairs, there being no organised sports. There seemed to be one topic of conversation: was there any truth in the officer's statement that if one put water in the wash basin and pulled out the plug, the water would revolve in the opposite direction after we crossed the equator? This was supposedly how the Captain knew the exact moment when we crossed the line.

Our next experience was crossing the date line; we went to bed on Sunday, 27th February and woke up on Tuesday, 1st March! Despite the loss of twenty-four hours, we were up early to see our arrival at Suva on the Fijian island of Viti Levu. The approach was across a large and very calm bay with a coral reef through which we had to pick our way. An earthquake had thrown up large quantities of rock from the sea bed and this had landed on top of the reef and was to be seen as great brown protrusions sticking up out of the water. To the east was a pair of flat-topped rocky islands and between these, we saw the sun rise, tingeing the grey water with pink and yellow, a group of palm trees on the very tip of Viti Levu black against the pink sky. Behind us to the west was a range of mountains, deep blue to purple in colour, looking rather menacing even in the lovely early morning light.

Upon arrival in the port, we decided to go on a morning motor tour in a taxi. We drove along the coast road, past the delightful Albert Park, Botanical Gardens and Government House. We turned inland and passed masses of banana and breadfruit trees, rice paddy fields and sugar canes. It was a pleasant undulating country with thick undergrowth and tropical flowers of all colours growing in the hedgerows. Our tour was to take us to the Rewa Hotel on the banks of the river, where we stopped for morning tea. The hotel appeared quite primitive with a long veranda on which we sat for our refreshments.

Our next stop was a Fijian village where we were surrounded by delightful, almost naked children. We were invited into one of the native huts where the bed occupied most of the space and was quite the show piece. The floor was covered with straw matting and everything was very tidy. The Fijian women wore European dresses with long, tight underskirts reaching their ankles.

We had driven out of Suva to the south-west, and now we returned from the north, looking down at a lovely view of the harbour with the rugged mountainous country beyond. We were set down at the local market and we spent the rest of the afternoon walking around the stalls piled with native work, and most fascinating of all, coral of every colour, shape and size. Like most other people, we went on board ship again carrying a green basket made of palm leaves with five large pieces of white coral.

On our way back to the ship, we met two small Fijian boys going to see our ship sail. They told us that English had to be spoken in the schools. We asked one what he was going to be when he grew up and he replied, 'A teacher.' When we asked the other, he said, 'I'm going to work.'

The farewell from Fiji was one of the lasting memories of the trip. We sailed in the early evening and the open quay was an ideal setting for the most colourful scene. The whole town seemed to have turned out to see us sail and the long stretch of open wharf in front of the Customs shed was a riot of colour from early afternoon. At the stern, a choir of native school children, all wearing brilliant jade green dresses were singing; at the bow, a party of Fijian braves performed strange war dances. At the bottom of our gangway stood two Fijian policemen in white skirts with jagged hems, scarlet belts, navy tunics with bare feet and legs. Then of course, there were all the hundreds of ordinary people who had come along either to wave farewell to friends on board or just to enjoy the excitement of a large liner leaving.

The next two days took us very quickly from the tropics and it became quite cool for our arrival in Auckland, New Zealand. It was a little misty as we sailed into Waitemata Harbour early in the morning, but we took a morning tour by bus through the city, up One Tree Hill and through Cornwall Park to the racecourse. Here, the bus drove us down the main drive in order to show us the beautiful gardens. We then left the city and drove up into the hills through bush country with enormous tree ferns everywhere. We had morning tea at a small café in amongst the lovely green hills; the sun was shining and the colours were just perfect. Morning tea consisted of a full Devonshire cream tea. The drive back into Auckland gave us a wonderful view of the two harbours of Waitemata and Manukau.

It was dark when we sailed and the harbour then presented a lovely sight with the bright lights of the shore and the mysterious dark water with the ghostly white of many small yachts out to see us leave, but we had heard rather gloomy reports of the behaviour of the Tasman Sea, so out came our seasickness tablets in preparation. Fortunately, it decided to be kind to us and the threatened hurricane which was supposed to be bearing down on us, never arrived.

For the next two days, the ship didn't seem quite the same. Many of our fellow travellers had left at Auckland, and to add to our feeling of sadness, a first-class passenger died and was buried at sea. It created a very eerie atmosphere on the ship when the engines were stopped for the burial just as darkness fell.

On Monday, 7th March at eight o'clock in the morning, we docked in Sydney Harbour and our welcome to Australia equalled that of Canada. We found people to be most helpful and friendly; especially so, as by this time our bank balance was down again to around thirty pounds and we needed to fast track our journey to Melbourne where Jane had a job waiting for her. Fortunately, we made our southward journey via bus without mishap, and to our amazement, I even managed to obtain a job within a week of our arrival and find a small flat. Actually, the advertisement for the flat read: 'Suit two gents', but little things like that didn't worry us, so we telephoned and asked, 'Would you consider two girls?' They did!

Jane's job was a temporary one and it lasted for fourteen months. During this time, we saw a great deal of Victoria, besides spending a very enjoyable ten days on holiday in Tasmania. Naturally, this wasn't enough for us, so in May we set out again, bound for Alice Springs and Queensland. At the time, travelling in central Australia was pretty expensive, so our itinerary was planned to take us from Alice Springs to Tennant Creek, across to Mt Isa and then up to Cairns. When people said that we would be tempted to go on to Darwin, we firmly said that we couldn't afford it.

Ayers Rock in the morning sun.

We just loved every minute of our two week stay in central Australia. The weather was perfect; very cold at night and brilliant sunshine during the day. We spent three nights under canvas in Palm Valley and four out at Ayers Rock[63]. One of our companions on the trip was 'Grandpa', a ninety-two

63 A large rock formation in central Australia now known as Uluru.

year old farmer from Seymour, Victoria, who had made the trip by train with his two grand-daughters. He participated in everything, but his comments were inclined to be along the lines of: 'I've seen this sort of thing before in my time.' All things said and done, he appeared to still be thrilled with all he saw.

One of our many memories of those two weeks was the animals. We saw literally hundreds of kangaroos, some emus, wild donkeys, brumbies and dingos. At Ayers Rock, the dingos howled around the tent and one night, a member of the party firmly said she woke to feel the warm fur of a dingo lying on top of her bed; there were pad marks in and around her tent the next morning too!

Jane and I with a koala.

Of course, our friends were quite right about visiting Darwin. Before long we'd decided to risk going there by service coach and this addition to our itinerary was nearly our downfall. It meant that we arrived in Cairns with about fifteen pounds left between us, but we weren't the least bit worried because we were quite certain that we would find work there. How wrong we were. It was the end of June and the winter season was in full swing. There were few opportunities for temporary seasonal work and those that were available had been filled a couple of weeks earlier. I think I might have stood a chance of a job in a fish bar, but this meant getting up very early in the morning to be there when the shop opened at eight o'clock. Jane put her foot down and said, 'Penniless or not, I can't have you coming home every night smelling of fish!'

We spent a day and a half walking the streets, and looking back, it was really a most humiliating experience. I went into a large chain store and was interviewed by a very young girl, who said straight away, 'Oh no, I'm sorry. We never need senior staff.' Next, I saw a very charming government official who had no vacancies in his department, but said he'd take my particulars in case he heard of anything. Very apologetically, he asked my age and when I told him he said, 'You carry your years well, don't you?' Finally, I went to a well-known Australian firm and here an elderly lady with pure white hair came up to me at the desk. 'You want office work?' she asked. 'Yes,' I said. 'I don't mind what I do.' Her reply almost made me laugh—'I'm sorry, dear. We have nothing. You see, all our staff stay until they get married.'

We decided that it was no good staying in Cairns so, together with what seemed like quantities of other girls obviously equally as unlucky, we caught the train to Townsville. We stayed at the People's Palace and the next day we were woken to the morning service over the house loud speakers at seven o'clock. To our amazement, the reading contained, 'Ask and it shall be given unto you; seek and ye shall find.' So we went out with high hopes, but soon found that the situation was no better. However, that night, we received an urgent phone call from one of the hotels we had visited earlier, asking if one of us would go along because their new waitress had let them down and dinner was to be served. I decided to go and I must have done alright as the manageress thought I was a trained waitress. I had always said I'd like to try my hand at it one day, just for fun. Fun! I certainly didn't think of it as that after that first night or even at the end of the first whole day when only two of us had coped with a dining-room of fifty people for dinner.

I started work the next morning at seven o'clock, so missed the morning service, but Jane said that again the message was most apt: 'Take no heed for tomorrow, tomorrow is here, the day you were worrying about yesterday.' Well, we were taking heed as our finances were getting worse and worse, and after paying a week's board, we found ourselves with only three pounds. However, we didn't really worry unduly, although we did spend quite a long time that night discussing which of our friends in Melbourne would be the best to write to and request a loan of sufficient funds to enable us to return, and how long we could safely wait before writing. We didn't want to write, not because we were too proud, but because we felt it would lessen our achievement. We decided we must give Townsville a chance, and after all, I had a temporary job which would just about pay our board. The hotel seemed quite willing to keep me, despite my inexperience and I soon realised that I knew more than some when I saw a young girl being asked by a guest for another piece of bread. She walked across the room to an empty table, picked up a roll in her fingers, returned to the guest and planted the roll squarely on his plate. I didn't do that sort of thing, even if I did occasionally forget how to order correctly, and yelled at the chef, 'Two pork on order!' when I really meant, 'Two pork waiting'!

In the meantime, poor Jane was trudging along to the employment bureau every morning and sometimes in the afternoon too, but there was never anything on offer. In between times, she'd sit on a seat outside the hotel waiting for me to come out during my brief periods off duty. For the best part of two weeks, her lunch consisted of six dry biscuits, a small piece of cheese and a banana. She said she would always remember walking, for what seemed like hours, around one of the chain stores, looking for the cheapest brand of face powder and soap with the least obnoxious smell.

Eventually, our luck returned. We'd decided to write to some of the hotels of the Great Barrier Reef islands and to our great delight, the management of Hayman Island phoned to say they had vacancies for two housemaids. We had no idea what we were in for, but at least it would be a roof over our heads. It turned out to be a perfect spot and we spent a very happy three and a half months there and saved more than we'd done in the last months we were in Melbourne.

The staff beach at Hayman Island.

We came back to Melbourne for the 1956 Olympic Games because I was lucky enough to get a job as Secretary to the Chef de Mission of the Kenya Olympic Team. I was much amused when I attended a reception given for the team and met two Federal Members of Parliament and their wives. They'd both been guests on Hayman Island and I'd been their housemaid. Isn't life fun?

By this time I imagine our travels were becoming rather a joke among our relatives and friends at home. Certainly I think some of them thought we would never return, but they were wrong. We began to feel that it was time we saw them. Nephews and nieces were growing up fast. We had new godchildren whom we had never seen, but again finances had a big say. We had saved a great deal in the short time we spent on Hayman Island, but we did not have enough to take us home by the direct route and anyway, that was far too orthodox for us! So we settled down in Melbourne again after the excitement of the Olympic Games to save sufficient money for our next move—home.

This time I went to work for a large English pastoral firm that owned seven cattle stations, eleven sheep stations and two sugar mills, as well as being very big wool brokers.

Me with my cleaning cart.

Not knowing anything about the wool industry, I was very keen to learn about the trade, so my employers arranged for me to visit their wool store and to the Wool Exchange to see a wool sale.

I went initially to the wool store, and while sitting with the manager in his office, I learnt my first very important lesson about the trade. It was never necessary to send representatives out to all corners of the world to try and sell the Australian wool clip. Instead, the world's buyers came to Australia, to the selling centres of Melbourne, Sydney and Brisbane, and what was even more amazing, they did all their buying in cash. In other words, something like 8 million pounds could change hands at Melbourne and Sydney's Wool Exchange during a four-day sale.

The manager then took me up to the third level, which was just one huge room called the show floor. The walls were painted a light colour and the room was very brightly lit. We came in at one end and in front of us was row upon row of bales of wool. Each row was in fact formed by large wire pigeon holes, or perhaps a better description would be miniature horse stalls, back to back. In each compartment was a huge bale, holding at least 250 pounds of wool. The top end of the bales opened along one side and out of it bulged the wool, falling into heaps onto the floor in front. It was wonderful to see the thickness of a really good fleece, like the Merino. The top of course, was dirty in colour, but underneath it was white and very silky. The wool was very oily to feel, some more so than others, and if you pushed your hands down into it for long, they came out very soft.

The bales were all grouped in lots, each lot having a number displayed on a round black disc behind it. Some growers had sufficient wool to fill five or more bales of one particular type. Lots of less than four bales were grouped together with similar wool and this was known as 'interlotting'. Then, there were of course, many different types of wool, and not even the tiniest curl was wasted; a bale, a fadge[64] or a sack would all fetch a price.

The manager then handed me over to a young man who was learning the trade, known as a cadet, and he took me around and explained the various types of wool. There were

64 Package of wool in a wool pack weighing less than 220 lbs (100 kg).

many intricate points to be taken into consideration when they classed or grouped the wool; the length and fineness of the strands (known as the staple) and the waviness of it (known as the crimp). Some looked as if though they had had a very tight permanent wave. Then too, the wool varied on different parts of the sheep. For instance, the back was usually less matted with burr than the tummy, and wool with a thick mass of burr in it would have to go through a special process before it was ready for weaving.

It was interesting to see the difference in colour between the wool from sheep on varying types of soil. This was particularly noticeable when the sheep came from a district where the soil was very red and dusty. The wool had a definite red colour, and if you felt it, you could feel the dust within it.

My visit to the wool store was during the morning of a sale day. The show floor was almost eerie as it was so quiet, despite the number of people walking up and down the rows. These were the buyers and very important people they were too. Some of them were quite young men and they all carried catalogues. These catalogues were clipped to a board about twelve inches by ten inches and on them the buyers made notes of the lots most suitable for their buying orders.

Our next call was to the level below where the classing was carried out. Here, all around the edge of the floor were piles of wool, varying in size from huge mounds to tiny ones which looked as if they must have come from the pet sheep who kept the front lawn mown for someone. Even the black sheep of the family sent in his contribution and there was a little pile of silvery grey too. This wool was examined and grouped by the Classer and then it was weighed and listed on the grower's card. Next, it went into a wire basket on wheels and was taken to one of many large cages in the middle of the room. These cages had three wire walls of about ten or twelve feet high and the fourth side was open. On the back wall hung a description of the type of wool. The basket of wool was added to the correct group and the owner's card was hung on a spike on the side wall. As the pile of wool got higher, the men had to throw themselves on top of the pile to push it down. Finally, when they thought that there would be 250 pounds of wool in the cage, it was placed into a bale, weighed, and if correct, it went into a huge press that reduced it to about half its size. The opening was sewn up and another bale was ready for the show floor.

The last area I was shown was on the ground level—the Shipping Department. I had seen the classing and I had seen the buyers at work on the show floor. They did their work throughout the morning, some starting as early as six o'clock. During the afternoon, while the sale was in progress at the Wool Exchange in the city, the workers started gathering up all the wool that they had pulled out of the bales, pushing it back in and fastening up the opening. Then the bales were taken to a trap door in the floor and dropped down to the Shipping Department. Here they were stacked in great piles from floor to ceiling. They again went into a huge press that decreased their size even further, a process that was known as 'dumping'. It compressed the bales so much that it made a difference in a ship's hold of nearly two bales in the place of one not put into the press. While in the press, three steel bands were put around each bale to keep it securely packed throughout its long journey.

Near the press was a large screen on which hung big stencils of all sorts—three diamonds, stars, letters and even a heart. These brands belonged to the wool mills of the world and seeing that the bales were branded correctly was an exacting job because some had to be placed on a particular corner, some in two different spots and so on.

Just as we left the wool store, the twelve o'clock siren sounded. The buyers went off to snatch a hasty lunch in the pleasant dining-room provided for them, while next door, the clients were also provided with facilities for a meal. The clients of course, were the growers who had come into town to look at their own particular clip, no doubt to compare it with others. I'm sure that they felt a great sense of pride at the wonderful result of their labours. The manager told me that sometimes the keen interest shown by the growers presented quite a problem on the show floor. Naturally, every effort was made to give the buyers freedom of movement up and down the narrow passageways between the bales, but this was not always easy when growers brought their whole families to see the wool. A baby in a pram had even been seen!

The day I was there, about 6,500 bales of wool were on show in that one room. At an average of ninety-two pounds per bale, you could work out the tremendous value of the contents on that one afternoon.

In the afternoon, I went to the wool sale. It's not easy to explain how the sale was carried out except to say that it was like an auction. It was terribly difficult to follow, partly because the bidding was all done in pence per pound and partly because of the speed; up to 400 lots could be disposed of in one hour. Roughly, this was what happened: the auctioneer called the lot number from his catalogue, say 32. Following this, he called the starting price for the lot in pence, which meant that it could not be sold for less than this amount, say 94 (meaning 94 pence per pound weight). The bidding then started, probably in farthings like this: 1 (meaning 1 farthing), 2 (in other words a halfpenny), three (3 farthings) and so on. The minute the bidding stopped without any pause as far as the amateur onlooker could tell, the auctioneer went onto the next lot, although he did name the final buyer each time. So the general noise sounded rather like this: 32, 94, 1, 2, 3, 95, 1, 2, 3, 96, 1, 2, 96½, Brown; 33, 101, 1, 2, 3, 101¾, Smith; 34, 91, 1, 2 and so on. To add to the difficulty, not only were the buyers of all nationalities, but some seemed to make coughing noises in their throats, so when the bidding got really exciting, the noise sounded more like geese honking.

The sale I went to had among its buyers, representatives from France, Japan, and the United Kingdom, as well as men from the local Australian mills. There was some keen competition between France and the local mills for one particular type of wool. All the time the sale was going on, young men (called runners) were hurrying from the Wool Exchange back to their company offices with the prices realised for the various lots. In the Accounts Department, the staff calculated the final result to the buyer and the grower, and where a bale contained wool from more than one grower, the total price had to be divided up between them according to the weight of their wool.

The Australian wool clip brought in over 465 million pounds in the 1956/57 financial year. I certainly couldn't help thinking what a tremendous responsibility rested on those buyers as they walked around the show floor, plunging their hands into the bales of wool, pulling out a few staples, examining them closely to determine its quality and trying to estimate how much wool would finally reach, for example, the mill in Yorkshire where it will be made into a new winter coat.

I greatly enjoyed my time at the pastoral firm; it was a fascinating place to work and I had learnt so much about the industry. I had made many friends there and I really didn't want to leave. Despite this, it was becoming obvious that we must start making plans for our return to England. Family and friends were writing to encourage our return as it had been so long since we had seen them all.

We decided that we wanted to arrive just in time for the summer, which would mean leaving Australia in autumn, but the great question was—how were we to go? A great deal of discussion then ensued and our flat was littered for months with little pieces of paper covered with calculations as we tried to stretch our funds as far as possible. We wanted to see New Zealand because we had only spent part of a day in Auckland on our way from the

United States and yet we also had a great desire to see something of the Far East. I mentioned this dilemma in a letter to Grannie, who was now ninety years old. She wrote to me by return mail. Her letter read: 'I read recently in a newspaper that New Zealand was short of young women. I think you should go there and I am sure the government would help you.'

Despite my grandmother's very practical suggestion, we remained undecided for some time. We had hoped that we would be able to travel to both areas, but we finally faced realities and decided that this was really too much to expect; we decided in favour of the Far East because it would be so different from anything we had seen.

So we came to problem number two: bookings. It was comparatively easy to get something seven months ahead on one of the liners sailing from Hong Kong to England, but it was not so easy to get from Melbourne to Hong Kong. The ships on this run were small cargo boats and were often booked up years ahead, but we made a tentative booking and were told that we would hear nothing until January or February, leaving only eight weeks before we hoped to leave. We were told this would still give us time to make air reservations, although this was something we did not want to do and what about all the luggage we had collected? How often we said, 'In future we will always travel light,' but how easy to say and how very difficult to do.

We were lucky and were allocated a two-berth cabin on a passenger freighter, its cargo being largely frozen meat for Japan. So in the middle of March, we said a very sad *au revoir* to our many friends in Melbourne and headed north.

After leaving our last Australian east coast port, we sailed up past the Celebes to Tarakan in North Borneo. Tarakan was a rich oil centre and we called there to refuel. From there we went to Manila in the Philippines and here, we were entertained like royalty by some students Jane had taught during her time at the College of Nursing Australia in Melbourne. When we arrived alongside the quay, a party of very lovely Filipino girls in national costume came on board with gifts of cigars for the men and sprays of tropical flowers for the women. Close behind them were Jane's ex-students, Oni and Pori. After greetings were exchanged, the first thing we said to them was, 'Please take us to a bank because we must get some Filipino currency,' to which they replied, 'You don't need money when you're with us. Just say what you want and we'll get it for you.' Their hospitality was like that all day.

We were shown all over Manila, even travelling in one of the brightly-painted jeeps that served as public transport. That night we were invited to go with them to a party being

Filipino nepa huts.

given at the Australian Embassy for some of the students who had studied in Australia. It was a lovely night and dinner was served in the garden with small lamps on each table. It was a buffet style meal and in the centre of the long table was a roast sucking pig. It was two o'clock before Oni and Pori finally said goodbye, and four hours later, on a perfect morning, we sailed out of Manila Harbour, across the bay and past the island of Corregidor, where General MacArthur made his famous stand in World War II.

We had been told the worst possible stories of the behaviour of the South China Sea, but it was very kind to us in our tiny ship on our way to Hong Kong. We had heard so much about this duty-free port and the fabulous bargains you could get, but it surpassed even our wildest dreams.

The Chinese were certainly clever salespeople. Take for instance, the tailor we had been told of in Melbourne. It was not an easy shop to find in Kowloon, on the mainland of China, and we arrived very hot and rather weary. Immediately when we entered the tiny shop, three smiling young men in immaculate dark suits came rushing up with chairs, while behind them came a girl with bottles of iced fruit drinks. Refreshments over, we got down to the business of choosing materials for some dresses. The walls were lined with shelves of the most glorious brocades, shantungs and cottons. While we were being measured, the owner of the shop asked if we would like to be taken for a drive one afternoon to see something of the New Territories. This was the stretch of land on the mainland opposite Hong Kong, which at that time, was leased from China. It was a most beautiful drive and took about four hours in a large chauffeur-driven car.

We spent eight packed days in Hong Kong marvelling at the colourful streets, shops and of course, the breathtaking view from the top of the Peak, looking down on the harbour.

View of Hong Kong from the Peak looking down on the harbour.

It was four weeks since we had left Melbourne and we had another four weeks ahead of us, but this time on a big passenger liner.

Our first port of call after Hong Kong was Singapore where we spent three days. Here again, we were lucky because we had been introduced to John Kee Soon Bee. We did not know until we met him that he was a member of the Singapore Olympic Water Polo team, and at the time of our visit in early May, he was busy training for the Asian Games in Tokyo at the end of the month. He very kindly took an evening off to take us out fishing Malay-style and we joined a party of his friends to spend the night out on a kelong.

Although rather hard to describe, a kelong was a small timber hut built on stilts over the water, anything up to a mile out from the shore. The fishing was done at night, with the fish attracted to the brilliant kerosene lights slung over the huge net suspended between stakes alongside the hut. The net was raised every two hours and the fish collected in baskets, sorted, packed into crates with layers of ice, and sent off to market at dawn. It was quite fascinating sitting looking down into the area of brilliantly lit water and watching the fish. Flying fish skimmed everywhere, some looking like butterflies with double wings, and there were garfish with bright blue tails, pink cuttlefish and many others.

Supper was set before us; a wonderful meal of freshly caught fish, and we were expected to use chopsticks to eat it. We did, but very inexpertly. We found that fish bones and chopsticks were very difficult to cope with.

As time moved on, we became sleepy and John brought along two young Chinese women to look after us. We were told that a tiny attic above the main hut was 'for ladies to sleep'. A rush mat was spread on the wooden floor and we were each given a small cushion for our head—and that was that! We never thought that we would be able to sleep, but we did, and in spite of the *click, click, click* coming from below where some of the men were playing Mahjong. We awoke with the new noises coming from the netting at two o'clock and went down then to have a look, but unfortunately, the catch that night was not a very good one. We hoped we were not the cause—John had mentioned earlier that our host was the only person in Singapore who would allow women to visit a kelong. Apparently there was a strong superstition that women brought bad luck and poor catches.

After all this activity, even the Mahjong players gave up and all was quiet until dawn when the Malay fishermen set off to shore with the night's catch. Gradually, as the sun came up over the horizon, the kelong came to life. The two fishermen left at the hut wound up the net and examined it for any holes, and some of the boys got out their fishing poles. It was a beautiful morning; the sun turned the timber of the hut a lovely golden brown and the sea was so calm that it seemed to have an oily sheen on the surface. We greatly enjoyed our visit to the kelong and was most grateful to John for organising it.

The kelong.

Later that afternoon, we returned to our ship and continued on our voyage, but each time we visited another new port, our enjoyment of it was tinged with apprehension as home was getting closer and we were unsure of our futures. We had left home in April 1953 and were now arriving home five years later, after only expecting to be away for one year.

From a finance point of view, we had arrived in Quebec City with exactly twenty pounds between us. When we had arrived back in England and had paid the duty on the projector we had bought in Hong Kong, we had six pounds between us. So our five years away really cost us seven pounds each, which was pretty wonderful I think.

Home Again!

1959–1970: What Do I Do Now?

During the 1960s, Formula One racing car driver Jack Brabham, occupied a room in the store-cum-workshop at Repco in Surrey where I worked. He used this area to prepare his racing cars. As many of the staff got to know him quite well during this time, we were all very enthusiastic about his race results and often went to watch him compete in his Brabham-Repco car.

I have a very happy memory of Jack and his wife coming to dinner with Jane and I at our second floor apartment in Pimlico. Jack almost climbed out the window to stick his decal on the outside of the large picture window. No window cleaner managed to remove it during the rest of our occupancy and I sometimes wonder if it is still there.

Memories of Formula One racing legend, Jack Brabham.

Shortly after returning to London, Jane and I decided that as we had lived together for so long whilst travelling the world, we might as well continue to do so. Finding an apartment in Pimlico, overlooking the Thames, we soon settled in, and then began looking for employment. Jane approached the London Hospital where she happily accepted her old post of Sister Tutor, and I approached my old secretarial college for advice. As I had never had to seek work since training as a secretary at Mrs Hoster's back in 1939, I thought they might be able to help me—and they did! The college had an employment agency and one of the first cards taken from their file was a position working with Repco Limited, as Secretary to the London Branch Manager. Obtaining an appointment with the firm, the interviewer commented that she felt I would be very welcome because I would know that it was not just a short bus ride from Melbourne to Sydney.

I thoroughly enjoyed my position at Repco and the many wonderful people with whom I worked and associated. In the 1960s, I had the pleasure of working with two executives who had been transferred from Melbourne to the London Office; Peter, and his wife Kath, and Jeff and his wife Jenny.

My office at Repco.

The summer of 1966 saw me again travelling to Melbourne to visit my many friends, including Elizabeth, who had been introduced to me by the Company Secretary of Repco. After spending a wonderful few weeks of much fun and laughter, I joined the ship *Rangitoto* on her farewell voyage across the Pacific through Panama to England. Amongst the passengers joining us in Auckland were friends Margot, Betty, Gill, Isobel, Jean and Jeanne. We were a merry group and found great pleasure in each other's company.

It was during this trip that I received a telegram from Repco offering me the position of London Branch Manager, which was a great thrill. I happily accepted the position and thoroughly enjoyed the new challenges the position brought.

Leave of Absence

1970–1971: Perth, Hong Kong, Japan, Taiwan, Nepal, India, and Greece

In March 1970, Jane and I decided that we needed a break. Being granted leave of absence from our respective employers, we spent a very happy year in Perth, Australia. We had planned, as usual, to stay only a year—and this time we stuck to it! We left Perth for home, making the journey via train to Melbourne where we had a wonderful time catching up with friends for the next three weeks. From there we boarded ship and cruised to Hong Kong via Sydney, Brisbane, Japan and Taiwan. We disembarked in Hong Kong and boarded a BOAC flight bound for Nepal, thoroughly enjoying our adventures in that country. Travelling on to India and Greece, we finally arrived home in March 1971, exactly one year later.

Finding accommodation did not pose much of a problem in Perth and nor did finding employment. Jane worked at the Royal Perth Hospital and I became Secretary to the Immigration Chaplain attached to the cathedral. Migrants from the United Kingdom were still coming by sea at this time and we welcomed a number of clergy and their families. I always remember one husband telling me that they were saving up to return home. When I showed surprise and sadness at his decision, he immediately told me they were very happy, but had decided that if they had the money in the bank, they would never want to return home. How sensible.

Our weekends and holidays during this time were taken up with visiting so many lovely places: Mundaring Weir with its lovely trees and the kookaburras—some of which were tame enough to come and share our picnic lunch; Canning Dam and the youth centre at Araluen, Rockingham, with its tree-fringed beach and calm waters; Yanchep National Park and the lovely coastline going north from Fremantle; and last, but perhaps our favourite place of all, the North Mole at Fremantle where we sat for hours at weekends watching the huge container vessels, oil tankers and passenger ships coming and going, intermingled with the small craft of all sizes and types.

Much of the year flew by and soon enough Christmas was upon us. It was so strange to be doing the last of our shopping in temperatures around 96°F. It was so different to the very cold weather back home at this time, but fortunately it dropped to 73°F on Christmas Day so that those who preferred a traditional Christmas were able to cook and enjoy the hot fare. The respite was short lived, however, and during the next week the temperature climbed back up to 96°F. From Boxing Day and for the next four days, the tennis enthusiasts had the chance to see many of the world's top women playing in the Federation Cup[65], and certainly one of our memories would be of poor Virginia Wade playing her singles match with the temperature on court said to be around 120°F.

The next two months went all too quickly and there just didn't seem to be enough time to see all our friends and to visit all the places we had grown to love so much. We finished our respective jobs on 26th February and two days later left Perth to spend ten days touring the south-west of the State. In all, we covered about 1,100 miles, driving leisurely and enjoying every type of scenery including the glorious coastline from Busselton to Augusta; we certainly would never forget the bath at Meelup Beach or the colour of the Indian Ocean at Hamelin Bay. Then inland to the land of the huge Karri trees (our thoughts went back to 1955 and the Californian Redwoods). On the way back from Albany, we spent two wonderful days with friends who were having a fishing holiday at Nornalup, overlooking the Frankland River. What could be more peaceful, even if the only fish we caught were maddening little things known locally as 'blowies'. There seemed to be literally millions of them just waiting to take your bait and then blow themselves up to look like a child's bath toy when you pulled them from the water. Definitely not edible!

Hamelin Bay.

65 The Federation Cup was the premier team competition in women's tennis, launched in 1963 to celebrate the 50th Anniversary of the International Tennis Federation.

Karri trees along a long stretch of road.

We had exactly a week in which to clean the flat, finish packing, sell the car, have various injections, and say farewell to many friends. What a week that was! How we ever made the train would always remain a mystery to us, but we did and there on the platform were many of our friends waiting to make sure we did get away. Our twin compartment was full of flowers, homemade biscuits, toy koalas, bon voyage cards, fruit and other gifts. Tears were certainly in our eyes that night.

The train journey from Perth to Adelaide took almost two days. Kalgoorlie was the last sizeable township we visited in Western Australia and we then had over 1,000 miles to travel to Port Augusta which included the famous Nullarbor Plain. Stretching as far as the eye could see, it extended for 420 miles and for most of the way, we saw nothing but barren country, red sand and low scrub. The only houses to be seen were those belonging to railway employees and these were grouped in tiny settlements of perhaps ten or twelve wooden homes, with a post office and a store. We were told that, at regular intervals, a provision train known as the 'Tea and Sugar' called at these isolated groups. There was often a 'welfare car' attached to the train which brought infant welfare sisters, dentists and clergymen to the settlements, and sometimes another car which contained a theatrette with the latest films.

On arrival in Adelaide, we quickly contacted a number of friends and so spent a very happy four days in the City of Churches. The weather was beautiful and we were outdoors most of the time. One friend took us on a picnic to Victor Harbour and others drove us into the hills and through the vineyards. We then boarded a train to Melbourne where we spent a hectic three weeks of visiting our many friends settled in this region of Australia.

From Melbourne, with the sun still shining, we set sail on 22nd April for the Far East. Our ship was the *Tjiluwah*, often referred to as one of the 'white yachts'[66]. Owned by the Royal Interocean Line, she had a Dutch captain and officers, while the crew were mostly Chinese. She carried 100 first-class and 118 tourist-class passengers and from the start it was clear that she was a happy ship. The majority of the passengers were Australians doing the round trip, but we also added New Zealanders, Japanese, Chinese from Hong Kong and Fijians as we went from port to port.

We spent four days in Sydney and one and a half in Brisbane, after which time we settled down to nine days of the Pacific Ocean with time to play deck games, sleep, eat, and unwind. It was a happy period, and for us, it went all too quickly because we knew that once in Japanese waters, the days would fly by and we would be leaving the ship before we had time to think.

Life on board ship.

Our first Japanese port was Yokkaichi and here we sighted the smog which cloaked so many of the cities, especially along the coast where industry was heaviest. We visited Mikimoto Pearl Island, where we were able to watch girls wearing long white robes and head scarves diving for pearl shells. The art of pearl culture was discovered in 1893 and became a thriving industry. It was fascinating to see the pearls being graded according to shape, size, colour, lustre and coating.

66 The *Tjiluwah* and her sister ship, the *Tjiwangi* were considered to be the most popular and beautifully proportioned passenger cargo liners seen in Australian waters during the 1950s and 60s. In 1963, both ships had their hulls painted white, after which they became known as the 'elegant white yachts'.

During the night, we sailed up to Nagoya, which was known as the Detroit of Japan. With a population of almost 2 million, it was the largest industrial city in central Japan. Here again, the dominant feature was the smog and drabness of the city, but as we drove inland, despite the low cloud and rain, the green countryside became attractive and it was amazing to see how every inch of ground was cultivated. Despite the weather, people were working in the rice paddies, and as we travelled along, splashes of brilliant colour caught the eye, produced, by streamers in the shape of fish flying from poles. It was a time of celebration in Japan—the Festival of Boys—when households celebrated the health of each male child and displayed a carp streamer *(Koi-Nobori)* for each male child. There was a great variety of colours and sizes and the fish were made of cotton, nylon or sometimes silk.

That day, we were taken to the River Kiso which was nicknamed the 'Japan Rhine', and in parts it certainly bore some resemblance to that wonderful river. For six miles we travelled in a long boat and the object of our jaunt was to shoot the rapids with the expert guidance of two boatmen, one in the stern and one in the bow. It couldn't have rained harder than it did during those six miles and so we could only huddle together under the tarpaulin covers, lifting them occasionally to release a cascade of water and to peer out at what must be lovely scenery on a hot, sunny day.

From Nagoya we sailed up to Yokahama, our most northern port of call. As we entered the huge harbour we saw Mt Fujiyama in the early morning sunshine, but at first we could not believe it was the great Mt Fuji because it didn't look like snow on the upper slopes and certainly not the dazzling snow depicted in pictures. However, we soon realised that once again the great enemy of the world was spoiling our view; the smog had caused a yellow haze to deaden its brilliance. Sadly, this was to be our only view of the mountain because the weather was not too kind during our visit.

Yokohama was the port for Tokyo and both cities seemed somewhat frightening. There was so much hustle and bustle, so many people and yet no signs—other than in Japanese—to help tourists find their way around. At each port, the Purser's Office provided all passengers with slips of paper giving the name of our ship and our berth written in Japanese so that we could hand this to a taxi driver in order to get ourselves back to the ship. In Tokyo, the Mecca for shopping was the Ginza, which at night was a riot of light. A feature of Japanese cities was the many underground shopping arcades and some of those stretched for what seemed like miles. We were taken into one in Nagoya and our guide was careful to tell us only to walk straight ahead or, he said, we would be completely lost and would not know how to get back to our meeting point.

There were high-rise buildings about, but nothing very spectacular and we were told that Tokyo experienced an earthquake shock on average once every three days, so people were presumably not too keen to live on the top floors of large apartment blocks.

During our stay in Yokohama, we were able to take two full day excursions. The first was to Kamakura and Hakone. Kamakura was thirty-one miles from Tokyo and was the initial site of the Feudal Government about 800 years ago. It was famous for the 700-year-old bronze statue of Buddha and the beautiful gardens of the Hotel Fujiyama, built in 1870, and displaying a mass of beautifully coloured azaleas.

Kamakura, Japan: the 700-year-old bronze statue of Buddha.

From Kamakura we drove on to Hakone which is known for its beautiful lake, formed from the crater of an extinct volcano. Boarding a small boat we were taken on a cruise around the lake where, we were told, you could obtain a good view of Mt Fuji. Unfortunately, as the weather was so bad, we could only see a faint outline of the mountain through the cloud and mist.

The second full day excursion was to the world famous Nikko National Park, a distance of ninety-three miles from Tokyo which we travelled by express train. This was by far the most disappointing day of our whole trip because it hardly stopped raining all day. The Park covered an area of 543 square miles, and because it was further north and fairly high, some cherry blossom was still in bloom and so gave us an idea of how beautiful those trees must be in the spring. Next, we were taken by coach to see Lake Chuzenzi, one of the largest lakes in Japan, and then up the tortuous road with over forty hairpin bends to visit the Toshugo Shrine which built in 1636 in a mixture of Buddhist and Shinto architecture.

From Yokohama, we turned south again to Kobe. We liked Kobe better than any of the other cities visited. It was well laid out, clean and set against a background of mountains. Here there were many street signs; all the direction indicators in the large underground shopping complex were in English as well as Japanese, so getting about was a much less hazardous affair.

On our first morning in Kobe, we were taken on a tour of the city and to Sorakuen Garden where the size and colours of the azaleas were quite beyond belief, making it a perfect setting for the Japanese women wearing gorgeous kimonos, still to be seen in fair numbers.

Sorakuen Garden.

On the Sunday, we went to see the famous Takarazuka Revue whose history, we were told, dated back to 1913. In an effort to boost sales, the president of Hankyu Railways began staging Western-style musical shows. The novelty of Takarazuka was that all the parts were played by women, like a mirror-image of Kabuki[67]. The first half of the program we saw was devoted to a musical play which was colourful and rather like an English pantomime. The second half was more of a revue, with twenty short scenes all related to the theme of 'joy'.

Our final day in Japan was spent visiting Kyoto. For ten centuries until 1868, Kyoto was the capital city of Japan and as such it had many wonderful shrines, the most famous being the Sanjusangendo, a Buddhist temple. Housed in one long building was a large statue of Kannon, the Goddess of Mercy, flanked on each side by 500 more life-sized Kannon statues standing side-by-side several rows deep and all wrought in gold. They certainly made an impressive sight! Another wonderful shrine was the Heian Jingu, which was dedicated to Emperor Kammu and Emperor Komei[68], beautifully lacquered in vermilion and surrounded by cherry trees. Here we saw many small bushes covered all over with knots of white paper. These supposedly brought good fortune to those who tied them onto the bushes. But perhaps the most beautiful shrine of all was the Kinkakuji—or Golden Pavilion—built first

67 A traditional Japanese form of theatre whose actors are all male.

68 The first and last emperors that reigned from Kyoto.

in 1397 and then rebuilt in 1955 in the same form. Each of the three floors was a different style of architecture and the building was surrounded by colourful gardens and a pool which mirrored the pavilion.

Later that evening we sailed away from Japan, leaving behind the rainy weather. It was good to be at sea again and to be able to laze away the hours in the sunshine, but I must say that I enjoyed learning about the Japanese culture and we found the people to be most courteous.

Our next port of call was at Formosa—or after its recent name change, Taiwan. Our first stop was Keelung, the port for Taipei, which was the capital. Getting ashore was not easy as our British passports were confiscated and, because we didn't have visas, special permission had to be obtained from the Chief Immigration Officer for us to go ashore. Our fellow Australian passengers had no difficulty, but at that time Australia had not recognised China whereas the United Kingdom had.

Keelung was unbelievably smelly, with open drains alongside the pavements and terrible hovels in the back streets, but the main thoroughfares displayed their prosperity by the many tall buildings and department stores in the process of being built, and gave the perception, on first sight, that this was a well to do little community. The drive to Taipei was pretty, and like Keelung, was quite impressive with a central square flanked by large government buildings. We were taken to lunch at a wonderful hotel a little out of the city, owned by Madame Chiang Kai Shek[69], where we were offered either a Chinese or Western-style meal. The service was excellent and everyone in the hotel was out to please and to help where necessary. We visited the National Palace Museum, an imposing building with a most attractive exterior and a marvellous collection of priceless Chinese relics. We also visited Yangmingshan Park and a china, pottery and porcelain factory. If only we had not been flying home from Hong Kong—what lovely examples of their work we could have brought home with us.

We spent the next day at Kaohsiung. Here the harbour was larger and the whole area was bristling with guns at the harbour entrance and on every vantage point overlooking the area. No photographs were allowed, and we were told that from time to time, Taiwan and China exchanged gunfire across the dividing water. We were taken for a drive into the

69 The wife of President Chiang Kai-shek of the Republic of China.

surrounding countryside during which we were lucky enough to see a funeral procession, which was most colourful and very happy! The mourners were delighted to be photographed as they danced along the road to the accompaniment of a band and waved to us as they passed. We stopped at another of Madame Chiang's hotels, this one more magnificent than the first. It had been opened only a matter of two weeks prior to our visit. The entrance was teeming with bell hops dressed in white suits and caps piped in red, but there was no sign of any clients. We had drinks in the coffee shop and were then taken up the grand marble staircase to see one of the bedrooms, which was fabulously furnished. The outside of the hotel was a symphony of red, white, green and blue carved woodwork. We hoped that the Taiwanese Government could persuade the world's big businessmen to visit their country and enjoy the luxury of these two hotels, both so in contrast to the poor homes of the local people just a stone's throw down the road.

So we came to our last day on board the *Tjiluwah*—a day that went far too quickly, and inevitably, saw us finishing our packing well after midnight. We sailed up towards Hong Kong and Kowloon early the next morning and quickly realised that great strides had been made since our last visit in 1958. Our first close up of the progress was when we left the ship and walked through the huge Ocean Terminal with its highly polished floors, corridors of shops, and restaurants. We were met by the Hong Kong Manager of Repco, who quickly drove us away to the hotel which he had chosen for our ten day stay. This was the Golden Gate in Austin Road, Kowloon. It was most comfortable, excellently run with a good dining-room, serving reasonable meals. We had a television in our room and a large bathroom with a bath and shower. In addition, it was within easy walking distance of Kowloon's main shopping area. We had no doubts at all that we would spend a very happy time at the Golden Gate.

Our first impressions were soon confirmed; Hong Kong *had* changed a lot since our last visit in 1958. There were fewer signs of poverty in the main streets of both Hong Kong Island and Kowloon, many more tall buildings had been built, and resulting from all this of course, prices had gone up considerably. Our tailor looked after us in the usual way; he put his chauffeur and Mercedes Benz at our disposal for a day. It was hot during our stay and rather sticky, but we nevertheless enjoyed visiting Repulse Bay, and Aberdeen, and also travelling by normal ferry service to the outer islands.

From Hong Kong we flew to Kathmandu, changing planes in Rangoon where we spent the night in the airport. This was quite an experience because we had no visas for Burma as

Jane and I with the chauffeur-driven Mercedes Benz in Hong Kong.

we only intended to wait the few hours in the transit lounge. It wasn't until we left the BOAC plane that we learned that even transit passengers needed visas, and there was a time when we thought we might be sent on our way to Karachi! However, the immigration officers took pity on us and allowed us to stay, saying, 'You do realise, don't you, that there won't be as many people in the airport as there are now? We do hope you will be all right.' Apart from a few cockroaches and the sight of a cat-sized rat, we were all right.

At dawn, we flew out by United Burma Airlines to Kathmandu. Our hotel here was in the centre of the city, with the occasional sacred cow wandering by or lying on the pavement outside the door. The Hotel Crystal was not large, but was comfortable with air-conditioned rooms and large private bathrooms. The food was quite good, although some of it was rather strange to us, but at least it did not give us any tummy trouble. The lights, however, were very poor and kept going on and off as if trying to send a message in Morse code.

The Nepal Tourist Office was a couple of minutes walk from the hotel and we were quickly around there to see what we could do during our short stay. The hotel staff were also anxious to arrange independent taxi tours for us. During our stay, we tried both. On the first afternoon, we went on a tour of Kathmandu itself. We visited Patan, the second city of Nepal and only about five miles from Kathmandu, and the Temple of Kumari Devi where the Virgin Goddess lived—a girl who had been chosen at eighteen months and would remain shut away from the world until she reached puberty. We were also driven a short way into the country to visit Swayambhunath, a Buddhist stupa[70], more than 2,500 years old. It was built on a hill two miles from Kathmandu and the view of the valley from the terrace, which

70 A type of Buddhist structure.

was shared with sacred monkeys, was breathtaking. During the afternoon we also visited a Tibetan community project and saw both men and women weaving rugs and singing a repetitive chant as they worked.

The next morning, we were up at half past three to drive in a Land Rover to see the sun rise over the Himalayas. The vantage point was at Nagarkot and it took us two hours to get there. The road was rough, particularly when we started to climb and we had to cling onto the seats to prevent ourselves being thrown in all directions. All the way we passed people walking in single file along the roadside, carrying vegetables or firewood in baskets on their backs and taking the weight by means of leather straps across their foreheads. They were on their way to market in Kathmandu and had probably been walking all night. In the villages, our driver had to avoid chickens, dogs and of course, plenty of sacred cows.

On arrival at Nagarkot, we were joined by a group of local children dressed in thin cotton shirts, woollen caps and with torn shawls round their shoulders. It was chilly and they shivered as they gazed at us and tried to carry on a conversation using phrases obviously taught to them by a succession of tourists. Gradually the sky lightened, and then imagine our amazement when we heard a cuckoo! Later we were to learn that it was the Hoopoe, whose call was identical to that of the cuckoo, but much more frequent. We had already been warned that May was not the time of year to see Mt Everest and so we were not too disappointed when we realised that neither Everest nor Annapurna were going to be visible that morning, but at least we saw the whole Himalayan wall, a dream we had both had for many a long year. First blue arid then dazzling white as the sun rose, it was a sight we would never forget and one which we hoped we would be lucky enough to see again one day but perhaps in November or December when the air was crystal clear and all the peaks visible.

The Nepalese utilise every inch of ground for cultivation.

The drive back was quite fascinating as we were able to see the way the Nepalese utilise every inch of ground by building sweeping terraces of paddy fields down every hillside, beautifully neat and all set against the fabulous backdrop of snow-capped peaks.

The next day we were to have had a day's drive to the border of China, but word came through that the Chinese, who had built the road for the Nepalese, were blasting in the area and it was not safe to go. We went instead for a lovely drive by taxi through the countryside and along the road into India. It was wonderful scenery, with hair-pin bends, high peaks, terraced farmland, with people working in the fields and laying their wheat on the road so that passing cars and trucks did the threshing for them.

We loved the Nepalese countryside and would have liked to have had longer to drive around and also to wander in the back streets of Kathmandu. We liked the people and wished we had more opportunity to talk with them.

From Kathmandu we flew to Delhi and on to Srinagar in Kashmir where we were to stay on a houseboat for four days. Srinagar stood on the Dal Lake and around it were terraced gardens laid out by the Moguls some 400 years ago; one of these was full of all the well-known English June flowers. Connected to a network of canals and the Jehlum River, the Dal Lake was the main thoroughfare for boat traffic and vendors in their shikaras[71] sold everything from vegetables and fruit to shawls, fur hats, jewellery, biscuits and toilet needs. From the lake, one could look away up the valley to the snow-capped Himalayas; or to the Hari Parbat Hill, crowned by an old fort; or towards the city and Shankaracharya Hill. We drank all this in as we were gently ferried across from the road to the *Athena*, our houseboat. We did not know what to expect in the way of accommodation, but we need not have worried. The *Athena* turned out to be a luxurious home comprising of a lounge and dining-room, both furnished with locally-made walnut furniture; three double bed-

Jane shopping on Dal Lake.

71 Similar vessels to Venetian gondolas.

The Athena.

rooms, each with its own bathroom; and a small kitchen where the houseboy prepared tea and coffee and kept meals hot after collection from the communal kitchen situated on land behind the vessel. And what delicious food it was! The grilled lamb chops, chicken curry and beautiful fresh vegetables, including lotus roots, would always remain a memory. The vegetables were mainly grown on the lake in floating gardens and large stretches of what seemed like peat-type soil, pegged to the lake bottom with stakes and solid enough for a man to walk about on. Our boatman landed on one to show us how he could walk on it, the sensation we thought, of being something like walking across a rope bridge.

We spent half a day visiting Srinagar, walking through one of the busy streets with its open shops, horse-drawn buggies and general bustle of people on bicycles and on foot. We visited a carpet factory; a store selling beautiful woollen and silk scarves, caftans and shirts; and another specialising in papier-mâché boxes, trays, wooden bowls and other local handicrafts. The real highlight of our stay was a whole day spent by the rushing mountain river at Pahalgam with the mighty snow-covered peaks looking down on us as we ate our picnic lunch and cooled our bottle of soda water in the river, and the next day when we drove to Gulmarg, a village 9,000 feet above sea level, where the mountains surround the highest golf course in the world. Yet another highlight was the boat trip by full moon, with our boatman quietly singing Kashmiri love songs, and another; the many kingfishers on the Dal, brilliant in colour, swaying on the reeds, but quickly winging away just before we could move close enough for a photograph.

We left lovely Kashmir the richer by a handsome rug and two caftans and flew back to Delhi where we stayed for three nights. It was unpleasantly hot and we had slight tummy trouble, both of which somewhat coloured our visit to this beautiful city. The magnificent government buildings still stood as memorials to the days of the British Raj, and our hotel with its huge circular dining-room and large bedrooms—furnished as drawing room and bedroom combined—almost echoed with the ghosts of the past, particularly when the band was playing in the dining-room.

We travelled by coach to Agra and were thrilled at our first sight of the Taj Mahal, although we agreed with a fellow traveller who said she thought some of the thrill was taken away by the fact that it was so exactly like the multitude of pictures one had seen of the Taj and that therefore, one had a feeling of having seen it many times before.

We felt sadness about leaving Delhi, but could not feel anything but a certain relief when we were finally our of the heat and on the KLM plane on our way to Greece. However, we decided that we would not mind returning one day when it was not so hot and when we would hope to be feeling one hundred percent fit instead of definitely off-colour.

The beautiful airport at Athens, with its shining marble, the brilliant blue sea seen through the glass walls of the terminal building and the friendly welcome of the Greek authorities was refreshing. 'You have a British passport? That's all right. Away you go—and welcome to Greece!' made a great impression on us.

In Athens, we clung to every minute of our five day stay, knowing that once this was over then 'leave of absence' would be over and we would be faced with the need to settle down again for a spell. This did not of course mean that we were not looking forward to seeing relations and friends again, but by the same token, it meant that many friends would, in future, seem to be a very, very long way away, and unless they were planning a visit to the United Kingdom, then there was little chance of our seeing them for perhaps another two or three years.

It was now early June and Athens was rather too hot for standing about in places like the Parthenon where there was little shade, so it became yet another place to return to one day. It was such an interesting and beautiful place that it would be an area not to miss if planning a trip to Europe. We stayed in an excellent hotel, The Amalia, perfectly situated almost in Constitution Square. The service was first class, the rooms comfortable, and in fact, we could find no cause for criticism in our short stay.

Our last real day of relaxation was spent cruising to Hydra. This was a memorable day, so too was our visit to Delphi, for no one could ever forget the view looking down to the valley stretching towards the Gulf of Corinth. Everything about our stay in Greece was memorable—the drive to Corinth, the visit to the Parthenon and to see the sound and light show, the sunset seen from the Temple of Poseidon at Sunion, and the fish dinner given to us by the local Repco agent on the quayside at Piraeus.

Me at the Parthenon.

Then came our final flight to London. We left Athens with the temperature rising into 90°F, but soon the pilot was warning us of rain at Heathrow Airport. The sun continued to shine and we began to think of putting our plastic raincoats back into our overnight bags, but when we started to land we suddenly came down through the clouds to a typical November day in London. The ground below was grey, shading to black in places. Huge patches of water showed where fields were flooded and soon the plane's windows were blurred with rain. We were home! Our white cardigans and blue crimplene skirts looked strangely out of place, but we had left our coats in Hong Kong to be sent on by post in order to reduce our baggage weight and allow us to bring with us a projector from Hong Kong and a tape-recorder from Japan.

If the weather was not welcoming, our friends' warm reception made up for it. In two cars, we were soon back in Pimlico and opening the door of our flat. It looked just as if we had been away on two week holiday. Our 'daily' had arranged for her husband to redecorate it and she had put everything back where it belonged. In fact, there was not a sign of the three separate tenants who had lived there during our year long 'leave of absence'.

A Road Well Travelled

Looking back through the beautiful bound book of memorabilia collected from my early years by my paternal grandparents, I think I have had a very varied life, leaving me with many memories and many friends. My tremendous appreciation goes to everyone who has helped to make these memories, but particularly to my dear friends Helen and Jane who travelled so many roads with me.

Pre-war holidays in Europe, war-time holidays in the United Kingdom, post-war holidays on the Continent, working holidays in Canada and Australia and holidays to many new places and the places I loved—I've seen so much during my lifetime, but that quotation still sums up my feelings admirably:

Travel gives a character of experience to our knowledge,
and brings the figures upon the tablet of memory into strong relief.

Afterword

1972–Present

In 1977, after a period of ill health, my dear friend and travelling companion Jane, died during open heart surgery. I appreciated the many friends who gathered around me at that time: my other dear friend of early travels, Helen; Frieda, Mary and Irène from my Cheltenham Ladies' College days; and Sheila, the Principal Tutor at the London Hospital and one of Jane's former work colleagues; all were of great support. Repco executive Jeff, representing his wife Jenny, flew over from Melbourne to be with me and remained for several weeks to help me in many ways.

Jane's contact with 'her' hospital remained until the end. Apart from her time in Canada and Australia, she remained at the hospital until her retirement in 1976. After this time, she maintained close contact with her many work colleagues and friends at the hospital. She was a very special person who cared more for others than for herself.

June 1978 saw me reach my twenty years of service with Repco and I received an award for service. At a special celebration in October, Tony Avery, the joint General Manager, presented me with a gold watch. It was strange to think that I had stayed in one place for so long after all my early travels.

I continued to work at Repco until my retirement three years later. Looking back at my twenty-three years of employment with Repco, I had made many friends, but I must particularly mention Tony Avery and his wife Valerie, and the Chairman of Repco, Sir Charles McGrath. Sir Charles and Lady McGrath and their family were so kind to me and I can remember spending many happy times with 'CG' and Madge at their beautiful home on Phillip Island.

In the next few years, I again visited three of my favourite travel destinations—Auckland, Perth and Melbourne—and it was while I was at a party in Melbourne that I met Rae.

Presenting me with my award for twenty years service, Tony Avery, joint General Manager of Repco.

Finding that we had much in common, we soon realised that we had even more; we had a mutual friend—Elizabeth[72]. So, it wasn't long before we became a merry threesome; they took me in hand and we toured all around Victoria and to parts of Melbourne that I hadn't yet seen. We had much fun.

This trip was a turning point in my life, prompting me to consider my future—did I wish to stay in England or did I wish to retire to Perth or Melbourne? Melbourne had always held a fascination for me and my many friends there made it seem very enticing. The decision was made in August 1981, when Rae and Elizabeth came over to England for a holiday. During this time, they invited me to join with them as a family—an offer that I happily accepted—and a couple of weeks later, after having arranged the sale of my home in Suffolk and letting my flat in Pimlico, I left England to come to my new home in Melbourne.

In 1982, I became a member of the Scots' Church Melbourne, a beautiful old Presbyterian Church in the centre of the city, at which both Rae and Elizabeth worshipped. Having worshipped in many and varied churches during my travels, I found that this church and its wonderful congregation suited me. As if to reinforce my decision to join, just three weeks later I was both thrilled and privileged to be among the congregation when Her Majesty Queen Elizabeth, attended the Sunday morning worship and Dame Pattie Menzies handed over her late husband's Order of the Thistle insignia for safe keeping at the church. As a great monarchist, this memory holds a special place in my heart.

72 I met Elizabeth in 1966 through the Company Secretary of Repco.

Over the next years, I found myself happy and content with my decision to move to Melbourne. I loved Australia and its wonderful people, and Rae and Elizabeth and their families were so very kind in accepting me, especially Rae's brother Harley and his friends Desmond and Allan. So in April 1990, after much discussion with my family, I made the decision to become an Australian citizen.

Her Majesty Queen Elizabeth II with Dame Pattie Menzies.

Today, Rae, Elizabeth and I still live together and to people who know of our situation, we are often referred to us as 'The Three Unclaimed Treasures'! To Rae and Elizabeth, who have given me so much happiness during these last twenty-four years, I give my loving thanks.

I have been able to return to England several times. On these visits, I have seen my cousin Jane and her sons Nicholas and Algernon; my friends, Mary and Irène, and their sons, Nicholas and Peter (both are my godsons); and Cedric and Elizabeth whose daughter Jane is my god-daughter and the great, great, grand-daughter of author Charles Dickens! I also keep in touch with relatives of my dear Jane, and have 'adopted' her two god-daughters Fiona and Angela. I hear regularly from another god-daughter who is here in Melbourne, Sarah, the granddaughter of Jack Mabbett, a Repco executive.

'The Three Unclaimed Treasures—trying our hats for a Buckingham Palace Garden Party. From left: me, Elizabeth and Rae.

Most of my spare time is spent doing voluntary work for The Scots' Church and I have found that I enjoy helping people. The wealth of experience I have gained in dealing with people the world over has stood me in good stead—and what better place could be found to put my talents to work?

Memorabilia

My parent's wedding in 1917.

Where it all started—Little Bookham Church.

To Frederick Percival & Violet Mary Boilleau Robinson

In Remembrance of the Baptism of

at

by on

"It is Your Parts and Duties to see that this Child be brought up to lead a Godly and a Christian Life."

"Train up a child in the way he should go and when he is old he will not depart from it."

"A child left to himself bringeth his mother to shame."

"Ye fathers, provoke not your children to wrath: but bring them up in the nurture and admonition of the Lord."

"If any man lack wisdom, let him ask of God, that giveth to all men liberally, and upbraideth not, and it shall be given him."

"As for me and my house, we will serve the Lord."

Teach Your Children to Pray. Pray for Your Children. Pray with Your Children.

My baptism certificate (1918).

The family grave at Little Bookham Church. Buried there are my great grandfather, Bun-pa, Grannie, and Uncle Lestock.

Dedication by Bun-pa of the installation of the electric light into Little Bookham Church in memory of my mother.

Uncle Lestock.

Four generations. From left: my second cousin Nicholas, Cousin Jane, Uncle Lestock and Grannie.

Ann Elizabeth Pollen Robinson (Me)

Violet Mary Boileau Robinson (Mother)

Sir Frederick Percival Robinson, KCB (Father)

Grace Amy Willock-Pollen (Grannie)

Henry Court Willock-Pollen (Bun-pa)

Kate Frances Robinson (Gran)

Frederick Authur Robinson (GP)

Jane McCreath

Helen Gibson

Photo of the Royal Family taken for Christmas 1937.

George R.I

George the Sixth by the Grace of God of Great Britain, Ireland and the British Dominions beyond the Seas, King, Defender of the Faith, Emperor of India and Sovereign of the Most Honourable Order of the Bath to Our trusty and well beloved Frederick Percival Robinson Esquire Companion of Our said Most Honourable Order Secretary Ministry of Works

Greeting

Whereas We have thought fit to nominate and appoint you to be an Additional Member of the Civil division of the Second Class or Knights Commanders of Our said Most Honourable Order of the Bath We do by these presents grant unto you the Dignity of an Additional Knight Commander of Our said Order and hereby authorise you to have hold and enjoy the said Dignity and Rank as an Additional Member of the Civil division of the Second Class or Knights Commanders of Our aforesaid Order together with all and singular the privileges thereunto belonging or appertaining

Given at Our Court at Saint James's under Our Sign Manual and the Seal of Our said Order this First day of January 1944 in the Eighth year of Our Reign

By the Sovereign's Command

Henry.

Great Master

Grant of the Dignity of a Knight Commander (Civil division) of the Order of the Bath to Frederick Percival Robinson, Esq., C.B.

The certificate my father received upon being granted a Knight Commander of the Order of the Bath in 1944.

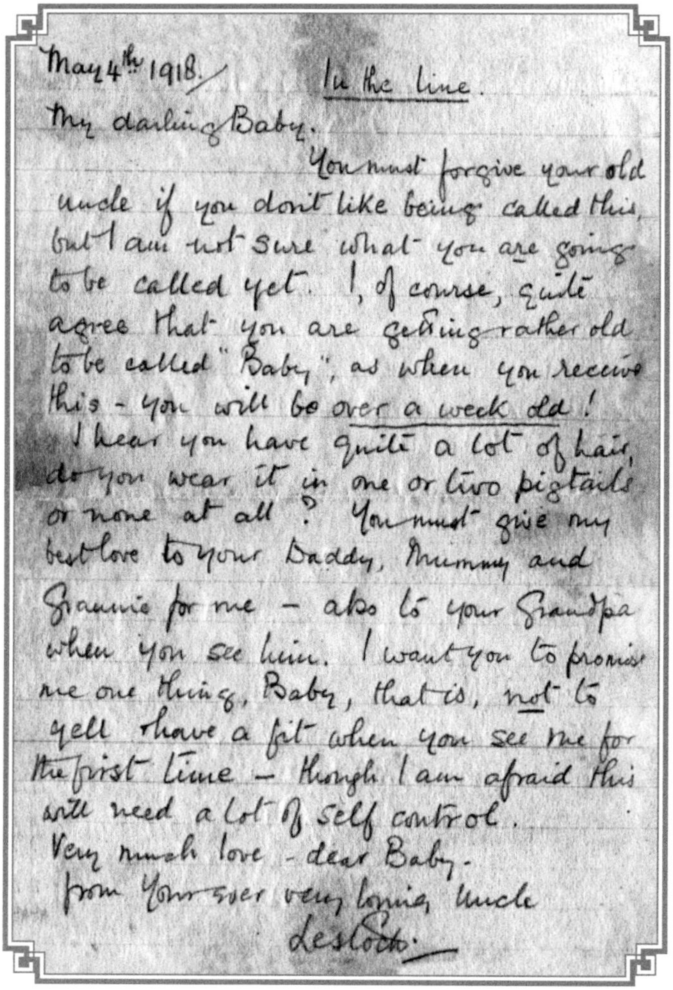

May 4th 1918. In the line.

My darling Baby.

You must forgive your old uncle if you don't like being called this, but I am not sure what you are going to be called yet. I, of course, quite agree that you are getting rather old to be called "Baby", as when you receive this - you will be over a week old!

I hear you have quite a lot of hair, do you wear it in one or two pigtails or none at all? You must give my best love to your Daddy, Mummy and Grannie for me - also to your Grandpa when you see him. I want you to promise me one thing, Baby, that is, not to yell & have a fit when you see me for the first time - though I am afraid this will need a lot of self control.

Very much love - dear Baby.

from Your ever very loving Uncle

Leslock.

Letter written to me by my Uncle upon my birth.

My bear family.

View of Lossiemouth, Scotland near my Grannie's home.

Me dressed up as a Christmas tree in 1927.

Left: One of my artworks. A woodcutting of Sheen Cottage.

Right: Celebrating my Australian citizenship in 1990. From top left: Rae's brother Hadley and Rae. Bottom left: Tip (my friend from Quebec), me and Elizabeth.

Left: Me with our dogs, Kirsty and Angus.

FAMILY TREE

OF

Pollen, Boileau, Willock and other Families, Descendants of King Edward III.

KING EDWARD THE THIRD,
Founder of the Most Noble Order of the Garter
Died 1372

John of Gaunt—Catherine de Roet,
Duke of Lancaster | Daughter of Sir Payne Roet, Kt.
Died 1393 | Died 1403

Joan de Beaufort—Ralph Nevile,
Daughter of John of Gaunt, Duke of Lancaster | Earl Marshal of England
Died 1442 | Died 1440

Richard Nevile—Alice Montacute,
Earl of Salisbury | Daughter of Thomas, Earl of Salisbury
Died 1460

John Nevile—Isabella de Inglethorpe,
Marquis Montacute | Daughter of Sir Edmond Inglethorpe
Died 1471

Lucy Nevile—Sir Anthony Brown,
Standard Bearer of England

Elizabeth Brown—Henry Durrant,
Earl of Worcester
Died 1565 | Died 1547

Lucy—John Nevile,
Daughter of Earl of Worcester | Lord Latimer
Died 1582 | Died 1577

Dorothy Nevile—Thomas Cecil,
Earl of Exeter
Died 1608 | Died 1622

Lucy—William Paulet,
Marquis of Worcester
Died 1614 | Died 1628

Charles Paulet—Elizabeth
Third son of Marquis of Worcester
Died 1654

Jane Paulet—Sir John Huband, Bart.
Died 1710

Jane Huband—Edward Pollen of Andover
Died 1732

Edward Pollen—Elizabeth Walsh
Of London
Died 1775 | Died 1760

Revd. George Pollen—Mary,
Rector of Little Bookham | Daughter of W. Goode of Worcestershire
Died 1812 | Died 1816

Henrietta Pollen—John Peter Boileau
Died 1817 | Died 1837

Major Charles Lestock Boileau—Margaret Stirling,
Of Castelau, Barnes | Daughter of W. Stirling of Brompton, Middlesex
Died 1889

Mary Elizabeth Boileau—Henry Davis Willock
Died 1919 | Died 1903

Henry Court Willock-Pollen—Grace Amy Martin,
Daughter of S. H. Martin
Died 1934 | Died 1958

Violet Mary Boileau Willock-Pollen—Frederick Percival Robinson
Died 1927 | Died 1949

Ann E. Pollen Robinson

Henry Lestock Boileau Willock-Pollen—Dorothy A. Sharland
Died 1969 | Died 1968

Jean M. Boileau Willock-Pollen (Jane)—Richard G. Williams (Bob)
Died 1970

Piers N. M. Williams (Nicholas)—Margaret E. Bzikot

Richard A. M. Williams (Algernon)—Celia S. Milln

Alexander B. M. Williams

Lydia A. M. Williams

For Jane

Jane came from a large family living in Maybole, Ayrshire. Her grandfather owned a boot and shoe factory in Maybole and his three sons inherited the business upon his death. Jane's father, while keeping a vested interest in the family business, became an insurance agent for the Prudential. He served throughout World War I and Jane's mother kept his job open for him, cycling all over Ayrshire, keeping in contact with his customers.

As soon as she was old enough, Jane travelled down to London to start her training as a nurse at the London Hospital in Whitechapel, becoming a Staff Nurse, Sister and finally, a Sister Tutor. Sadly, she died on 7th March 1977 in the hospital during open heart surgery.

On 19th March, a Thanksgiving Service for Jane was held in a country church in East Anglia. The Rector, the Reverend David Mathers gave the following address.

Service of Thanksgiving—19th March 1977

This is a very happy occasion. For those of us at Golders Green Crematorium, last week the field of most beautiful purple and yellow crocus spoke of resurrection and new life—now after the winter. We are full of joy today because we have been privileged to know and to love a most wonderful person in Jane McCreath. We rejoice that, after the winter's sleep of this mortal life, she has awakened to the summer of immortality. So our music and our flowers help us to forgot our sadness; the sadness of the loss of one we love, the sadness as we miss tremendously, Jane's warm and friendly presence with us, and to make us also remember that Christ, for Jane, has come again to receive her unto Himself, that where He is, there she may be also, and that in His presence is fullness of joy and at His right hand are pleasures for evermore.

I have been fortunate enough to know Jane for nearly four years. Almost all of you have known her for very much longer. Some of you remember her from the early days of training at

The London Hospital. You who are her brothers and sisters grew up with her as a child, but all of us, and Ann most of all, knew her to be someone who to be with was a tremendous delight; someone who could always cheer and revive one with a keen sense of humour; someone who thought of others more than of herself. We thank God today for these lovely qualities in her. We thank God today for Jane.

We have just sung these words:

Just as I am, of that free love
The breadth, length, depth, and height to prove,
Here for a season, then above,
O Lamb of God, I come, I come!

Jane was a person who had experienced that free love of God in his own Son Jesus Christ. We can echo these words of St Paul: 'She loved because He first loved her'.

Now her season here has passed and she is above with the Lamb of God. May we allow these words to speak to us, to speak in this manner to us as they spoke to Jane? May we so come to trust in Christ who taketh away the sins of the world so that we are conscious of coming to Christ and finding our lives transformed by of the power of His Spirit and feel in new measure that love and joy and peace.

Someone, when speaking to me of Jane as a nurse, said that to her it was the patients, and especially the young, who were important. One had complete faith in her and knew that in her care and concern for the sick and for the nurses training under her, there was attention given to the smallest detail. This is not something which comes without trying, and for those to whom it seems to come effortlessly there has been great self-discipline and hard work. For the Christian—nurse or patient, woman or man, adult or child, there is only one real answer—so to respond to the love and forgiveness of Christ that one's life is changed into a life of service to Him and through Him to others. Jane and her memory are a living testimony that what I say is true.

For Helen

I first met Helen in September 1936 when she was nineteen years old and we were both attending the Chelsea School of Art. She was a wonderful artist and calligrapher and worked for The Ashmolean Museum of Art and Archaeology for more than thirty years. In fact, one of her paintings was exhibited in a gallery in the Mall, London and many others were exhibited over the years in Eynsham. Her fame as an artist also reached Australia where we have five of her pieces in our home in Melbourne.

It was with great distress that I heard of Helen's sudden and unexpected illness two days before Christmas last year. Sadly, she died a week later on 30th December 2005. *The Ashmolean* published the following tribute to her.

In Memoriam

Helen Gibson was the calligrapher at the Ashmolean for over thirty years. She started in the Department of Antiquities in 1947, writing labels and drawing plans to illustrate displays. She later added the calligraphy for the Department of Western Art to her responsibilities and finally moved into the Department of Eastern Art as a part-timer. She retired from the museum in the late 1970s. In her time all labels were hand-written, and there are still samples of her beautiful hand on the mounts of some prints and drawings, as well as her illustrations of newly acquired objects in the Accessions Books. She is especially warmly remembered for the lovely hand-painted labels on Perspex that she produced for the sword-furniture display in the Department of Eastern Art, where she was also required to produce posters for temporary exhibitions. She was born in 1917 and died at the end of 2005.

The Ashmolean No. 50, Spring 2006, p.29.

The following eulogy was delivered by Jeremy Gibson, Helen's nephew, at her funeral held on Wednesday, 11th January 2006.

In Memoriam

Helen Gibson died after a mercifully short illness over Christmas, brought on by a stroke and heart attack. As the oldest long-term resident in Church Hanborough, nobody who lives in the village can remember it without her. However, she is just the last of three 'Gibson Girls' who have contributed so much to our village and parish over seventy-three years.

On New Year's Day, two days after Helen died, at the early communion service which uses the traditional Book of Common Prayer, Tim, our Rector, had very appropriately arranged for the Epistle and Gospel to be read from the traditional Authorised Version of the Bible. The actual volume had been given to 'SS Peter and Paul Hanborough, To the Glory of God and in memory of Winifred Margaret Gibson, 1897–1958' by Helen's mother, Hester, and Helen herself in memory of our aunt, who all who knew her remember as 'Winnows'.

Winnows first came to Church Hanborough in 1932, when she leased 'Mylors' from the Mansells, Helen Gale's grandparents. Thus whilst we can claim some years of Gibson presence in the parish, we are very much newcomers. The will of a Roger Mansell of Hanborough was proved in 1546!

Winnows lived at 'Mylors' for the rest of her life, dying far too early in 1958 at only sixty-one. But in 1942, Hester and Helen came to join her at 'Mylors'. Hester and Helen have been far longer lived; Hester, like her sisters, into her nineties, dying in 1980. Helen's brother, John, on Vancouver Island is still robust at ninety. I feel Helen will be very irritated not to have made it so far, but at least she retained all her faculties and physical capabilities until just a week before her death. Not bad for eighty-eight and three quarters.

In Winnows, Hester and Helen, Hanborough has benefited from three most dedicated parishioners whom I know have added greatly to the quality of Christian life over the many years they have lived here.

Helen's own contribution to village life has been self-effacing, but it is typical of what keeps our community going. For many years she was Secretary of the Parochial Church Council, and Treasurer of the St John Ambulance Brigade. I well recall the pain and grief the preparation of the minutes and accounts brought her, as I typed them up for her! Her annual sale at 'Mylors' of plants, food and the inevitable bric-a-brac, in aid of the parish church and her favourite overseas charity, St James Hospital, Mantšonyana, Lesotho, was an important date in our calendar. She was an expert calligrapher, and her work is evident in many places in the parish. As an artist, a good many of us have examples of her work.

As a close and familiar relative, one takes one's family members for granted. It is only when they have gone that you realise how important they have been to their friends and neighbours over what on this occasion was sixty-three years. The packed parish church and subsequently packed 'Hand and Shears' testified to the friendship and love she had inspired with so many in Hanborough and Freeland.

The following sermon was delivered by the Rector the Parish, the Reverend Dr Tim Naish, in St Peter and St Paul Church, Hanborough on Wednesday, 11th January 2006.

In Memoriam—Helen Olivier Costeker Gibson 1917–2005

Not long after my arrival here, Helen found me at a quiet moment here in the church and asked me, in that characteristic tone of gentle concern, if I was happy using the words 'world without end' with which so many of the prayers in the Book of Common Prayer end. She was very relieved when I said yes; most of you will be able to envisage the content bowed twinkle with which she went away. For apparently Colin, my predecessor, was uncomfortable with these words: he believes the world does end. It seems to me appropriate today to dwell on this question for a moment because Helen, as we know, would prefer a sermon the principal focus of which was on something of the Christian faith, and not on herself. I think I understand part of Colin's reasons but I believe that for the most part Helen was right.

We cans see arguments for both points of view in the reading we have just heard: 'I saw a new heaven and a new earth… Behold I am making all things new.' There is an end in that there is something new. In that sense the world perhaps does end. But there is also a continuity: the new is recognisable as heaven and earth. It is a new heaven, *a new* earth, *a new Jerusalem and in that sense the world is not ending, it is being changed. Elsewhere in the Bible, Paul writes about creation groaning as it were in labour pains longing to obtain the freedom of the glory of the children of God. Not then an end but a transformation: world without end, but changed. And it is in that light surely that Helen saw her own life and would wish us to see it.*

There is sort of end to her life, the reality of which this casket and our grief betoken. We shall miss that faithful presence in service to country, community and kin: to country, of which she was quietly proud, having served as a land girl during the Second World War—she was regularly, if not frequently, urging me to pray for the Queen; to community because most of us here know how much she gave to neighbours, to friends, to those whom she loved and who loved her; and to kin—I remember the quiet delight with which she told me about the gathering which Jeremy has just mentioned. We shall miss too her artist's eye and hand, demonstrated in her years at the Ashmolean; her beautiful calligraphy scattered in various places around this church and St Mary's Freeland; her delight in nature and liturgy and all that was beautiful. And we shall miss her unobtrusive devotion—not my phrase but one pinched from one of Helen's cousins earlier in the week. It seems to me to sum her up—unobtrusive devotion to God and to the church of this parish. I have had to put an extra item on to next Monday's PCC meeting agenda about all the tings that Helen quietly did of which we were probably unaware and which will only gradually emerge in the months ahead. Who will we find to replace her unobtrusive devotion?

And yes, all of that has come to an end because this body got worn out and we are glad that after its collapse it only lasted a week. And so in some sense a world, Helen's world, our world with Helen has *come to an end. But in the much more important senses, Helen was right and would want us, through our tears today, to rejoice in her 'world without end'. The Christian assurance in which Helen's life was deeply grounded is that the life and death and resurrection of the Christ, whose coming we have just celebrated, revealed eternal life. And so she lives eternally with Him not just in our memories of her graciousness and goodness and in the ways in which she has inculcated some of that in us, though that does foreshadow it, but in the more solid reality of the spiritual, the divine life that we often sense, reach out to and, through God's grace, make our own.*

Of course, we only have picture language to describe it, like the pictures of which we have just read: tears being wiped from eyes, the one seated on the throne, the water of life being perpetually available for the thirsty… Picture language that speaks of something we can but imagine, God the maker of heaven and earth, longing for its turning back to him and its perfection. World without end, eternal life, is not so much about quantity, length, but about quality. And it is that life that is without end as we see it and receive it in Jesus Christ. And we rejoice more with Helen then.

She lived, did she not, but such faith. With her unobtrusive devotion, she declared it much more by what she did and who she was than by anything she said. But she believed it was my job, and she told me so from time to time, to declare that faith audibly on her behalf, that faith in the Word made flesh. So I would ask today, those of you who have rejected the faith that was hers, those of you who are agnostic about it, and perhaps especially those who try not to think about it to make up their minds: on Helen's behalf, I'd ask you to consider the claims of Christ and of God's kingdom for which she lived. Of course, she would graciously accept those who with integrity cannot have such faith. But I believe that she would hope that you were willing, at least for today, to suspend your disbelief sufficiently to rejoice with her in the glory she now shares in greater fullness, the glory of the Father, the Son and the Spirit, to whom be honour and praise, now and for ever,

World Without End.

Amen